Dread Jesus

William David Spencer is a theologian of popular culture. Born and brought up in an inter-racial urban centre, his lifelong interest is global theology. Attracted to Rastafari's dynamic use of the Bible in song lyrics in 1976, he began studying its biblical themes while collecting hundreds of reggae songs and Rasta writings and interviewing many of its thinkers and performers. A song writer himself, he studied English and Education at Rutgers University.

He is an ordained Presbyterian Church (USA) minister and received Master of Divinity and Master of Theology degrees from Princeton Theological Seminary, and his Doctorate of Theology from Boston University School of Theology. He has served in urban street ministry, college chaplaincy, adult literacy, graduate seminary education, and pastoral ministry. He teaches theology courses for Gordon-Conwell Theological Seminary's Boston Center for Urban Ministerial Education and the Caribbean Graduate School of Theology in Kingston, Jamaica.

He is the recipient of several awards, including the Earl Award for excellence in writing from the Popular Culture Association. He is the author or editor of nine books and seventy articles, poems, stories. He is happily married to the Reverend Dr Aída Besançon Spencer, and they have a son, Steve, in university studying video productions.

By the same Author

Mysterium and Mystery: The Clerical Crime Novel

Chanting Down Babylon: The Rastafari Reader
(ed. with N. S. Murrell and A. A. McFarlane)

The Global God: Multicultural Evangelical Views of God
(ed. with A. B. Spencer)

God Through the Looking Glass: Glimpses from the Arts
(ed. with A. B. Spencer)

The Prayer Life of Jesus: Shout of Agony, Revelation of Love
(with A. B. Spencer)

2 Corinthians: A Commentary
(with A. B. Spencer)

Joy through the Night: Biblical Resources for Suffering People
(with A. B. Spencer)

The Goddess Revival
(with À. B. Spencer, D. G. F. Hailson and C. Kroeger)

DREAD JESUS

William David Spencer

First published in Great Britain in 1999
Society for Promoting Christian Knowledge
Holy Trinity Church
Marylebone Road
London NW1 4DU

The author and publisher acknowledge with thanks
permission to reproduce the following material:

Patrick 'Tony Rebel' Barrett for signed permission (8 November 1993) to quote lyrics
used in the following songs:

'The Voice & The Pen' (by P. Barrett, M. Bennett)
'Creator' (by P. Barrett)
© 1993 Rebellious Vibes (BMI), collected on Tony Rebel,
Vibes of the Time (CHAOS/Columbia: OK 53455, 1993).

Ras Michael Henry for signed permission (14 July 1993)
to quote lyrics used in the following songs:

'New Name' (by Ras Michael (Michael Henry)),
collected on *Kibir Am Lak: Glory to God* (Jamaica: Top
Ranking, no number, no date), also © Ras Michael Henry, 1985,
collected on Ras Michael and the Sons of Negus, *Rally Round*
(Ho-Ho-Kus, NJ: Shanachie: 43027, 1985).

'He is Risen' (by Ras Michael), 'Marriage in Canaan'
(trad., arranged with new lyrics by Ras Michael Henry),
© Ras Michael Henry, 1989, collected on Ras Michael,
Know Now (Newton, NJ: Shanachie: 64109, 1989).

Victor Essiet for signed permission (5 October 1995)
to quote lyrics used in the following song:

'Thanks and Praises' (by Victor Essiet)
© by V. E. Music, administered by 58/59 Music Publishing,
EMI, collected on The Mandators,
Power of the People: Nigerian Reggae (Heartbeat: 156, 1994)

'Time Will Tell'
Words and music by Bob Marley
© Copyright 1978 by Bob Marley Music Ltd,
PolyGram International Publishing, Inc.

British Library Cataloguing-in-Publication Data

A catalogue record for this book is available from the British Library

ISBN 0-281-05101-1

Typeset by David Gregson Associates
Printed in Great Britain by
The Cromwell Press, Trowbridge, Wiltshire

For my dear wife,
Aída Dina Besançon Spencer,
with lifelong gratitude

Angel of Death, Lay Down Your Sword

Angel of death, lay down your sword.
Peace, dreadful warrior of the Lord.
For your commander, great and strong,
a gentle babe is born.

Hold, great winds, vast stores of rain.
Ring, lofty mountains, echo plains,
From terrible heaven's armory
flows softened melody.

Peace in heaven, peace on earth.
The hosts proclaim a joyful birth.
Great God, forsaking majesty,
has come to you and me.

William David Spencer (1982)

Contents

Preface

'Judas sold Jesus for 30 pieces of silver ... Your same friend that eat and drink with you will eliminate you, it's true', sings Jamaican Junior Murvin.[1] 'Who is he that shared his blood at Calvary? Who is he?', sings another, Judy Mowatt, former back up singer for Bob Marley and the Wailers and now a musical statesperson.[2] 'Sweet Jesus, what a wonder you are', sings a third, the great Lincoln 'Sugar' Minott.[3] 'He is risen! Christ is risen!', declares a fourth, master drummer Ras Michael Henry.[4] All of these have called themselves Rastafarians, the healers of the nations, the renovators of Christianity, the true followers of Jesus the Christ.

Although Rastafari see their movement as instituted by God before the creation of the world, Rastafari itself first appeared after 1930 when Jamaican street preachers began declaring that the former Ras Tafari Makonnen, newly crowned as Haile Selassie, emperor of Ethiopia, was either Almighty God come to earth or the return of Jesus Christ as black in a new dispensation.

Two millennia ago on the road to ancient Jerusalem, where he would be raised up on a Roman executioner's cross and put to death, Jesus the Christ prophesied, 'If the Child of Humanity be lifted up, he will draw all people unto him.' Echoing across the centuries, his words have penetrated into lands then undiscovered to draw to this quintessential victim and victor nations yet unborn. These multinational peoples' adaptation of the faith of Jesus in turn has and is impacting Christianity. Such is the case of the Rastafarians.

The story of how Jesus was 'liberated' from dominant cultures, fitted out in locks and set at the head of a two thirds world movement which today is global in its impact – and of the prior claim the gospel of Jesus Christ holds on that movement – is a true detective story as exciting as anything I researched when I hunted down the elusive mysterium of God in the modern mystery novel in *Mysterium and Mystery*. In one sense, it is also the next stage of the quest for the power of Jesus that I began in the book I coauthored with my wife, Rev Dr Aida Besançon Spencer, *The Prayer Life of Jesus: Shout of Agony, Revelation of Love*. And it represents the main fruit of my studies, from which the book *Chanting Down Babylon: The Rastafari Reader* developed with N. Samuel Murrell, Adrian McFarlane, Clinton Chisholm, and many others, as a by-product.

Besides *Chanting*, a number of good books, some readily available, some not, some hopelessly obscure, have been written on Rastafari and its dissemination through the lyrics of reggae. Most of these touch on the theology of Rastafari, though they focus elsewhere. None, however, centre on the bridging figure of Jesus. What follows, therefore, is not a rehash of what they have done. It is a Christological study that attempts to place Rastafari in the context of the history of Christian theology – to give it a much-needed theological reading in addition to the sociological, ethnological, historical, musical, anthropological and political readings that ordinarily have been done. I think what is happening in Rastafari raises significant questions for the future of global Christianity. Is Rastafari simply a bizarre Christian cult, destined to fade if the emperor's self-denial of divinity proves true by his non reappearance or resurrection? Or, is it destined to become a vibrant two thirds world reform movement within the parent faith, recalling Christianity to its original, non-oppressing gospel for all people, elevating the poor and dispossessed, while humbling the erring and oppressive rich?

In the more than two decades I have been researching this book, I have been introduced to a wide variety of Rasta theological configurations, especially altering as the flow to Africa ebbs back to Jamaica. Ultimately, I focused on the figure of Jesus and the variety of Christologies, or views of Jesus, within Rastafarian culture.

My research was done between 1976 and 1999 in Jamaica, elsewhere in the Caribbean, in the United States, in the United Kingdom, and to a lesser degree in Europe and the Near East; but information was provided me by a network of Rasta and Christian thinkers, academic colleagues, fellow researchers, and a host of interested well-wishers, from Hawaii to Mali, Ghana to Germany. Many people, therefore, deserve warm credit for helping me amass the information I assess in this book.

Among the principal, I owe an inestimable debt to Timothy Erdel, former librarian of the Caribbean Graduate School of Theology and Jamaica Theological Seminary in Kingston, for his tireless photocopying of primary source material from the Zenas Gehrig Library. He turned up not only what was published, but also what was not. And his securing of scarce material, dissertations, unpublished interviews and papers and other ephemera helped enrich this work beyond being just another review of the secondary literature. I am also grateful to my 'family' in Jamaica: President Dieumeme Noelliste, Dr Anthony Oliver, Dr Carleton Dennis, Dr Jean Lee, Dr Zenas Gehrig, Ms Gloria Noelliste, Mrs Cecelia 'Madge' Spencer, and the staff and students at the Caribbean Graduate School of Theology (CGST) and the Jamaican Theological Seminary (JTS) in Kingston, my home base in the Caribbean where my wife and I teach adjunctively.

All fresh material is drawn from my own interviews and song assessments, and all translations from the Greek, Hebrew and Spanish are my own (unless otherwise noted). A previous version of the poem, 'Angel of Death, Lay Down Your Sword' appeared in the 17 December 1982 issue of *Christianity Today*, p. 24.

Rasta theology, of course, is being continually created, and at the forefront of its formulation are the musicians who take the Rasta message and develop it for the world audience. This is fitting for the theology of a mostly oral culture. Therefore, I invested a good deal of interest in a review of Rastafarian reggae and of interviewing those who considered themselves 'reasoning

Rastas'. Since Rastas, in common with Christians, expend energy debating about who is 'true Rasta', some readers may grumble over some of my inclusions. Within Rastafari, exhortations like Burning Spear's 'Jah Kingdom' and Sugar Minott's 'A Just Rasta' plead for 'inity' (unity) among the 'bredrin'. If interviewees declared themselves Rastas, I accepted their word, agreeing in this case with the King James Version's rendering of Proverbs 23.7a, 'For as he thinketh in his heart, so is he.' I honoured self-identification as I sought out those who were recognized by all as serious Rastas who were dealing with the figure of Jesus. Since so much of the study fell into the hybrid area of theomusicology, many of those were musicians. Particularly (though in no special order), I want to highlight those whose insights had a profound effect on the book and the people who helped me reach them: Barbara Blake Hannah, Byron Antonio Beckford, Somala of Dominica, the Abuna Paulos, Patriarch of Ethiopia, Ras Siam and Ras Isha of Negril, Lloyd Knibbs, Majek Fashek, Oluwole Peku Ojitiku, and the Prisoners of Conscience, Lucinda Fleurant of Interscope, Neil Lifton, the staff at Loon Mountain Park, particularly Gloria Rainwater and Ron Seiko, Joseph Hill of Culture, Djate Richards and promoter Lisa Jones, Ras Michael Henry, Tracy Singleton and the Sons of Negus, Mykal Roze (Michael Rose), Junior Taylor, Toby Goldberg, Derrick 'Duckie' Simpson, Garth Dennis, Euvin 'Don Carlos' Spenser of Black Uhuru, Louie Rankin, Angela Lang of Mesa/Blue Moon, David 'Ziggy' Marley, Kathy Gillis of Virgin, Andrew Tosh, Samantha Glynne, Bunny Wailer, Bo Edwards, Donohue of Kingston, Ansel Cridland and the Meditations, Charlene at Free World Music, Clement 'Bankie Banx' Banks, Marvin Gilmore of the Western Front; Patrick 'Tony Rebel' Barrett, Pam Turbov, Winston 'Pipe' Matthews and the Wailing Souls, Imani Tafari-Ama, Pamela J. C. Hart, Julie Michailow, George Michailow and Rikki Betts of Fast Lane Productions, Dean Ellis at All Tone Records in Brixton, Ras Seymour McLean, Sister Maniah Mani, Stanley Byfield at World Vision for Christ Bookstore in Brixton, Bishop Joe Aldred of The Centre for Black–White Christian Partnership, Selly Oak Colleges, Billy Bennight of Frontline, Manley 'Big Youth' Buchanan, Mike Caccia, Frederick the Maytal 'Toots' Hibbert, Garrett Vandermolen, Heartbeat Records, Mortimer Planno, Ras Alan Martin of the U.N.I.A., Lindon 'Half Pint' Roberts, Russell Gerlach, Anthony 'Anthony B' Keith Blair, George Golding, The Original House of Blues and staff, Cambridge, MA, Billy Graham, Miss Stephanie Wills, Alvin 'Keith' Porter of the Itals, Victor Essiet and the Mandators, Roger Steffens, Andrew Tosh, Meirwyn Walters, Susse Chalet of Cambridge, Dr George Eaton Simpson, Tafari Products of Montego Bay, Cuthbert Gustave of St Lucia, Nicola Willams and the Boonoononos staff, Susan Cummings-Maroni, Tommy Cowan, Carlene Davis, the Rev Che Cowan, Dr Samuel Vassell.

Particularly, I would like to thank Judy Mowatt for sharing her astute insights and providing the taped interviews with Haile Selassie. Brother Marcel Goffe provided great insight and alerted me to the declaration of the Prophet Gad, which Dwight Smith retrieved from the Internet.

Dr Edward Osei-Bonsu in Ghana and Dr John Aboyeji and the Rev Femi

Adeyemi of Nigeria supplied some helpful insights and Andrea Madden some wonderful reggae from Mali.

In Jamaica the Rev Clinton Chisholm first helped me find my way around Kingston. He also located for me the copy of Leonard Howell's *The Promised Key* (which we published under separate cover in *Chanting Down Babylon: The Rastafari Reader* (Temple University Press, 1998)), *The Holy Piby*, and the *Plain Talk* articles, on which I draw in this volume. He is a never failing source of friendship and encouragement. His own analysis of Rastafari in his widely circulated cassettes is a model of scholarship.

On the home front I am grateful to my dear friend and colleague Kevin Aylmer, who helped me interview many of the groups, along with providing friendship and camaraderie. Scholar, friend, and filmmaker Jasmin Sung has been supportive since the beginning, loaning books, sending articles, and introducing me to her own superb film *Rasta Women: Daughters of Zion* (USA, 1986). Stu Berns, director of the American School of Music (Peabody, MA), advised me on musical matters and Benjamin Herman graciously supplied the journal articles on the examination of the Turin Shroud.

Again, the superb library staff of Gordon-Conwell Theological Seminary, under the skilful guidance of Dr Freeman Barton and Dr Meredith Kline, Jr, hunted down a wealth of material. Heidi Hudson and Marcella Charles gave typing and scanning assistance, Richard Jordan rescued several lost interviews with his computer wizardry, Dr William Mounce graciously translated my Macintosh chapters to IBM use with lightning skill, and the Rev Kukzin Lee carefully formatted the final draft onto MS Word.

My Gordon-Conwell Master of Divinity students in PR 261 'Theology and the Arts' contributed some fine responses to my lecture 'Liberation Theology and West Indian Music', as did both the students at Eastern College in the classes of Professor Nathan Corbitt and those of Jamaica Theological Seminary in the class of Tim Erdel. As well, our students over the years at the Caribbean Graduate School have contributed many rich perspectives and insights as have our colleagues on the faculty and staff.

Particular effort was made by Sarah C. Jones, former editor of *Network News*, who corrected the manuscript on disk. Key support for the project was provided by Academic Dean Dorothy F. Chappell and Provost Mark Sargent of Gordon College.

In order to find the select songs I analysed here, I reviewed thousands of reggae songs, quite a few of them introduced to me by the delightful staff and programming of WERS, Emerson College Radio (Boston).

Above all, I wish to thank my wife, Dr Aida Besançon Spencer, for the constant support and excellent advice and original insights she continually provides and for her astute primary editing of the present work, and my son, Steve, for great companionship running down music around the world. Particularly, I want to thank Naomi Starkey, former commissioning editor at SPCK and presently with the Bible Reading Fellowship in Oxford, who first championed this project, my very supportive final editors Alison Barr and Mary Matthews, along with Sheena Daley, George Taylor, Philip Hillyer and the delightful SPCK staff. I am also indebted to my friend, colleague, and co-editor of *Chanting Down Babylon*, Dr Nathaniel Samuel Murrell, who carefully critiqued the first three chapters of the manuscript and helped pare away the dross. My dear friend Dr Edwin Yamauchi also reviewed chapter one.

Other editors of my earliest versions included the astute Kenneth Arnold, Prema Cutrona, and the good Richard DeBacher. To the Otis Carl Edwards, Jr. xerox enterprises I dedicate the Further Reading, plus gratitude for duplicating to Cherry Gorton.

And, ultimately, I thank God for the inexpressibly gracious gift of Jesus the Christ, the true healer of the nations.

Introduction

On 2 November 1930, in the ancient city of Addis Ababa in the country of Ethiopia, a man named Tafari Makonnen was crowned emperor. That coronation sent a theological shockwave through a rising pan-African consciousness movement a world away in the Caribbean. Some Jamaican preachers proclaimed him earth's rightful ruler, the fulfilment of biblical prophecy, the presence of God on earth. Many reared in Christian denominations began to leave their churches and proclaim the former Ras (prince or field marshal) Tafari (creator) the expected Messiah. Interpreting his coronation as an historical sign of the dawning of the age of the Apocalypse, some even armed themselves for the battle of Armageddon. Soon they were clashing with police. Hundreds walled themselves into a former planter's mansion in the hills of Jamaica's St Catherine parish, soon adding cannabis sativa, called ganja, and long braided hair to their distinctive lifestyle. In the streets of Kingston's slums (called Trenchtown, Back o' Wall, the Dungle), their street preaching was fervent. At first they avoided drumming as pagan because of its wide use in syncretistic worship. But, as years went by, they began to proselytize others through the use of infectious, inverted pulse beat rhythms with exquisitely beautiful, globally popular melodies and often unforgettable biblically-based lyrics.

Through the centre of this apparently new religion, now dubbed Rastafari after the original title and first name of the Ethiopian emperor, ran the atavistic thread of a prior Christian theology. As the years went by, that thread, appearing again and again in Rasta reasoning, proved a strong bond linking the two faiths in inseparable, though at times acrimonious, embrace.

Today, over half a century later, Rastafari impacts the world. Russian, Israeli, Japanese, Scandinavian, Nicaraguan reggae bands pump out a 'Rasta' message that at times would be unrecognizable to the founders of the faith. In Africa Rastafari and Christianity are being wed into a hybrid 'Rastafarianity', exalting the emperor but rejecting his divinity. Jesus too has taken on a new significance, freed from his blond-haired, blue-eyed western captivity and wedded to African images of a black liberating Christ.

As the centre of Christianity continues to shift to the two thirds world, the ebb and flow effect rebounds back on western Christianity, already altering its self-understanding in a global perspective.

How will Christianity understand itself in the twenty-first century as the effect of its two thirds world incarnation continues to impact it? What will the figure of Christ become as new definitions replace older, increasingly obsolete western images? Further, what is the place of a movement like Rastafari within the history of Christian orthodoxy?

Through examining the shared figure of Jesus, this book assesses Rastafari's intriguing theologies, placing them within the context of Christian doctrinal history. In pursuing the theological figure of Jesus Christ from its transformation into the Black Christ on into its appropriation in the fascinating Christologies of Rastafari, we may be able to glimpse what the contribution of Rastafarian theologies of Jesus Christ might mean for the future of Christianity as a global religion and an ethical way of life.

Our sources to explore what some might term this 'folk theology' necessarily comprise oral materials (lyrics and interviews, called 'reasonings'), as well as written sources. Written statements of such popular theologies are not more valid than sung statements or spoken statements. Rather than an academic discipline, a popular theology is built on a religious experience of everyday, workaday people. Rather than arriving like Buddhism did, worked out by the scholarly Siddhartha Gautama, whose experiences followed a vigorous period of philosophical study and hands-on exploration of the ethical lifestyle potentiality of Hinduism, or Scientology in our own day, which is a new religion worked out by writer L. Ron Hubbard, a theology of the people does not begin with academically trained intellectuals. Rather, it begins with a believed encounter with the divine, a mixture of experience and reaction, thought, and subsequent action and reflection. All statements in any mode, as any theology, should be examined and evaluated to establish their validity.

Rastafari, as a largely oral popular theology, is a mutating body of thought and an ethical way of life being created out of the materials of Christianity, African heritage, diasporan black experience, among other sources.

This book is a sustained theological analysis of the central figure of Christianity, Jesus Christ, as he traverses Rastafari, and it evaluates the images and significances emerging. The results are historically located and assessed within the theological history of the source faith: Christianity. Particularly, the study seeks to set these results in a theological context within the history of theological thought.

Of course, in a new faith, people's views often mutate. While in a study like this, adherents' recorded responses become frozen in time, responders live on and change. Perhaps we should have borrowed a subtitle from William James and dubbed this: 'Varieties of Rasta Religious Experience in Views of Jesus'. But what the book does do is gather up from over twenty years of listening and interviewing, five decades of recorded Rasta music (beginning in the 1950s), and over sixty years of published material (commencing with Leonard Howell's *The Promised Key*) substantiated perspectives about Jesus that Rastas have held and do hold.

One insight which emerges from this study is that for outside observers to misunderstand what Rastas believe is extremely easy. Rastafari may look like a massive cultic monolith to the fearful outsider – all full of beards, dreadlocks, revolutionary rhetoric, worshipping a half-barbaric, long-dead

African potentate, whose main objective was to call all the children of former slaves back to Africa to safety while he destroyed the white races, or, better yet, marshalled them into an army to do it for H.I.M. (His Imperial Majesty), while trouncing on Whites' worn-out confession of a mythical Jesus – and all of this forged in a bizarre and dazing cloud of lethally potent ganja. Such a reductionist view is simply wrong. Within Rastafari is a multiplicity of faith stances that run a full gamut from a Nicaean Creedal, Garveyite, afrocentric orthodox Christianity to a new religion centred on the reluctant shoulders of Ethiopian Emperor Haile Selassie I, a highly educated, sophisticated, forward-thinking political statesman who led his country into the modern world. Some Rastas elevate his sizeable achievements to effecting the incarnation of God the Father or the reincarnation of Jesus Christ on earth. Some Rastas are exclusive, maintaining a hostility to Whites. Some Rastas have moved, as did Malcolm X toward the end of his life, to an inclusive openness to likeminded people of all races. Some Rastas themselves are white. Some Rastas wear beards, some long locks; some wear neither. Some embrace the use of ganja; some repudiate it fully. Some Rastas reject Jesus as a myth to subjugate people; others worship Jesus as Jah (God) among us. And this last point marks the terrain of our present study: to assess the place and significance of Jesus Christ in Rastafari.

To do so, we will begin by exploring the contextual background of the New World's Ethiopianism and 'Black Jesus' theology, the rise of Rastafari, the traditional Rasta definition of a Messiah constructed to oppose the white Jesus of the colonizers, the positing of Haile Selassie I of Ethiopia as that Messiah and the parallel attempts to assign a place to Jesus as returned in Selassie, a myth, a mere human, prophet, or an avatar. After examining pantheistic definitions, we will move on to examine a Rootsman or Roots Christianity, in its sub-Christian as well as its Nicaean formulations, that reasserts a view of Jesus that is not western, but is also eastern, both heterodox and orthodox. I contend that the image of Jesus Christ in Rastafari is a window into its theological progression: where it has been and why it began there; where it is now in its current state of rich flux; and where it may go and take its parent faith in the twenty-first century and perhaps beyond.

One final note to scholars who come to my study with the suspicion that attempting to systematize Rasta views on Jesus is an illegitimate enterprise since the decentralized nature of Rasta reasoning and the apparent resistance of the movement to requiring a confessional set of doctrines precludes just such an enterprise. One may well ask if any attempt to systematize religious experience from early Christianity to Soka Gakkai Buddhism is valid. Such is the central problem of all systematic theologians entering any faith arena. I understand systematic theology, however, as an integral part of a three-prong activity wherein experience becomes text to be explored through exegesis. The findings are ordered into a – hopefully – helpful system for inter-pretation. The principles thus derived are then applied to action. The final judgement of legitimacy does not really rest with us scholars, but with the people whose experiences and reflections on those experiences we are attempting to explain. If they find the results accurate and illuminating – then it is legitimate. With this view as my hermeneutic, I have kept my material before the Rastafari, submitting interviews and interpretations to those interviewed for correction before publication. At every turn Rastas have given me warm encouragement along with their constantly helpful correction. Barbara Blake Hannah affirmed the plethora of Christologies I was turning up with a hearty, 'Yes, of course, they're all different!', assuring me that the result would prove most helpful of all to Rastas to be able to see each others' views. Don Carlos encouraged me, 'The world needs those kind of teaching right now. I remind you.' Derrick 'Duckie' Simpson ordered, 'You must please write the book. You must write the book: Rasta and Christianity ... Just write the truth, man.' To the best of my ability, that is what I have tried to do.

1 The Black Jesus

RAS JESUS

JAH would never give the power to a baldhead.
Run come crucify the dread.
Time alone, oh! time will tell.
Think you're in heaven, but you living in hell

sang Jamaica's musical superstar, the Honourable Robert Nesta 'Bob' Marley, capturing the heart of the Rastafarian view in his anthem 'Time Will Tell'.[1]

God, known to the elect by the secret name 'Jah', would never give the divine spirit to a member of the white oppressor race, the 'baldhead' who lets a barber cut his hair and does not let it flow down in long, natural locks. The one who was crucified and who is worshipped across the world as saviour must have been a member of the oppressed black race who was sacrificed at a Calvary in Africa thousands of years ago. Eventually, history will prove that the oppressors' 'Christian' Church that claims it has the ticket to heaven is but the gateway to hell. This idea is at the core of traditional Rastafarian theology.

The vision of a dreadlocked black Jesus whose passion of suffering and work of salvation was played out in Africa is the culmination of a developing vision from the very roots of pre-Columbian culture. It persists through the attraction and repulsion of 400 years of colonial 'Christianity' into the conscious Christological contextualizing of great Caribbean Christians from slave missionary to Jamaica George Leile through the Jamaican national hero Marcus Mosiah Garvey. It continues into the current afrocentric attempt to recast contemporary Christianity into a faith appropriable by the 'have-not' descendants of slaves by positing Christianity as a faith begun in Africa. Jesus, 'the man for others', is being appropriated from the heirs of Jamaica's plantocratic aristocracy by the children of its slaves and hirelings. Today, through a strange song in a strange land, reggae music, the reclaimed image of Jesus in several variations is proclaimed around the world. As a substitution, it further seeks to change the image of the object of faith of the West's dominating cultures' own white children, singing now themselves of a black two thirds world Jesus within the pulsing rhythms of a compelling global music of protest.

To begin this journey we must choose an entrance. Rastafari is based on an afrocentric cosmology of history. The position explored by archaeologists and popularized by such books as Robert Ardrey's 1961 *African Genesis* was from the outset an essential tenet of Rastafarian belief. In its beginning in the early 1930s, Leonard Howell, one of its founders, proclaimed, 'Ethiopia is the crown head of this earth field since heaven has been built by His Majesty Ras Tafari, the Living God',[2] 'His Majesty King Alpha and Queen Omega being the keepers of the tree of life',[3] since 'long before this world was Ethiopia's glory has been running Cotrillions of centuries ago'.[4] But, 'Owing to the universal rend of our ancient and modern Kingdoms we are at this juncture of our history scattered over the Globe into little sectional groups'.[5] Such a position is still staunchly maintained over a half century later, as Ras John Moodie noted in 1992: 'It has been said, Africa is the birthplace of civilization. The Bible shows her to be the Garden of Eden'.[6]

What happened in this 'universal rend' has been explained in music by a premier talent of Rastafarian reggae, Michael Rose (Mykal Roze), in one of his most intriguing songs, 'The World Is Africa'.

The song identifies the entire 'world' as having originally been Africa but now being 'divided into continent states', Today, split from their original motherland, nations suffer hostile cities, ignorant violent people, and the murder of their black inhabitants.[7] As Michael Rose explained the concept of the song to me:

> You see, a lot of people is confused. They don't know God. They don't know who is Jah. You understand what I'm saying? So is like, because 80 million people has been lost, we the ones who are so far away from Africa and know the truth. You know, it's like we are relating it to the younger ones who are coming up. Because, like the elders, they don't want to hear it. They're lost. Did you know that Ethiopia was the first civilized city throughout the universe? ... Did you know that there wasn't any life throughout Europe and the West come back to America, Jamaica, everywhere? There was no civilization. In civilization in the unheard of time. Do you understand what I'm saying? It's like the whole world was Africa, right? Like my hands [puts his hands together, fingers spread out]. And of like earthquake and earth movements [splits his hands apart to show continents drifting apart from one another]. So, this is why we have like Germany over there and we have like America over here. [So, the whole world] Is Africa, because of earth movements. And it's because of the vibes of the people.

In the vision of Rastas like Michael Rose, the actual splitting of continents was due to human wickedness impacting nature:

> It's like the life. If you get up every day and you pray and pray, you get rainfall, you get crops, you get everything that's blessing. But, if you don't pray, the rain won't fall, you won't get good food, you won't get nothing. You see what I'm saying? So, because the vibes of the people is not right, it cause by nature earthquakes, earth movements, so people separate. So, it separation in terms of the people to settle. Because once they're together, they keep fighting. Once they're together they keep fighting: rule and divide, rule and divide. Who wants power? Power! Power! Everybody wants power! And there's only one power on the earth: Jah.

This concept of a primal Africa, torn apart by dissension and elemental disaster, naturally determines the colour of Jesus, because Jesus, coming from the land of the Bible, must have come from Africa: 'In the first place, Jesus is a black man. Out of all the nation comes. Out of the black comes all nations'. Did Whites come from Blacks? According to Michael Rose, 'Yes . . . out of the black race come all nations.' Rose's viewpoint is one held historically by many Rastas and is reflected in Rastafarian preaching, musical lyrics, books, poetry, artwork. This afrocentricism is part of the search of New World Blacks for their heritage, stolen since the days of slavery. The movement is called 'Ethiopianism' and it will be our point of departure into the territory of the Rasta view of Jesus. After examining the context of Ethiopianist views of Jesus, we will travel through its search for a black incarnation of God in Christ, as it looked for an image of Christ inclusive of Blacks and freed from the depicted white exclusivity of the Euro-Western Christ. At the chapter's conclusion we will assess the significance of the emerging image within the context of the Bible and of greater global Christianity.

ETHIOPIANISTIC CHRISTOLOGY

On Mount Montserrat in Catalunya in Spain is an image of the Madonna and child that dates from the end of the 1100s. Many explanations for its appearance have been proffered, the effect of humidity, a chemical reaction, oxidation of a former silver plate covering, or, perhaps, it was done intentionally, but the 'Moreneta', as it is affectionately called, is the statue of a black virgin bearing a black Jesus. It is among the earliest of many depictions of a Jesus who is depicted black extant in the world today.[8]

In 1700, a young Congolese woman named Beatrice (Beatrix) Kimpa Vita believed she had been inspired to shed light on the true colour of Jesus that such statues as the 'Moreneta' suggested. She declared that Christ, identifying with the oppressed Africans, had manifested as a black man in São Salvador, Congo and had chosen black apostles.[9]

In the Americas on 13 February 1829, a free man named Robert Alexander Young declared in his book *Ethiopian Manifesto*:

Ethiopians . . . submit with fortitude to your present state of suffering, relying in yourselves, from the justice of a God, that the time is at hand, when, with but the power of words and the divine will of our God, the vile shackles of slavery shall be broken asunder from you, and no man known who shall dare to own or proclaim you as his bondsman.[10]

For Young, history was poised for the entrance of a liberator. Who was this 'man we proclaim ordained of God, to call together the black people as a nation in themselves'? Young reported he was someone who appeared white but was descended from mixed parentage:

We say, in him will be seen, in appearance, a white man, although having been born of a black woman, his mother. The proof is strong, and in Grenada's Island, Grand Anta Estate, there, some time ago, did dwell his mother – his father then owner of the said estate. The church books of St. Georgestown, the capital of

Grenada, can truly prove his birth. As another instance wherein providence decreed he should appear peculiar in his make, the two middle toes on each of his feet were, in his conception, webbed and bearded. Now, after the custom of the ancient order of men, with long and flowing hair, by like appearances may he be known; none other man, but the one bearing the alike marks, and proving his identity from the island on which he was born, can be the man of whom we speak. To him, thou poor black Ethiopian or African slave, do thou, from henceforth, place a firm reliance thereon, as trusting in him to prove thy liberator from the infernal state of bondage, under which you have been so long and so unjustly laboring. To thee he pledges himself, in life to death, not to desert thee, his trust being in the power of the Almighty, who giveth not the race to the swift nor the battle to the strong, but decrees to all men the justice he establishes.[11]

Further, on September 28 of that same year David Walker made his *Appeal in Four Articles; Together with a Preamble, to the Coloured Citizens of the World*, reminding suffering slaves of the western hemisphere of their true identity as free Africans, true citizens of a homeland from which they had been cruelly kidnapped and transported to the Caribbean. The Rastafarian roots harmony group, the Meditations, still mourn that captivity in Winston Watson's 'Tin Sardine' in their noteworthy collection 'For The Good Of Man' (Heartbeat).[12] In this poignant song they lament that like animals, like fish caught in a net, like sardines in a tin, their African ancestors were kidnapped into New World captivity through the 'racial discrimination' and 'vulturistic' sins of the 'pirates, thieves and murderers' of the Nina, the Pinta, the Santa Maria, and the S.S *Jesus*. The lyrics cry over and over again, 'The S.S *Jesus*!' 'I can't believe it!' 'Slave traders' transportation.' 'The S.S *Jesus*!'

That the name of Jesus, the great spiritual liberator of humanity, should be shamelessly emblazoned on a ship comandeered to enslave is unfathomable. As the violent once bore away this liberator himself to death on the cross, now, hiding behind his name, violence against the innocent continues, for as the Meditations' 'churchical chant' 'Tin Sardine' points out so poignantly, for the first slaves, 'Jesus' was the name of a ship given by Queen Elizabeth I to John Hawkins to commence British participation in the slave trade.

What was needed was an exodus deliverance, as the Rastafarian Patrick Barrett, who performs his outstanding dancehall-style chants under the name 'Tony Rebel', articulated in a piece he wrote with Mikey Bennett, 'The Voice and the Pen', keying off the great spiritual 'Go Down Moses':

When Israel was in Egypt's land
Suffering, suffering, suffering
Oppressed so hard they could not stand
The more things change a the more they remain the same
Suffering, suffering, suffering
And God said, go down Moses
Way down in Egypt's land
We say pharaoh but you know them name . . .

'Cause I will be the voice, I will be the pen
I will be the Moses weh come back again
And if it cost me me wealth, cost me me fame
I will wear the next X behind my name

'Cause big speech mouth sweet big promises a make
And all now mi no see weh poor people a get
A pure blood and tears and whole heap of sweat
And that cause sufferation and a whole heap of death
How could you be sitting there, telling me that you care
Promise people good things and by the Bible you swear
Now is the time to make you speech
because the right time come.[13]

Looking for the 'right time' for a liberator, any liberator, to end enslavement pulsed at the heart of early Afro-American consciousness. For David Walker the end of suffering and slavery would be effected by none other than Jesus Christ, himself. Walker, Young and like-minded thinkers were engaged in forging a pan-African 'Ethiopian' identity for all the kidnapped Africans of the western diaspora. Each new thinker augmented the intense expectancy of imminent divine liberation that was already abroad. Who the liberator would be varied between the writers. But the dual answer represented by Walker and Young set in motion twin streams, as we shall see, that have flowed through Ethiopianistic theology into the mighty oceans of contemporary black theology.

David Walker declared:

Remember, also to lay humble at the feet of our Lord and Master Jesus Christ, with prayers and fastings. Let our enemies go on with their butcheries, and at once fill up their cup. Never make an attempt to gain our freedom or natural right, from under our cruel oppressors and murderers, until you see your way clear – when that hour arrives and you move, be not afraid or dismayed; for be you assured that Jesus Christ the King of heaven and of earth who is the God of justice and of armies, will surely go before you. And those enemies who have for hundreds of years stolen our rights, and kept us ignorant of Him and His divine worship, he will remove.[14]

For David Walker, Jesus would return, delivering and vindicating those humans who God 'pleased himself' to create 'darker than the white'.[15]

Similarly, Robert Alexander Young also envisioned a liberating messiah, a messiah his *Ethiopian Manifesto* was intended to herald. But his messiah, he explained, was not the returning Christ:

As came John the Baptist, of old, to spread abroad the forthcoming of his master, so alike are intended these our words, to denote to the black African or Ethiopian people, that God has prepared for them a leader, who awaits but for his season to proclaim to them his birthright.[16]

God was about to provide succor from a brown liberator who, bridging black slave and white overlord, was ordained to end oppression.

While Young's already arrived Grenadan messiah may not have achieved the physical liberation he prophesied, still Young's anticipation did provide some key elements that a hundred years later would produce a climate of welcome when Ethiopianism peaked, seeing a monarch rumoured to be descended from a Semitic father and a Sabean mother ascending to the throne of Ethiopia itself. All through the Americas Ethiopianism was creating hope – and tension.

For example, on Sunday afternoon, 20 June 1920, violence erupted in front of a restaurant at 209 East 35th Street in New York City when Grover Cleveland Redding, a 'prophet' of the 'Abyssinian Order' from Chicago, ended a parade he was leading by burning a United States flag. The 'Abyssinians' had been distributing a leaflet with the Ethiopian royal lion set between two flags. One of these was a flag of Israel. What the leaflet proclaimed, ten full years before the ascendancy of Haile Selassie, is provocative:

THE LION OF JUDAH
TREATY
BETWEEN THE
KING OF ETHIOPIA
AND THE
UNITED STATES
His Majesty Menelik II., King of Kings of Ethiopia
TO REGULATE
COMMERCIAL RELATIONS
BETWEEN THE TWO COUNTRIES
Signed at Addis-Ababa, December 27, 1903.
Ratification advised by the Senate, March 12, 1904.
Ratified by the President, March 17, 1904.
King of Ethiopia notified of Ratification, August 12, 1904.
Proclaimed, September 30, 1904.
BY THE PRESIDENT OF THE UNITED STATES
OF AMERICA

A PROCLAMATION

Whereas a treaty of commerce between the United States of America and His Majesty Menelik II., King of Kings of Ethiopia, was concluded on the twenty-seventh day of December, one thousand nine hundred and three, the original of which treaty, being in the Amharic and French languages, is word for word as follows:

The text of the trade treaty followed. When the Abyssinians burned a second flag, a gun battle ensued. Several protesting Whites were shot and killed. Captured, Redding was hanged.[17] But the conviction that the time had come to switch allegiance to a black Ethiopian monarch was burning. And that flame was fanned in the Caribbean by fiery preachers like the Rev James Morris Webb in his book, *A Black Man Will Be the Coming Universal King, Proven by Biblical History* and in his famous Liberty Hall speech in September 1924. Webb declared:

> The head of Great Britain will do as the Kaiser did and attempt to rule as universal king. Then the nations which were Great Britain's allies in the World War – Belgium, France and America – will join to crush Great Britain. The universal black king will then appear and dominate all. He will tear down all their claims . . . The world cannot realize this now. It will take time. When the prophetic part of the Bible is preached the world will realize that the universal black king is coming.[18]

Such a proclamation ignited a fervent expectancy of apocalyptic dimensions. In Jamaica, a number of figures, most notably Isaac Uriah Brown under the name 'Royal Prince Thomas Isaac Makarooroo of Ceylon' and Cyril Linton Mitchell, who took the title 'Prince Shrevington (or Shervington) Mitcheline', put forth their claims to be that expected black monarch. While these were largely ignored, the most successful, Prophet Bedward, as we shall see, did achieve a measure of acceptance.

'Ethiopianist' preachers' descriptions of the coming king were as varied as those who applied for the title. Young, for example, prophesied the black ruler would have a webbed and hairy foot, a reference, perhaps, to the Islamic legends surrounding Selassie I's traditionally claimed ancestor the Queen of Sheba as having the hairy legs and foot of a donkey.[19] The Koran may preserve a touch of this legend (or the legend may embellish the incident) in Sûra xxvii ('The Ant') 43–45, wherein Solomon tricks the Queen into raising her robe and uncovering her legs, by making her cross a glass floor she believes is water, though no more details are given. Further, though more remotely, the Grenadan liberator was to have long and flowing hair, a style later affected by Rastafarians. So messianic eschatological prophecy like that in Young's *Ethiopian Manifesto* provided an ideological and theological archetype for the eventual emergence of Rastafari. From all these apocalyptic speculations emerged two initial strains within developing Ethiopianism: to look for deliverance either to Walker's 'white' Jesus Christ or Young's more 'black' messiah. Eventually these strains began to fuse into one. People began to look to a black Christ as their Messiah. By 1898, the great Bishop Henry McNeal Turner of the African Methodist Episcopal Church was declaring that Jesus Christ was in actuality a 'Negro' messiah. He declared:

> We have as much right biblically and otherwise to believe that God is a Negro, as you buckra, or white, people have to believe that God is a fine looking, symmetrical and ornamented white man. For the bulk of you, and all the fool Negroes of the country, believe that God is whiteskinned, blue-eyed, straight-haired, projecting-nosed, compressed-lipped and finely-robed WHITE gentleman, sitting upon a throne somewhere in the heavens.

Bishop Turner's assertion came as part of a heated newspaper editorial debate between white and black controlled presses, fuelled by the heated response to the legalized segregation of *Plessy* vs. *Ferguson* (1896), strong anti-black sentiments in the United States, and lynchings by the Ku Klux Klan. But, as a trained theologian, he was careful to point out that depicting God was subjective to all races. He argued:

> Every race of people since time began who have attempted to describe their God by words, or by paintings, or by carvings, or by any other form or figure, have conveyed the idea that the God who made them and shaped their destinies was symbolized in themselves, and why should not the Negro believe that he resembles God as much so as other people? We do not believe that there is any hope for a race of people who do not believe that they look like God.[20]

That both he and the white press were engaged in projection, Bishop Turner was more than willing to admit. As he explained:

> Yet we are no stickler as to God's color, anyway, but if He has any we would prefer to believe that it is nearer symbolized in the blue sky above us and the blue water of the seas and oceans; but we certainly protest against God being a white man or against God being white *at all*; abstract as this theme must forever remain while we are in flesh.[21]

Referring to Genesis, he argued, 'Blackness is much older than whiteness, for black was here before white, if the Hebrew word, coshach, or chasack, has *any* meaning.'[22]

What Turner concluded had far reaching implications for Christian blacks: 'Whenever we reach the conclusion that God or even that Jesus Christ, while in the flesh, was a white man, we shall hang our gospel trumpet upon the willow and cease to preach.'[23]

By the turn of the century, Ethiopianism in the Caribbean islands had become an intense movement. A Jamaican, the Rev Fitz Balintine Pettersburgh, drew up *The Royal Parchment Scroll of Black Supremacy*, which he described as an Ethiopian 'Bible-Text' or rulebook for an 'Ethiopian Western Repository'.[24] The Anguillan Robert Athyli Rogers even produced a new Bible for black people, *The Holy Piby*, and a new church, the afrocentric Afro Athlican Constructive Church. Moreover, Rogers' outlook on the messianic question added a new element to the mix, looking to the Bible for another person to incarnate the divine presence besides Jesus. Jesus Christ is honoured in *The Holy Piby* as a messenger and 'Prince of the Kingdom of God' (Aggregation 1.7). Rogers writes:

> Q8. Do the Athlians believe in Jesus Christ.
> A. As a true servant sent by God to seek and to save the lost house of Israel. (Questions And Answers: Q8, A8).[25]

As a 'colleague' of 'Athlyi' (Rogers himself), Marcus Garvey, and others, Jesus joins them in coming 'to save' 'the down-trodden children of Ethiopia that they may raise to be a great power among the nations and in the glory of their God' (Questions And Answers: Q9, A9). But the actual incarnation of

God for Rogers was not Jesus (though God was his 'Father' and he is identified as 'his divine highness' (Aggregation 1.7; 3), but another biblical character:

1. And it came to pass that God entered the body of an unknown dead and the dead became alive, then did he walk about the earth in person.

2. He dwelt among men and wrought many miracles so that the kingdom of heaven might be verified.

3. He suffered persecution and privation as an example of what ministers of the gospel must suffer to maintain the kingdom of God among men.

4. And it came to pass that God gave his name Elijah, and he called upon the name of the Lord God even though he himself was God.

5. Now when the time had appeared for God to return, the supreme angel commanded the chariot of heaven to meet him.

6. And when the chariot appeared unto Elijah, he ascended and returned to his throne in heaven where he reigned from the beginning and shall unto the end, king of kings, and God of gods.

7. Had the men in the days of Elijah's visit on earth taken a right record of his administration, long before this day the inhabitants of this earth would have known him as God of all men.

8. For in Elijah do the heavenly host worship as God of the universe and in him do I, Athlyi, believe as the only God.

9. He is the Lord of righteousness and of love, an industrious God, jealous, brave, omnipotent, omnipresent, a king of sympathy and of justice, giver of power and salvation, upon this God, and him only, his Law and the Holy Ghost shall the Athlians build their church.

10. We shall endeavor to please and serve him, for he is our God. We shall worship him with all our hearts and with all our souls, for unto us there is none so good as the Lord, our God.

11. When the Lord God of Ethiopia is with us in the battle for that to which we are entitled, show me the foe so powerful to set us down? Verily I say unto you there is none. (Athlyi 2.1–11)

An angel named Douglas from this 'throne of Elijah, God of heaven and earth' (Facts of the Apostles 3.4) proceeds to establish a new order to deliver oppressed Blacks:

Q.12. What is the difference between God's holy law to the children of Israel and God's holy law to the children of Ethiopia?

A. There is much difference, the holy law to the Israelites was given to Moses, but God's holy law given to the children of Ethiopia was handed to Athlyi by a messenger of the Lord our God, notwithstanding in the law given to the Israelites there are ten commandments, but in the law given to the children of Ethiopia there are twelve.

Q.13. What Church is already established on God's holy law given to the children of Ethiopia?

A. The Afro Athlican Constructive Church.

Q.14. By what other name shall this church be known?

A. The House of Athlyi. (Questions And Answers: Q12 – A14)

Neither the fulfilment quotient of Shepherd Athlyi's prophetic powers nor his impact and influence upon the Divine Will proved particularly potent when he prophesied:

> The following morning after Athlyi's vision, Athlyi looked towards the rising sun and cried out saying, my God, my God, what shall happen to the apostles of the Twentieth Century? Father if it's me, even I that shall pass from the presence of men grant that the Piby live forever that the children of Ethiopia, through the teaching of the Afro Athlican Constructive Church, may obtain salvation forever. (Facts of the Apostles 4.1)

Today *The Holy Piby* has been relegated to obscurity along with its Afro Athlican Constructive Church. The law of Deuteronomy 18.22, that a prophet is authenticated only if his prophecy comes true, may have been levied on the Shepherd Athlyi, but one insight rang truly: Rogers' declaration that Marcus Garvey was 'God's foremost apostle' of Ethiopianism (Facts of the Apostles 1.4).

Jamaican national hero Marcus Garvey was indeed the greatest Ethiopianist preacher of all. By echoing the sentiment of Bishop Turner and avoiding the theological dead end into which Rogers had blundered with his zombie apotheosis theory, Marcus Garvey explained his pro-African image of God as black in this way:

> If the white man has the idea of a white God, let him worship his God as he desires. If the yellow man's God is of his race let him worship his God as he sees fit. We, as Negroes, have found a new ideal. Whilst our God has no color, yet it is human to see everything through one's own spectacles, and since the white people have seen their God through white spectacles, we have only now started out (late though it be) to see our God through our own spectacles. The God of Isaac and the God of Jacob let Him exist for the race that believes in the God of Isaac and the God of Jacob. We Negroes believe in the God of Ethiopia, the everlasting God – God the Father, God the Son and God the Holy Ghost, the One God of all ages. That is the God in whom we believe, but we shall worship Him through the spectacles of Ethiopia.[26]

Clearly, like Bishop Turner's before him, Marcus Garvey's definition of a black God was symbolic. It countermanded the co-opting of the image of God by Whites. Garvey based his theology on a biblical understanding of God as colourless spirit.

Nevertheless, in response to what the white races had done, he conversely depicted God in the image of black humans, the Creator reflecting the created. Garvey, of course, was completely conscious and open about what he was doing. God had no colour, he agreed. But, since one segment of humanity had made God reflect solely itself and therefore excluded others from God's image, African peoples were reappropriating God as black.

Claiming God, and thereby dignifying God's reflective black human images, was the *telos*, or end point, of Ethiopianism. It found one of its most potent expressions when Leonard Howell, a world travelling Jamaican with mystical interests that had put him afoul of Garvey's United Negro Improvement Association in New York, responded ideologically to the coronation of Haile Selassie I as emperor of Ethiopia. Returning to Jamaica, Howell, along with Joseph Hibbert, spurred a small group of preachers who began announcing that Haile Selassie I was the long expected universal king. Compiling his own book, *The Promised Key* (circa 1935), Howell proved an indefatigable champion of this new black messiah. By 1933 he had gained national attention, when the 16 December issue of Jamaica's largest newspaper, *The Daily Gleaner*, reported he had been on the streets of St Thomas parish selling postcard-size pictures of Haile Selassie as repatriation passes at a shilling each. A team from the University of the West Indies, later commissioned to study the movement by the Rastafarian eldership, learned he sold about 5,000 of these pictures.[27] Now that public attention had been drawn to him, Howell was not long in feeling its disapproval. On 5 January 1934 he was arrested at Port Morant and charged with fraud. Eventually, repeated persecution, disappointment, and his own sense of power altered Howell's message into preaching his own divinity. But in these early years his first declaration was a culmination of Caribbean Ethiopianistic theology, centring on Haile Selassie. Howell's message was focused and unequivocal:

The glory that was Solomon greater still reigns in Ethiopia

We can see all the Kings of earth surrendering their crowns to His Majesty Ras Tafari the King of Kings and Lord of Lords Earth's Rightful Ruler to reign for ever and ever.

Upon His Majesty Ras Tafari's head are many diadems and on His garment a name written King of Kings and Lord of Lords oh come let us adore him for he is King of Kings and Lord of Lords. The Conquering Lion of Judah, The Elect of God and the Light of the world.

His Majesty Ras Tafari is the head over all man for he is the Supreme God. His body is the fullness of him that filleth all in all. Now my dear people let this be our goal, forward to the King of Kings must be the cry of our social hope. Forward to the King of Kings to purify our social standards and our way of living, and rebuild and inspire our character. Forward to the King of Kings to learn the worth of manhood and womanhood. Forward to the King of Kings to learn His code of Law from the mount demanding obsolute Love, Purity, Honesty Truthfulness. Forward to the King of Kings to learn His Laws and social order, so that virtue will eventually gain the victory over our body and soul and that truth will drive away falsehood and fraud. Members of the King of Kings, arise for God's sake and put your armour on.

Dear inhabitants of this Western Hemisphere, the King of Kings warriors can never be defeated, the Pope of Rome and his agents shall not prevail against the King of Kings host warriors you all must stand up, stand up, for the King of Kings.

All ye warriors of the King of Kings lift high King Alpha's Royal Banner, from victory to victory King Alpha shall lead his army till every enemy is vanquished.[28]

Like Howell's prose, this specific application of Ethiopianism was incendiary and it ignited a fire that soon backdrafted on incumbent Christianity's object of worship: Christ himself. Assessing Mussolini's invasion of now sacred Ethiopia, Zion seat of God on earth, L. F. C. Mantle, writing in the 24 August 1935 issue of the popular journal *Plain Talk*, explained:

The Romans or Italians are the same people that had barbarously and brutally crucified our Saviour 2,000 years ago, and Mussolini is now haunted to give the Italian nation as a ransom for the sacred blood of Jesus For reference — Read Jer. 23:9. and you will see the inward impression of Mussolini. I am appealing to all Men and women of the Negro race to leave off idolatry and come now, and worship the true and living God of Israel. Be it understood that you are assisting the Romans to fight against yourselves even though we know that they cannot win. The Roman Catholic Church is a part of 'its' states and governments.[29]

Early Rastafarian street preaching went further, highlighting a relationship between Jesus and Selassie I. George Simpson, among the earliest sociologists to study the movement, recorded a series of Rasta street meetings by Joseph Hibbert's group in 1953. 'Do you see any resemblance between Jesus Christ and Ras Tafari?' asked one speaker provocatively. 'Haile Selassie is Jesus Christ reincarnated', spelled out another one. ' ... We are celebrating the coronation of Jesus Christ tonight, and for that we make no apology and no compromise. Mau Mau is a war between black men and white men. The white men throw bombs on the Mau Mau, but they can't hurt them because Haile Selassie controls the bombs. Mau Mau don't have guns; they use bows and arrows.' Then bringing the various religiopolitical dimensions of Ethiopianism together, the preacher concluded, 'The white man tells us to wait until Jesus comes, but we're not going to wait ... Our only hope is to go back to Africa. In the near future we are going back to our Homeland.'[30]

But before this programme of seeking black messiah figures centred on the emperor of Ethiopia, it had a crucial focusing. Ten years before the coronation of Haile Selassie, previously multi-focused Ethiopianist expectancy was gathered up in Jamaica and focused on one commanding and charismatic individual. And though this precursory Caribbean messiah failed, in effect, he prepared the people to expect the imminent return of a Christ figure.

JAH INCARNATE

Evening had fallen, 31 December 1920, in August Town, St Andrew, Jamaica. The followers of Prophet Alexander Bedward were disappointed. The prophet had gathered a sizeable following around him, healing, preaching and claiming that he would ascend to heaven in the manner of Jesus. The day passed. He did not. Eventually, the prophet was arrested for sedition and led away to an asylum. But the fervor the Bedwardites had imbibed went on bubbling just below the popular religion of the people, effervescing with the awakening pride of Ethiopianism and the free-floating expectancy that something momentous was about to occur, an expectancy lately focused on Prophet Bedward.

Soon the former Bedwardites were caught up by the fiery vision of Marcus Garvey for a United Commonwealth of Black Nations created out of West Africa,[31] and electrified by returning missionaries from Ethiopia, David and Annie M. Harvey, who arrived in Jamaica contending the diasporan sons and daughters of Ethiopia were really 'Israelites'. And they were soon intrigued when preachers like Robert Hinds, one of their number, two Masons, Joseph Hibbert and H. Archibald Dunkley, and the returning Leonard Howell converged on Jamaica in the early 1930s. The time seemed ripe for another appearance of a messiah, but the claims of Jamaican Prince Edward Emmanuel paled against those of an authentically Ethiopian monarch, the reputed 225th successor to the line of King Solomon of Israel, crowned with the titles 'Haile Selassie' (Might of the Holy Trinity), Elect of God, Lord of Lords, King of Kings, Conquering Lion of the Tribe of Judah.

The country bearing the biblical name of all Africa, Ethiopia, had declared this king the 'Power of God'. Could he be the Christ who was to return? wondered the Caribbean Ethiopianists.

Searching the Bible for proof that God could indeed be black and appear incarnate in Africa, Ethiopianist preachers came up with what they felt to be two significant discoveries. First, the King James Version seemed to have an unheralded name of God tucked into Psalm 68.4, 'Sing unto God, sing praises to his name: extol him that rideth upon the heavens by his name JAH, and rejoice before him.' They concluded, reasonably, 'JAH' must be the true name of God, and therefore a true follower would obey this Scripture and extol God by that name.

Untrained in Hebrew, the preachers had no idea they were looking at a partial transliteration of the Tetragrammaton, the first two radicals (consonants) in the common name for the Lord, normally translated 'the LORD'. The four letters JHWH, partially transliterated ('JH') in Psalm 68.4, were felt by rabbis to be too sacred to be pronounced in daily use. Therefore, when the Masoretes added vowel points to the text, they substituted the vowel points for the word for 'Lord' (*Adonai*) for whatever had been the original vowels. When an observant Jew reached the name of God, the reader simply sounded out the vowels and substituted *Adonai* for the name of God in the text. Even today, orthodox Jews follow this practice and the present writer, when learning Hebrew in company with several orthodox Jews, was taught to do the same, a practice he still follows out of respect for orthodox Judaism thirty years later.

After the rise of modern biblical criticism in the 1700s, scholars attempted to reconstruct the original vowels, guessing that 'a' and 'e', the most common vowels and ones able to be supported by the consonants, were the eliminated original vowels. The softer German pronunciation 'Yahweh', rather than 'Jahweh', came to be employed by scholarship. In popular religion an attempt to sound out the impossible combination of the vowel points for *Adonai* with the consonants of the Tetragrammaton had produced the nonsensical rendering 'Jehovah'. This occurred as far back as the 1600s in the formative years of the King James Version and that reading lent itself to such movements as the Jehovah's Witnesses in the late 1800s/early 1900s. We have noted two early founders of Rastafari, H. Archibald Dunkley and Joseph Nathaniel Hibbert, were members of the secret Egyptian Masonic order, the Great Ancient Brotherhood of Silence or Ancient Mystic Order of Ethiopia.[32] The Masons had consciously adopted the name Jah from Psalm 68.4 and built it into their composite name for God 'Juh-buh-lon'. As Mason Malcolm C. Duncan explained in his manual *Duncan's Masonic Ritual and Monitor*, the ritual of giving 'the Grand Omnific Royal Arch Word' is concluded by three Masons raising their right hands above their heads and giving in a 'low breath' the words 'Jah-buh-lon, Jehovah, God', the pronunciation of the syllables being divided between them. Duncan details in the following note an eastern origin for this composite name, an influence that we will see in a later chapter has carried over to a strong segment of Rastafarian Christology:

> This ineffable name (in INDIA) was Aum, which, in its triliteral form, was significant of the creative, preservative, and destroying power, that is, of Brahma, Vishnu, and Siva . . .
>
> JEHOVAH. Of the varieties of this sacred name in use among the different nations of the earth, three particularly merit the attention of Royal Arch Masons:
>
> 1. JAH. This name of God is found in the 68th Psalm, v. 4.
>
> 2. BAAL OR BEL. This word signifies a *lord, master, or possessor*, and hence it was applied by many of the nations of the East to denote the lord of all things, and the Master of the world.
>
> 3. ON. This was the name by which JEHOVAH was worshipped among the Egyptians.
>
> I have made these remarks on the three names of God in Chaldaic, Syriac and Egyptian, *Baal, Juh, and On*, in the expectation that my Royal Arch Companions will readily recognize them in a corrupted form.[33]

If the ultra-secret Egyptian Order of Masons followed a similar practice (as Jonathan Blanchard notes its parallel use in *The Scotch Rite Masonry Illustrated*),[34] the new Rastafarians Hibbert and Dunkley would have been already disposed to use the name 'Jah'. Further, Leonard Howell had claimed to have travelled in Africa. Some African Christians, such as the Jah Jehovah, Jah Jiri churches in Nigeria, for example, also use the name 'Jah' for God. In addition, Joseph Hibbert had been in Costa Rica directly before returning to Jamaica and beginning his preaching and Leonard Howell also claimed to have travelled in Panama, being what Jamaicans call a 'Colon' man, emigrating to work there. For centuries, the Spanish equivalent of the King James Bible, the version of Cadiodoro de Reina (1569), revised by Cipriano de Valera (1602) and again in 1862 and 1909, was the standard Bible in use in Latin American churches. In this translation the name 'Jah' for God was prominently displayed, not only in Psalm 68.4, but also in others. Psalm 150.6 reads, 'Todo lo que respira alabe a JAH. Aleluya' ('May all that breathes praise Jah. Praise Ya'); Psalm 147.1, 'Alabad a JAH' ('Praise Jah'); Psalm 122.4, 'Y allá subieron las tribus, las tribus de JAH' ('And to there go up the tribes, the tribes of Jah'). 'Jah' is also used in Psalms 118.5, 17, 18, 19; 115.17, 18; 102.18; 94.7, 12. Such practice would bolster the new views of the proclaimers of 'Jah'.

The second discovery these preachers made was that Jeremiah 8.21 seemed to declare that, just as so many Ethiopianistic preachers had proclaimed before them, God was indeed self-revealed as black: 'For the hurt of the daughter of my people am I hurt; I am black; astonishment hath taken hold of me'. Unaware of Hebrew, they did not know that the word *qadar*, translated 'black' here, means to be 'soiled' or 'dark' in the sense of wearing mourning dust heaped on one's head, to be 'gloomy', to 'mourn'. They exulted that, just as they had hoped, the Scriptures did reveal God as black.[35]

Then picking and choosing with an exegesis based on the hermeneutic that all that affirms blackness in the Bible is canonical, all that does not is interpolated, or added, the Rastafarians commenced their approach–avoidance relationship with the King James Version. The United Kingdom's world-renowned diasporan Rasta band Steel Pulse captures the ambivalence in its song 'Not King James Version'. Writer and composer David Hinds extols a 'version' that identifies the Garden of Eden as having been in Africa and the biblical characters Daniel, David, and Abraham as 'black and bold', which, he claims, is information the 'King James Version' hid from him in order to deceive him.[36] A similar sentiment can be found in Junior Delgado's 'King James', which states King James has kidnapped black people with the 'holy book' and calls for a 'black man version' to liberate them.[37] Perhaps the most extreme statement of disapproval I encountered was from British Rasta Maniah Mani, who, holding up a Bible, declared, 'And you know this book? It's like a pornography book!'

The 'Missionaries' Bible', Rastas felt, had been used to oppress Blacks. Yet, for them, the KJV contained within it the testimony of JAH. So Rastafarian hermeneutics set about to decipher the true tales of these black forerunners of the Bible whose stories had been, as one might say, bleached by Whites.

A Rastafarian sect calling itself the Twelve Tribes of Israel is built on this premise. A Twelve Tribes belief posits that the true Jews, whose history is

recounted in the Bible, were Africans and black and a diaspora (dispersion)
has left them in captivity in places like Jamaica. So, for example, Neville
Livingston, original member of the definitive Rastafarian musical group, the
Wailers, who performs under the name Bunny Wailer, lists Jeremiah, 'Iziah',
Moses, 'Elijha', Joshua as Rastas 'come from Zion' in his song, 'Rasta Man'.[38]

As the brilliant and articulate Rasta spokeswoman Barbara Blake Hannah
explained to me: 'Christ is a terrible stumbling block for black people. All
their lives they have been presented a white Jesus – a blond haired, blue-
eyed Jesus. The Leakeys have proved that man originated in Africa. Jesus was
an African.'

When I replied, 'I think God chose a race different from Whites and Blacks
to show Jesus as unique but also all inclusive. When I see a Jew, I don't see a
Caucasian. I see something different – a Semite. When you see one, you see
something different, so for both of us there is uniqueness but there is the
inclusive too', she responded: 'When you say "Jews" you don't mean those
people living in Israel right now? They aren't true Jews!'

For Rastafarians like Barbara Blake Hannah and Bunny Wailer, true Jews
are Nazarites of African descent who follow the Levitical law and the Hebrew
code of the Nazarite found in Numbers 6.1–8:

> And the LORD spake unto Moses, saying, Speak unto the children of Israel, and say
> unto them, When either man or woman shall separate themselves to vow a vow of
> a Nazarite, to separate themselves unto the LORD: He shall separate himself from
> wine and strong drink, and shall drink no vinegar of wine, or vinegar of strong
> drink, neither shall he drink any liquor of grapes, nor eat moist grapes, or dried. All
> the days of his separation shall he eat nothing that is made of the vine tree, from
> the kernels even to the husk. All the days of the vow of his separation there shall
> no razor come upon his head: until the days be fulfilled, in the which he separateth
> himself unto the LORD, he shall be holy, and shall let the locks of the hair of his
> head grow. All the days that he separateth himself unto the LORD, he shall come at
> no dead body. He shall not make himself unclean for his father, or for his mother,
> for his brother, or for his sister, when they die: because the consecration of his God
> is upon his head. All the days of his separation he is holy unto the LORD (KJV).

Devout Rastafarians have been serious about keeping these precepts. To cut
the locks from a locksman, as is sometimes done in prison, is to profane him.
The extent of that sacrilege, in Rasta perspective, not only interferes with
their vows to the Old Testament Nazarite rule, but interrupts as well their
imitation of Christ, who Rastas believe must himself have been a locksman.

I met Bunny Wailer for the first time in a Kingston car park and asked him
his opinion of Jesus. The legendary singer shot back, 'I've never seen a bald
head Jesus yet!', summarizing the first line of his own song that keys off the
old gospel stomper 'Old Time Religion'. The song explains this view: Jesus is
a Nazarite (called Nazarene in the song). That is why he is always depicted
with long hair. If one does not 'put away' the 'old [Testament] for the new',
but studies 'Numbers 6', one will understand that Christ and every 'opostle'

was a 'dreadlock bearded man'. Therefore, all true followers of Christ should eschew the barber shop and grow dreadlocks.[39]

Like Barbara Blake Hannah and Bunny Wailer, many Rastas with whom I spoke sincerely and fervently believe that Jesus was in reality a dreadlocks who in history (or 'black my-story') was crucified on a Golgotha in Africa centuries ago, before that sacred land split off and shifted to form part of the separate land mass we call 'Asia' today.

2 Significance of the Black Christ

THE BLACK JESUS AS INCLUSIVE

Within Christianity, a similar programme of positing Jesus as black has been in progress in black theological circles as well, spearheaded by such prominent and distinguished scholars as James Cone, Cain Hope Felder and Albert Cleage. The Reverend Cleage electrifies congregations by proclaiming, 'When I say Jesus was black, that Jesus was the black Messiah, I'm not saying "Wouldn't it be nice if Jesus was black?" or "Let's pretend that Jesus was black", or "It's necessary psychologically for us to believe that Jesus was black." I'm saying that Jesus WAS black.'[1] How does he establish that conclusion? He follows the same line of reasoning that Jamaican national hero Marcus Garvey did when he declared:

> Never admit that Jesus Christ was a white man, otherwise he could not be the Son of God and God to redeem all mankind. Jesus Christ had the blood of all races in his veins, and tracing the Jewish race back to Abraham and to Moses, from which Jesus sprang through the line of Jesse, you will find Negro blood everywhere, so Jesus had much of Negro blood in him.[2]

Since Jews, like Arabs, in Albert Cleage's view, are a national mixture of Chaldeans, Egyptians, Midianites, Ethiopians, Kushites, Babylonians and people of Central Africa, he concludes Jesus should be considered black, 'If God created man in his own image, then God must be some combination of this black, red, yellow and white.' Therefore, he argues, 'In America, one drop of black blood makes you black. So by American law, God is black.'[3] In Kelly Brown Douglas's perceptive *The Black Christ*, she puts black Christology into the context of black liberation. In her perspective:

> Fundamentally, a proper understanding of the Black Christ ought to refer to both Christ's physical appearance and to Christ's relationship to the Black freedom struggle. The Blackness of Christ then is not determined by images or actions alone. A defining assumption of this book is that to call Christ 'Black' suggests something about both Christ's appearance and actions.[4]

This too is the crux of the concern for Rastafarians. A 'black' Christ is one liberated from the blond-haired, blue-eyed captivity of slave master Christianity and returned to all oppressed people. The Jesus who preached good news to the poor and liberation to the captives is himself liberated from the golden shackles of corporate ecclesiasticism.

But Rastas go one step further than these Christian theologians in appropriating Jesus. For many Rastas the 'black' God is reflected in the 'black' Jesus who is reflected in the 'black' Haile Selassie. And this is a conclusion built from afrocentric premises, as Ansel Cridland, articulate spokesman for the respected Rastafarian group the Meditations, explained to me:

> The world began in its details in Africa. That's where the world began. All these people that you see, they are grandchildren that are scattered all over the earth. Seen? That's where the world began. Seen? And you know that Africa is the part for the black, seen? Black supreme. And the little knowledge them — I've just always seen, you know? I've just always seen that God is a black man, you know? It said a part of Ethiopia. That's where the world really started.

Yet, ironically, despite the sincere devotion Jamaicans have paid to him, Haile Selassie I returned unopened Marcus Garvey's invitation to attend a world leadership conference for black leaders. Garvey was enraged at what he considered an affront to all black people worldwide and retorted:

> There must be a real recognition of the Negro Abyssinian. He must not be ashamed to be a member of the Negro race. If he does, he will be left alone by all Negroes of the world, who feel proud of themselves. The new Negro doesn't give two pence about the line of Solomon. Solomon has been long dead. Solomon was a Jew. The Negro is no Jew. The Negro has a racial origin running from Sheba to the present, of which he is proud. He is proud of Sheba but he is not proud of Solomon.[5]

The pragmatic Garvey objected to claims of rising Rastafarian belief in this 1936 editorial in *The Black Man*. First, he sneered at the descent from the Semitic Davidic line claimed by Selassie I, a claim on which Rastas built their theology of Selassie I's divinity. Second, he attacked the idea that Blacks are Jews, the natural follow through of Rasta Afro-Israelism. Conservative Rastas to whom the present author has spoken part company with Marcus Garvey at this point, explaining that just as John the Baptist, near the end of his life, doubted Christ and sent his disciples for proof (Matthew 11.2–15; Luke 7.19–23), so did Marcus Garvey, who, though an honourable prophet, was still merely a man, near the end of his life doubt Selassie I who was divine. Of course, some Black Christian theologians take strong exception both to the Rasta position and that of Cleage. The historian Chancellor Williams in his provocative *The Destruction of Black Civilization: Great Issues of a Race from 4500 B.C. to 2000 A.D.* (1976) believes:

> That a 'little learning is a dangerous thing' is also indicated among the relatively few who preach about the Jews being a 'black people,' Joseph and Mary being 'black' and Jesus Christ — also 'black' etc ... A group of American Negroes recently went to Israel, claiming that they were the 'original' Jews, the 'Lost Tribe of Israel,' and that, therefore, the country belonged to them. Movements of this kind would not deserve even a sentence here if they were not indicative of the frustrations and confusion, and the frantic pulling in different directions which

further bind the race in chains difficult to break. They are mental chains as well as blinders.[6]

While black Christian intellectuals debate the proper approach to interpreting or interpolating blackness in history, among Rastas too a surprising variety of views of Jesus' colour exists. Such a plurality of views came out during a discussion I had with Derrick Simpson, Euvin 'Don Carlos' Spenser, and Garth Dennis, Michael Rose's former colleagues in Black Uhuru. Duckie Simpson began to tell about an alleged theophany, or appearance of God, he had read about in a magazine:

> You know what I saw the other day? And I was trying to tell some good friends of mine? The soldiers in Somalia – there was an article in one of those magazines saying that a soldier – there was a sandstorm – and a soldier happened to take a picture of the face of the image of Christ inna that sandstorm. The picture was so visible – you understand? Of the picture of Christ – a caucasian looking person. So I take the picture and look on it closely. You know, fe a sandstorm and thing and a picture and a face of a man. It's supposed to have a little body that the folks saw. The rest of the picture – the people, you know, some looking at the plane. Part of a plane come in and things. Some of them look upon the plane. Some of them look upon some soldier. Some are look at something like that going on. Everybody. It's supposed to be of so! You understand me? So have to change what them announce them see. All them countries, people can now read between the lines. Something like that happening in a sandstorm like that. You better run for cover or you supposed to look from both doors and that's good.

To this Don Carlos smiled assent, 'Yeah, you could find a mystery.' The mystery of Christ appearing perhaps white, perhaps black, or of having both black blood and white blood, makes many Rastas inclusive and their vision of Rastafari as open to all.

Don Carlos added, 'Every race bow to Rasta. You ain't gonna find a white guy in the (Black) Moslem. You ain't gonna find white guy in voodooism or other matter, but in Rasta you find everyone.' Would you indeed find a 'white guy' in Rasta? All three members of Black Uhuru were unanimous. 'Why not?' asked Derrick Simpson and Garth Dennis. 'Why, yes?' Don Carlos replied, 'Japanese, Philippines, nations, Chinese, one world! Rasta is for everyone. One world!' As Duckie Simpson encapsulates their vision, 'There's a dread, there's a Rasta in every race.'

The 12 Tribes' intellectual Marcel Goffe affirmed this growing Rastafarian inclusivity to me when he objected to even identifying Rastafari as an 'afrocentric' movement:

> You use the word 'afrocentric' ... For me, based on my studies of the Scripture, Christ is a Shemitic person, neither black nor white. Yes, that's what 'Shemitic' means ... When it comes to Rastafari, me, as a Rastafarian – I don't see things in black and white. I see things in black, white, and brown ... So, for me, I don't look on it as yourself as a new development for the 'afro' – you used that word,

right? ... The 12 Tribes of Israel is all over the world. There's branches of the 12 Tribes of Israel all over the world. So, we have long, long ago gone past skin color ... I see myself as an Israelite. I tell you that. Some of Abraham's seed. Is not Abraham's seed based upon the faith? You have those who are Israelites of faith differing from the ones who are genetically Israelites.

In such views these Rastas actualize Albert Cleage's anthropomorphic ideal for God: The One who is some combination of black, red, yellow and white. Or, in a transcendent sense, the One whose image is reflected in a combined multiplicity of people.

Such a perspective may be taking certain Rastas toward the position of anthropologists like Frank B. Livingstone, who applied the work of biologists to the human species to conclude that 'the concept of race' itself is outmoded. Observing that genetic characters cease to differentiate in 'composite or mixed' populations, so that 'as the number of characters increases it becomes more nearly impossible to determine what the "actual races really are" ', Livingstone decided, 'There are no races, there are only clines', adding that 'the theoretical analysis of clines has barely begun but there seems to be no need for the concept of race in this analysis'.[7]

Indeed, for many contemporary Rastas, as for the early Christians, neither the ethnological background nor the appearance of Jesus are of ultimate significance. Particularly, this is true for Rastas who function within the larger global community. Jesus as the one for all who by word and deed calls all to obedience to God and kindly actions towards humanity is what finally counts most. The dreadlocked Anguillan poet Clement 'Bankie' Banx put it well, when I asked him, 'Do you think that Jesus had dreadlocks?'

Oh, I don't think it's important, you know? ... I mean, the image of Jesus, the image of God is nothing to me. You don't need to put a face on God for me. If you begin to say that Jesus has dreadlocks, you begin to say he's not white. Is he black? Is he yellow? Is he Chinese? God is God. And I think that's not important. And I think God wants us to know that. That his race, creed, class had nothing to do with it. I would easily say that God was a dreadlocks just because of the times. Because it was way back and all that we see of Jesus he has long hair and he has a beard, so a nazarene is what we call it. And he's a man who lived in the wilderness, so naturally he would live like that way. He didn't have a comb. A guy who lived out in the wilderness forty days and forty nights. I think Jesus was just a guy who was really, really smart and felt God and he lived naturally. He had the things that God put up next to him, you know? And he, you know — I don't think the dreadlocks question is part of what it means. You know, you can be a Rastafarian without dreadlocks. It's not important.

Further, for some Jamaican Rastas the crucial issue is not even what name you worship in, that of Jesus or the new name of Selassie I, but what you do. Explaining an African symbol of Christ as a connector between the two faiths, Black Uhuru united the devout of each belief together on sincerity of thought and action not on externals like appearance. And they also drew the inverse point: cruelty destroys that unity. True belief in Jesus connects with true Christianity. As Don Carlos observed, 'They're the same thing. But only different name. Jesus is only in the ancient time.' But evil actions of enslavement and pillaging destroy that unity. Derrick Simpson explained, 'These guys went down to Africa. Did what they did. You know? Took away the Ark of the Covenant, stole the Black Christ, you know? Like Windsor Castle that got burned down the other day? A lot of stuff got lost in that fire. Yeah, what they stole from Africa.' What was the 'Black Christ'? Garth Dennis noted, 'There's a Black Christ that they used to take into war. Ethiopia. And they always took it into war with them: Like a madonna. A black one. The British, they have stolen a lot of things from us.' But right actions could unite Christians and Rastas in Black Uhuru's perspective, because, in Derrick Simpson's view, Eastern Orthodoxy has the claim of precedence. 'The orthodox was the oldest church in the world. Even before the Catholics. It was a formation.' Garth Dennis agreed, 'The first Christianity. All them thing a part of the documents.' So, in essence, Black Uhuru would see Christianity and Rastafari as basically the same thing. When I asked, 'Would I be a Rastaman, if I am a true Christian?' Don Carlos replied, 'If you fix your heart, yeah. If you have a God's heart.' When I observed, 'Of course, I can't grow the locks', Don Carlos replied, 'No, well, doesn't matter.'

This inclusive view of Jesus and of blackness for all 'kindly hearts' is one being developed in Caribbean pan-African theology according to Professor Donald M. Chinula in a footnote to his article 'Jamaican Exocentrism: Its implications for a Pan-African Theology of National Redemption'. Current Jamaican pan-African theology, according to Chinula, sees some people as black 'biologically', some 'politically', some 'symbolically':[8]

> 'Symbolical blackness' is used to describe blackness as a symbol of oppression. In this sense, the Israeli people of Pharaoh's Egypt were black. 'Political blackness' refers to how one chooses to identify politically. It answers the question: Out of all humankind, which grouping of people most closely share a sense of peoplehood or personhood with me?[9]

In his view 'redemption' means 'the restoration, in Jesus' name, of the majesty of the black Jamaican humanity disrupted and debased or never allowed full blossom by Euro-American racism which deprived it of those human freedoms promised by Jesus of the cross and resurrection.'[10]

Chinula's view articulates what for victims is the significance of a 'black' Jesus. He is a God who preaches release to the captives (Luke 4.18). How that release is achieved, of course, becomes the locus of debate: in what ways can the rule of Christ, which he informed Pilate did not come from this world (John 18.36), right this world in a manner commensurate with Christ's own actions?

Such thinking is the essence of what the black Christ meant for Marcus Garvey and for many black intellectuals and what it means for numerous Rastafarians.

And, as we shall see, it sheds some insight on what Jesus revealed about himself in one of his most searing sermons: that chilling prophecy recorded in Matthew 25. But it also raises the question, how legitimate is the enterprise which attempts to see God 'through one's own spectacles'?

GOD IN OUR IMAGE

When Winston Churchill's granddaughter, the sculptor Edwina Sandys, unveiled a four-foot bronze statue of Christ on the cross at a Maundy Thursday service of Manhattan's Episcopal Cathedral of St John the Divine, the church went into an uproar. Christ had become a woman. The 'Christa', Sandys explained, was created to show women that 'the church still has power and that people do care'. While some parishioners found it 'not at all blasphemous', seeing 'Christ as our mother', others fumed, 'It's disgraceful. God and Christ are male. They're playing with a symbol we've believed in for all our lives.'[11] Christian watchdog journal *The Wittenburg Door* quoted Cathedral Dean James Parks Morton as arguing the portrayal was legitimate since 'Christ has always been portrayed in a form comfortable for worshippers, like Black Christs in Africa, Oriental Christs in China, and chubby Christs in Italy.' *The Door* criticized Sandys and Morton, complaining that with such reasoning we should also have 'statues of Georgia Washington, Tammy Jefferson, Dwyla Eisenhower! ... The Door thinks there must be a better way to speak to the issues of women besides putting tah-tah's on everyone.'[12]

How legitimate is an activity like Edwina Sandys': to take historical persons who are objects of faith and alter their portrayal radically for the purpose of sending a message about the faith each represents? Should Jesus be portrayed as a woman, as sculptor Sandys has done, in order to send a positive message to women about their place in Christ's Church? Should Jesus be portrayed as black as the Rastafarians, as heirs of Ethiopianistic theology, are doing and as African iconography has done for centuries, giving black Christians a sense of claim on a church that was nurtured in its earliest years in Palestine and North Africa?

Should Jesus be portrayed as Oriental as the great Japanese Roman Catholic writer Shusaku Endo has done in *Silence* (1976), his heartrending masterpiece about the Nagasaki martyrs, or painter Luke Hasegawa in his painting of a madonna and child in their honour? Should Jesus be seen as Chinese as in the scenes from the life of Christ painted by such artists as Lukas Ch'en, Lin Ho Pei, Lu Hung-Nien or Japanese as by Yoshikazu Kimura? And what about the Korean Jesus as in the painting of Ki-Chang Kim, or Australian aborigine as by Malanggi, New Guinean by Hiskia or by Qokomâi, Filipino as by Galo Ocampo, Indian as by V. S. Masoji or Govindan Raman, Indonesian as by Wajan Turun or Bagong Kussudiardja, Burmese as by Aung Soe, Sri Lankan as by Tissa Ranasinghe, as a person of Bangladesh as depicted by Dilip Barai? Should Christ have been represented as Greek, Slavic, Russian, as Eastern Orthodox iconographers have done for centuries?[13] Or, for a different purpose, should Christ have been portrayed as an animal(!) as C. S. Lewis did, imaging Christ in the lion Aslan in his Narnian Chronicles or as Robert Siegel did, portraying Christ as a whale in his fantasy novel *Whalesong* (1981)?

To phrase the question differently, why has Jesus been literally portrayed as a blond-haired, blue-eyed male Caucasian for centuries? Why is this portrayal considered correct but all the others deemed incorrect? Was Jesus in fact blond-haired and blue-eyed?

The blond-haired, blue-eyed Christ

Despite the Rasta suspicion that we noted earlier that King James rewrote the Bible to disguise the blackness of its characters, the first attested historical depicting of a blond-haired, blue-eyed Jesus antedates Britain's conceited, nervous monarch by hundreds of years.

In the early 700s, at the height of the battle over whether the use of icons in worship was blasphemous or not, John, a Christian civil servant under the Moslem caliph of Damascus, quit his job and became a monk at St Sabas Monastery near Jerusalem. Throwing himself with zeal into the battle on the side of revering images, he researched and compiled a book called *The Fountain of Knowledge* and in it presented a description of Jesus.

Prior to John of Damascus, Jesus' likeness had appeared sporadically in various catacombs and other places in the style called 'fresco', painted water colours on wet plaster. In frescoes, and a few sculptures Jesus appears now with short hair, now with long hair, bearded and beardless, tall and lithe, short and stocky. Sometimes his features appear Semitic, other times they are designed like the classic Roman features of a pagan god. One of the most famous of these early representations was the statue of Jesus that the woman healed from chronic haemorrhaging (Mark 5.24–34) erected in her home town of Caesarea Philippi. Eusebius, the early church historian, travelled to Caesarea Philippi during the 300s, while researching his book *The History of the Church from Christ to Constantine*, and visited the woman's home to view the statue. His description is intriguing – a woman kneels before a standing man, whose hand is stretched out to the woman. Then Eusebius writes, 'This statue (*andrias*) the likeness (*eikōn*) of Jesus it was said to bear' (Eusebius 7:18). *Eikōn* literally means 'the image' or 'likeness' or 'appearance', a term often used, for example, for the description of the emperor's head on a Roman coin. As residents explained to Eusebius, and later to Augustine, the healed woman had the sculptor copy the exact features of Jesus. But though Eusebius and countless others saw it with their own eyes, none of these – no more than the gospel writers before them – ever bothered to tell posterity what those features were. This was more a Gentile concern. As Eusebius observed:

> It is not at all surprising that Gentiles who long ago received such benefits from our Saviour should have expressed their gratitude thus, for the features of His apostles Paul and Peter, and indeed of Christ Himself, have been preserved in coloured portraits which I have examined. How could it be otherwise, when the

ancients habitually followed their own Gentile custom of honouring them as saviours in this uninhibited way?[14]

For the writers of the Gospels and for their disciples, however, representing what Jesus looked like might have been considered blasphemous or was of little importance – who he was as God among us and what he did to liberate humanity from sin being what really mattered.

Instead, recording a description was left to the 700s when John of Damascus described Jesus as tall, handsome, round faced, pale olive in complexion with arched eyebrows that met in the middle of his forehead, beard and slightly curled hair the colour of 'ripe corn'. His bright eyes were sunken, his sweet sonorous voice full of love and wisdom. John of Damascus was reportedly following an earlier tradition that we have extant in a strange document from the twelfth century that is related to a letter claiming to be from one Publius Lentulus. Lentulus was purported to have been a contemporary of Jesus and, some posit, the predecessor of Pontius Pilate as the Roman proconsul of Judea. This letter was allegedly written in the first century CE at the time Jesus was ministering in and around Jerusalem. Its description is remarkable:

> A singularly virtuous man has arisen and is living amongst us; those who follow Him call Him the Son of God. He heals the sick and raises the dead.
>
> He is tall and attracts attention, His form inspires both love and fear. His fair hair is long, flowing down to the ears and from thence to the shoulders; it is slightly crisp and curled, parted in the middle and falling on either side as is the custom of the Nazarenes. His cheeks are somewhat rosy, the nose and mouth are well shaped, the beard is thick and the colour of a ripe hazel nut, like the hair; it is short and parted in the middle. His look reveals both wisdom and candour. His blue eyes, at times, flash with sudden fire. This man usually so gentle in conversation becomes terrible when he reprimands, but even at such times there seems to emanate from his person a safe serenity. No man has ever heard Him laugh but often men have seen Him weep. His voice is grave, reserved and modest. He is as handsome as a man can be. He is called Jesus, the son of Mary.[15]

Art historian Giovanni Meille suggests this tradition forms the basis for the 'Emerald Portrait' of Jesus, said to have been ordered by Tiberius Caesar, though that particular origin is dubious. While the portrait may very well be dependent on this description, that the austere old soldier Tiberius even noticed Jesus among the multitude of Jews and others executed during his lifetime, not to mention ordered Jesus' image on an emerald (!), seems extremely unlikely. However, that 200 years later Emperor Alexander Severus would commission an image of Jesus to be placed next to Abraham and Orpheus, when Jesus was being revered as a demigod by some pagans, seems truer to form. Greek magical papyri have been unearthed using such Christian terms as 'son', 'life', 'Iao' (for 'Iesu'?), even 'John' for talismans.[16] Also more likely would be the interest of King Abgar of Edessa, a contemporary of Jesus, in commissioning a portrait of Jesus, since the King claimed to be the recipient of a correspondence with Jesus concerning an illness he wished healed, a correspondence which Eusebius travelled to Edessa to record from the governmental archives. The Edessan government is reported to have inscribed Christ's letter on its city gates to ward off invasion.

Despite such fervent Gentile interest in the features of Jesus, neither Jesus' family nor the twelve disciples who knew him most intimately have left us a clearly attested description or depiction of Jesus of any shape, form or hue.

No graven image

Why were the earliest followers of Jesus so reluctant to tell posterity what Jesus looked like? The main reason that the earliest Christians preserved no universally attested portrait of Jesus is because they were Hebrews and strictly adhered to the second commandment, which ordered them not to make any graven images. The aforementioned Tiberius discovered Jewish loyalty to that divine imperative only too well when his procurator Pontius Pilate brought images into Jerusalem to an uproar of protest. Even many Gentiles who joined the primarily Jewish church reacted against their pagan backgrounds, often refusing to chip out images of Christ on the grounds their new doctrine was so spiritual.

When Gentile converts did finally make portraits of Jesus (legend even attributing one to Luke the beloved Gentile physician and Gospel writer), Tertullian, the second- to third-century North African lawyer and defender of the faith, grumbled they bore no resemblance at all to Jesus. In point of fact, there were as many early portraits of Jesus with jet black eyes and gaunt swarthy face, as those portraying him with a fair and ruddy image. The former artists were faithfully following such suffering servant passages as Isaiah 53.2–3, 'His was not an attractive figure and there was no splendor. And we looked and did not see a sight that delighted us. He was despised and forsaken by others, a man of suffering and one who knew pain.' The latter were attempting to capture the image of the God/human who glows with glorious, majestic grace in Psalm 45.2, and is extolled, 'You are extremely handsome among Adam's sons'. The interest for both schools was theological, to depict the divinity shining through the humanity. By the early 400s Augustine was complaining in his *Confessions*, 'The image of Christ according to the flesh has been created and modified by countless conceptions, all varying. His true likeness is unknown to us.'[17]

Even in the catacombs these two images of Jesus coexisted, bolstering the persecuted with different aspects of Christ. In the Catacomb of Domitilla, Rome, for example, a fourth-century youthful, curly-headed, light-haired Jesus with ruddy red cheeks and a host of what appears to be young disciples behind, backing him up, reaches out a hand of comfort to the refugees. This light-haired Jesus found its way into the fifth-century mosaics, where Jesus fluctuated between being blond and light-brown-haired, bleaching particularly in the Italian renaissance until the great Italian masters like Gentile da Fabriano in the fifteenth century finally made Jesus and his mother Mary close to being platinum blondes.

On the other hand, artist Thomas Heaphy, in the middle of the nineteenth century, copied and published in folio a very Semitic looking Jesus with Hebrew nose, black hair and black beard from a fresco on the ceiling of the catacombs of Saints Nereus and Achilles. Heaphy dated the likeness in the second century. One scholar, Vicar Cyril C. Dobson, arguing on the grounds of first-century burial customs, which had an image placed over a grave, championed its dating in the first century and published a popular book claiming this fresco bore the exact face of Christ. Other scholars have not endorsed his earlier dating.[18]

But oddly enough, the light-haired Jesus of the Emerald Portrait and the dark-haired Jesus of the catacombs of Saints Nereus and Achilles bear a striking resemblance to each other when one compares them. Both depict a thin, pointed face and long Semitic nose. As for colouring, most of the catacomb depictions, according to classicist Catherine Clark Kroeger, show a brown-haired Jesus, neither blond nor black. By the late 400s, early 500s when Theodoric the Great, ruling Italy under the name of Patricius Romanus, commissioned twenty-two mosaics at Ravenna, these showed a black-eyed Jesus with light brown hair, somewhat of an historical compromise.

Decidedly black or African-appearing depictions of Jesus, however, as plentiful as they are in Africa today, have not been unearthed from the earliest years. The first instances of dark-skinned biblical figures do not appear until after the 300s when Coptic Christianity spread across Northern Africa to evangelize what today is Ethiopia, Eritrea, Djibouti, Somalia and the upper Sudan. Churches in Nubia, however, regularly featured paintings of darker church leaders, but lighter depictions of Jesus, Mary and Joseph.

Therefore, just as for white Europeans, who, as we have seen, apparently created legends for a white blond-haired, blue-eyed Jesus, so too what archaeology fails to discover, Rasta cosmology supplies. Speculation in Ethiopianism of a black Adam and Eve begetting the black biblical figures, as we have seen, was consciously developed in Marcus Garvey's philosophy. Then out of Garveyism flowed two streams: Rastafari and the Black Muslim movement. Both of these posited a black Israel. Like the Moslem creed, 'We believe in the truth of the Bible, but we believe that it has been tampered with and must be reinterpreted so that mankind will not be snared by the falsehoods that have been added to it',[19] so do Rastas posit a primordial African Israel whose tale is hidden in the Bible. That African Israel bears a direct relation, in Rasta theology, to all black people.

CHRIST IN THE LEAST OF HIS BRETHREN

Could Jesus have had dreadlocks? Can we know for certain what Jesus really looked like? Like Rastas, Christians have longed to look into the face of Jesus.

In the 1980s, Church of England artist Curtis Hooper stunned the world, when, using the Shroud of Turin as a model of what a crucified first-century Jew looked like, he painted a portrait of a dark-haired, angular, swarthy, oliveskinned, Semitic Christ from a life-sized clay model. Hooper had constructed the model during seven years of research, working from enhanced photographs and computer images of the minute details of the facial remains of the corpse. Studying racial anthropology in Israel, with special attention to the Bedouin, who some scientists believe resemble most closely the Jews of Jesus' day, he reconstructed the hair, skin and features in consultation with pathologists, plastic surgeons, morticians, as well as the scientists assigned to the Shroud.

For centuries people had been revering this fourteen-foot piece of linen, which is kept in the cathedral of St John the Baptist in Turin. Such reverence was especially enhanced in 1898 when a photograph by Secondo Pia etched out from the shadows a crucified man whom medical examiners observed had been whipped on both sides by a Roman *flagra*, the pellet-tipped whip in use in the first century, and nailed through the wrists in Roman custom. When the legs were observed to be unbroken in an omission of Roman custom, and a wound in the side was observed, many of the faithful concluded it was Christ's image, but just as many doubted.

Puzzled themselves, church authorities permitted the Shroud to be subjected to carbon-14 dating. From the moment the Shroud had been introduced by a knight named Geoffrey de Charney in Liray, France, at the opening of a new church in the 1350s, church authorities had been sceptical. The Bishop of Troyes immediately branded the Shroud a fake produced by a local artist, but the laity disagreed. In 1978, using every nondestructive test available, the Shroud of Turin Research Project concluded, with the exception of one member, Walter McCrone of McCrone Associates in Chicago, that the Shroud could be authentic. Finding particles of a vermilion developed in the middle ages, McCrone agreed with the Bishop of Troyes. As the controversy remained alive, in 1987 church officials allowed the new tandem accelerator mass spectrometry (TAMS) dating method to be employed, as it needed for analysis only a minute part of the Shroud. This time the scientists at the three selected laboratories – Oxford University in England, the University of Arizona in the United States, and the Technical University of Zurich – concluded the Shroud was a medieval forgery produced circa 1260–1390 CE.

But, still some scientists disagreed. The journal *Analytical Chemistry* reports that most of the investigators took exception to Walter McCrone's conclusion that the Shroud's image was a 'painting', agreeing 'that it looks just like a photographic negative – produced centuries before photography was invented'.[20] Most intriguing of the dissidents is Thomas Phillips of the

High Energy Physics Laboratory at Harvard University who argues that the inexplicable photographic quality of the image came about when the body encased in the Shroud suddenly resurrected, scorching the image into the cloth. It also radiated light and/or heat, generating a burst of neutrons. Under such conditions, neutrons captured by carbon-13 nuclei would convert them to carbon-14, generating such a high proportion of the radioactive isotope that it would distort the dating findings.[21] The dating team disagreed, but could not itself explain the effect.

But of saviour or sinner, hoax or resurrection proof, this image of a crucified sufferer forced artist Hooper into a study of racial anthropology which uncovered a pan-scientifically pieced-together profile of a first-century Jew. The resulting depiction, though starting from the disputed Shroud, used these outside scientific data to yield a portrait whose image still confirmed what many of those earlier catacomb depictions had shown, a long-haired, bearded sufferer with a Semitic nose and deep set eyes with large pupils: the portrait of a first-century persecuted Jew.

Such findings should come as no surprise to anyone. Whether blond-, brown- or black-haired, blue-, brown- or black-eyed, Jesus of Nazareth was what the Bible claims he was: a first-century Semitic Jew. He looked like a first-century Semitic Jew and speculations on the exact detail of his physical appearance are limited by the parameters of what first-century Semitic Jews looked like. But in one of his most enigmatic and apocalyptic sermons Jesus said this about himself:

> But when the Child of Humanity comes in his glory and all the angels with him, then he will sit upon his glorious throne. And all the nations will be assembled before him, and he will set them apart from one another, just as the shepherd sets apart the sheep from the goats. And he will place the sheep out at his right, but the goats out at his left. Then the Ruler will say to those at his right, 'Come, those blessed of my Parent, share in inheritance the governance made ready for you from the time the world was prepared. For, I hungered and you gave to me to eat; thirsted and you gave me a drink; I was a stranger and you welcomed me; naked and you clothed me; sick and you cared for me; I was in prison and you visited me.'
>
> Then the righteous will answer him, 'Lord, when did we see you hungry and provided you with food, or thirsty and we gave you drink? And when did we see you a stranger and we welcomed you, or naked and we gave clothes? And when did we see you sick or in prison and we came to you?'
>
> And, answering, the Ruler will say to them, 'Truly, I say to you, inasmuch as you did it for one of these insignificant members of my family, you did it for me.'
>
> Then he will say also to those out on his left, 'Get away from me, you damned, into the eternal fire prepared for the evil one and his messengers. For, I hungered and you did not give me to eat, thirsted and you did not give me drink. I was a stranger and you did not welcome me, naked and you did not provide clothes for me, sick and in prison and you did not take care of me.'

Then they will also answer, 'Lord, when did we see you hungry or thirsty or a
stranger or naked or sick or in prison and we did not provide for you?'
Then he will answer them, 'Truly, I say to you, inasmuch as you did not do it
for one of these least significant, neither did you do it to me'. (Matthew 25.31–45)

Jesus was a first-century Semitic Jew, but the Christ can be found in the eyes
of his oppressed brothers and sisters: the starving, the foreigner, the
dispossessed, the ill, the inmate for the sake of righteousness, the victimized.
The Christ is in the faces of those who suffer.

Marcus Garvey understood that fact, so he encouraged his followers to
make pictures of a black Christ, black angels, black prophets, a black
madonna, modelled on the faces of those they saw suffering. For Garvey,
Jesus was a human for all humans, in whose veins ran the blood of all
humans. But, at the same time, Garvey was reacting to the white exclusionist
depiction of Jesus as a human for some humans only.

This is also the point of the intentionally depicted black Christs of the
Ethiopian Orthodox Church (which are so appealing to Rastafarians), both in
Ethiopia and Jamaica. These are constructed for educational purposes. As the
first priest appointed to Jamaica, Archbishop Yesehaq, the Abuna, explains:

> Many efforts have been made toward the religious education of the black child;
> however, the black child has little to grasp from the traditional Western schools, as
> these curricula originated after the pattern of Western perceptions. For instance,
> the traditional picture that is painted of Christ is through Western eyes. Thus a
> black child would find it difficult, if not impossible, to identify himself with such an
> image, thereby causing Christianity to become irrelevant. For this reason it is
> desirable to project Christ's image as black to the African child. It is appropriate
> that each nation projects God according to its particular color, which is most
> relevant to the life of the individual. The ancient Ethiopian (African) Christian
> church with a great educational tradition will be of help in the education especially
> of the Afro-Caribbean and Afro-American child.[22]

But what the abuna, Henry McNeal Turner, Marcus Garvey and other
thinkers regarded as the concretizing of an abstract idea, the Rastafarians
sank as a new concrete cornerstone back into history as its foundation and
then piled current beliefs upon it as historical fact.

For neither of the two streams that flow from Ethiopianism and Marcus
Garvey did this speculation remain simply speculative. The year 1930 proved
to be a watershed for both the Nation of Islam and Rastafari.

For the Black Muslims, Elijah Muhammad writes, 'We believe that Allah
(God) appeared in the Person of Master W. Fard Muhammad, July, 1930; the
long-awaited "Messiah" of the Christians and the "Mahdi" of the Muslims.'[23]

For the Rastas too, the appearance of a black Christ figure, returned to
earth to set up his millennial reign, did not remain as a mere speculation or
an inference from a word in Psalm 68.4 or a phrase in Jeremiah 8.21 in the
King James Bible. When on Sunday, 2 November 1930, a living and breathing
Ethiopian monarch was crowned emperor with the messianic titles 'Might of

the Holy Trinity', 'Lord of Lords', 'King of Kings', 'Elect of God', 'Scion of David', 'Conquering Lion of the Tribe of Judah', some disappointed followers of Bedward and Garvey rejoiced that prophecy seemed to be fulfilled before their very eyes. And taking on that emperor's former names, they declared themselves the 'Ras Tafarians'.

3 Selassie I as Jesus Returned

THE SECOND COMING OF CHRIST?

On 21 April 1966 an aircraft landed at Kingston's international airport. The emperor had come. On tour of the Americas, the former Ras Tafari Makonnen, now Haile Selassie I, had accepted an invitation to visit Trinidad and Tobago. On learning of this, a number of Jamaican organizations intercepted the entourage and begged the emperor to include a four day visit to Jamaica. The reception was tumultuous. Some 100,000 people are estimated to have crammed the airport, straining to get a glimpse of the plane. A half hour passed and the airport was so thronged with people the emperor could not disembark. Finally, a delegation, including the prominent Rastafarian Mortimer (Mortimo, Martimo) 'Kumi' Planno, worked its way up the ramp, met the emperor, then demanded the crowd clear a path for him to descend. To those who met him, the visit was unforgettable.

Ras Michael Henry was one of those faithful:

> When he went up to Villa Royal, when he came through, we were all standing in line. Yes, in 1966 at Villa Royal I met him when he came down and, you know, bowed and said, 'Ababajoni,' which means, 'Father Majesty.' And when I looked up he just looked at us, you know, and looked at me and was smiling. Yes.

What was Ras Michael's impression of Haile Selassie I?

> Well, it was as this woman who spoke about His Majesty. When she met him, she said she felt as if she were in the presence of Christ. So, that's how I felt. Yes, and you know, he smiled and all so dignified in all his approaches, you know what I mean? So humble, yet so great.

Many Rastas had 'Just a Passing Glance (of Rastafari's face)', as Don Carlos sings, but it seemed to them 'a passing touch of freedom'.[1] Only the merest glimpse of the emperor's face amid the pressing throngs, only the briefest shake of his hand for a favoured few in that whirlwind visit, but the impression was indelible.

One future Rasta moved by the event was Michael Rose (Mykal Roze). A dozen years later he captured the excitement of that visit and its lasting impact in one of his most famous lyrics to a song co-written with Black Uhuru colleague Derrick Simpson: 'I Love King Selassie'. In this major piece that appears on numerous Black Uhuru and Michael Rose studio and live recordings, the emperor is presented as human (a 'man in flesh') into whose eyes one cannot 'look'. Having the attributes of Christ ('divine', a 'lamb'), he is yet a land-based 'monarch'. The song warns against seeking God's 'spirit' by prayer, since the 'spirit' is in each person's flesh, but observes enigmatically that some people attempt to 'work Jah to the bone'.[2]

I asked Michael Rose, 'What exactly does that mean: "You can't work Jah to the bone"?' He replied, 'Most people feel like Jah – he is in the form of a man, but he is not equal to man. That means you can't get rid of him, so you can't work him to the bone.' While the spirit of God is elusive (an 'elusion') for Michael Rose, the flesh and blood reality of Selassie I is not. In him God is seen as walking again among God's people. The Christ has returned, but with a new role now. To him, Jesus and Haile Selassie are related because they are in 'the same line'. Are they the same person? He assents, 'Well, if it's the same line, it's the same person. Can you understand what I'm saying? If it's the same line that comes down to the throne.' Further, he does not see Haile Selassie as merely a descendant: 'No, it's the same person.' Such a contemporary Rasta perspective continues the position of respected elders like the aforementioned Mortimer Planno, the man who cleared the way for the emperor to disembark, travelled to Africa with the official delegation to explore the possibility of repatriation, exerted key influence in Bob Marley's decision to convert to Rastafari, and served as spiritual guide in the Wailers' early career. After a speech at the University of the West Indies on 'Bob Marley, Christ, and Rastafari', he summarized his Christological position by assuring me that to him Jesus and Selassie I are indeed 'the same person'. What, then, distinguishes Jesus Christ and Selassie I? Rastas like Michael Rose see their roles as being different: 'So, it's like Jah come this time as "The Conquering Lion". And the Lion is to devour and the Lamb is to slaughter.'

What are the implications of this statement? For Rastas like Ras Siam and Ras Isha (Elijah), elders of the Rastafarian community in Negril, this means that the functions of Jesus and Haile Selassie will now be different. As Siam explained:

> You see, Jěsus was on earth, him use a small morsel of food and feed multitudes. He raising the dead from the grave. Yet, them still crucify him, So, listen, he was no more Lamb to the slaughter, you understand? When His Majesty come in his kingly character this time, he never come to raise dead from the grave no more. No, he didn't come to do that. Different formation. Yes, he doesn't raise no more dead.

Jesus and Selassie I have different roles. Do all Rastas view them as still the 'same person'? No, as we shall see. Why not? In a provocative and controversial article 'Hindu Influences on Rastafarianism', two scholars at the University of the West Indies, Mona (Jamaica), Ajai and Laxmi Mansingh, suggest an intriguing reason. Publishing their findings in a 1985 *Caribbean Quarterly* monograph on Rastafari, they distinguish two views of Jesus present among the founders that have been preserved in current Rasta theologizing on Jesus. Leonard Howell and early Rastas with a 'deeper knowledge' of Hinduism view Haile Selassie as a manifestation of God (similar to the Lord Rama, the first manifestation of Vishnu as human) rather than a reincarnation of Jesus. According to the Mansinghs, 'This concept refuses to share Haile Selassie's "divine soul" with any one, least with the Europeans' Christ.'[3] On the other hand, those like Joseph Hibbert, who are more Bible-based, see Selassie 'as a re-incarnation of Jesus Christ'. These Rastas posit a 'divine soul' that can be incarnated in any number of avatars (incarnations of Vishnu). Proof of their position comes from their personal interviews with Joseph Hibbert himself in 1982 and their observations of the Eastern leanings of Leonard Howell (e.g., his adoption of an 'eastern sounding' title (and persona) at his Pinnacle Hill commune and as a pseudonym for *The Promised Key*).

While many of the current Rastas with whom I spoke are not as defined in their distinctions, mixing together these positions, others have a clear christological preference, some along the lines of the Mansinghs' insight, some, as we shall see, with views outside the schema.

But for nearly all Rastas, a 'new name' in the new dispensation that indicates a God who uses divine power to take the side of the oppressed is what is most exhilarating. As Ras Michael Henry chants in the anthem 'New Name':

> A new name Jah got and it terrible among them. Heathen no
> like Jah name . . .
> For when I call him 'Rastafari' watch the wicked tremble.
> Heathen no like Jah name . . .
> For it's a new name, precious name, new name – Jah
> Rastafari![4]

While Ras Michael himself is very respectful to the old name, as we shall see in the next section, preferring to use 'Jesus' and 'Rastafari' interchangeably in his songs, others are less impressed.

Selassie the Lion and Jesus the Lamb

Why are some Rastas less impressed with Jesus Christ than with Haile Selassie? For these Rastas Jesus is not so much an example of a conqueror, but of the conquered: life's quintessential victim. Junior Murvin put this viewpoint well in his song 'Judas and Jesus' when he cited Jesus' being sold by Judas for thirty pieces of silver as his distinguishing mark. The song warns that, as Peter denied Jesus, a friend may 'plot against' one or even 'eliminate' one, so one needs to 'keep an eye' on one's friends.[5]

While many of these may even believe Jesus was sacrificed to atone for human sin, remaining a mere sacrificial lamb seems of little contemporary value. For these heirs of the oppressed, Jesus is more to be pitied than to be relied upon for succour. Therefore, one current trend, particularly in white Judeo-Christian theology, to present an immanent God who suffers along with people, leaves these Rastafarians cold. A process theology approach, like Rabbi Kushner's, seeing God as wanting to help, but limited, is eschewed by Rastas who prefer a deity who is 'Over-All', who calls all to repentance. A conquering lion can tear the whip of oppression out of the hand of the descendant of the slave driver. A sacrificial lamb merely exposes another back.

Michael Rose points out that the crucifixion meant humanity rejected Jesus:

> It's like in the time of Jesus when Jesus used to walk earth. It's like he was 'The Lamb to Slaughter.' So, they nail him to a cross. And it's the same people who claims that they need the leader. They need someone to pray to. And they nail him! Do you know what I'm saying? To a cross! So, what kind of people are these people? Do you know what I'm saying? Yeah, and they're the same ones who nail him to the cross. So, you know, it's like sometime I think, you know, what is it these people are after?[6]

So in his view, Christ makes a new manifestation, a new incarnation, this time not in meekness but in power:

> His Imperial Majesty Emperor Haile Selassie I is Jah, King of Kings and Lords of Lords. It's in the Bible. We didn't make up these things. It's naturally. Follow me? Okay, 'King of Kings and Lords of Lords' is a title. It's in the Bible. And it's a tribe. Like the root of David. Yes, so it's history. So, it's not like we Jamaicans made it up. And he is the one who comes as 'The Conquering Lion' and not 'The Lamb to Slaughter.'

So now in his perspective the same 'person' plays a dual role in history, first coming to die for sins and redeem humanity, then to rule the earth. All the praise due to 'Earth's Rightful Ruler' is thus bestowed by Rastas on Haile Selassie.

As Millard Faristzaddi summarizes the emperor's wealth of titles in the first volume of the *Itations of Jamaica and I Rastafari*:

> JAH, Faada, Son, and Spirit ... the Mighty Redeemer, JAH, Bright and Morning Star, I an I, Father Almighty, Most High, JAHOVAH, RASTAFARI, HIS IMPERIAL MAJESTY EMPEROR HAILE SELASSIE I, Negus of Ethiopia, Might of the Hola Trinity, Shiloh of Judah, Beginning without End, King of Kings, Lord of Lords, Prince of Peace, King Alpha ... Melchizedek, Iesus, Adonai, King of Salem, Hola One of Israel, Conquering Lion of the Tribe of Judah, Repairer of the Breach, Root of David, Elect of Himself and Light of this World, 225th King of the 3,000 year Royal Solomonic Dynasty, Ascendant of King Solomon and Queen Makeda of Sheba, Protector of all Human Faith and Ruler of the Universe.[7]

How can such lavish praise be heaped upon any living male? In this schema, since Selassie I is seen as 'Iesus', he is considered to have earned the right to be praised by previously offering himself as a sacrifice to be slaughtered for humanity's sins. Since, in this 'new dispensation', he is also seen as the Father 'Jahovah', he deserves all praise from what he has created. All the 'Might' of the Holy Trinity has been focused in him, for this is the translation of his title 'Haile Selassie': Might of the Holy Trinity.

Perhaps no contemporary Rastafarian, holding this perspective, has explored such a relationship more thoroughly in the lyrics he chooses to sing than the great burra drummer Ras Michael Henry, whose concerts at colleges, museums, and universities encapsulate an historical sweep of Rastafarian music. In song after song Ras Michael connects Jesus Christ and Haile Selassie. One of his favourite techniques is to alternate the two names. In Al 'Ras Judah Selassie' Walker's 'Kings of Kings', for example, he sings about 'a man', identified as 'God Almighty', who rules 'creation'. This man is from 'Mount Zion', but also from 'Ethiopia'. After listing H.I.M.'s coronation titles, the lyrics extol 'Haile, Hail-He! Rastafari, His Majesty'. Then, travelling backwards chronologically from 'Revelation to Genesis', they switch to proclaiming 'Jesus Christ, His Majesty', alluding to Jesus' words in Matthew 6.33, about seeking 'His Kingdom' first.[8]

In this way, the problem of Jesus' suffering unto death is solved by Jesus' return in Selassie I. Therefore, he sings in Al 'Ras Judah Selassie' Walker's 'I and I Praise Rastafari' that talk about Jesus' death, resurrection, and ascension is 'a lie', for 'the Lamb that was slain' is 'the Conquering Lion' ruling 'this world'. Therefore, in order to praise Jesus, 'I and I praise Rastafari.'[9]

Therefore, Ras Michael can place the following greeting on an insert in his 1988 *Zion Train* album:

> Greetings in the name of I n I Divine Light and Savior Jesus Christ who has now revealed H.I.M.self unto I n I in His Kingly Character and no other than His Imperial Majesty, Jah, Rasta Far I. Emperor Haile Selassie I. Almighty God! Whom is, was and forever shall be the wonderful counselor.[10]

For Ras Michael, the proof that Jesus Christ has risen again exists in his return as the living emperor Haile Selassie I. Since Christ is the one who first created the world, therefore, upon his return in Selassie I, he is naturally earth's rightful ruler. Ras Michael draws the theological parallel in his rephrasing of John 1.1 / Genesis 1.1 in his song 'He Is Risen':

> In the beginning was the word
> and the word was Jah and the word is God
> In the beginning God created the heaven and the earth
> and the earth was without void or form
> thick darkness was upon the face of the deep
> and the spirit and the word of the Lord moved upon the water
> and Jah divided the waters above from the waters beneath
> and Jah said let there be light and there was light
> he has risen
> Christ has risen
> Jah has risen
> He has risen from the dead![11]

The way Ras Michael has resolved the distinction between Jesus and Selassie I is to posit that Jesus, revealed as the Son of Jah, demonstrates for us perfect sonship. Haile Selassie comes as a king and perfectly represents the kingly quality of Jah. So, both aspects of the triune Godhead are represented by the same person from the same line of David.

As Ras Michael himself puts it, 'I would say, Jesus is the name of which all ChrIstians – ChrIstians people – be redeemed through and is represented through the biblical roots of His Imperial Majesty Haile Selassie.'

When asked if Jesus and Jah would be different or the same person, he is quick to answer, 'You see, no, God is ever one. Three in one.' Since Jesus and Selassie I share the same spirit, Jesus is the Son 'at that moment of time'. But asking if Haile Selassie was ever the Son at a moment of time is the wrong question. For Ras Michael, 'He came in the Fatherly manifestation.' So both a distinction and a unity exist in Ras Michael's Christology. Trying to draw out any distinction, I asked him, 'So, 2,000 years ago, Jesus comes down and says, "I'm the Son," and points back to the Father. Just as in 1930 the Father comes in Haile Selassie – is that what you're saying?' Ras Michael replied, 'Right, all right, the Father and the Son is one. So, His Majesty came through the biblical roots and show himself unto us as the Root of David, the Conquering Lion, so all we saw him as the Father.' Does he represent the Father, or is he actually Jah himself? To Ras Michael, 'The Father and the Son is one.'

Therefore, Ras Michael consciously depicts that 'oneness' in his reworking of an old favourite gospel adaptation of Count Ossie and his predecessors, 'Marriage in Canaan':

> There was a Marriage in Canaan
> Jesus and his mother was there . . .
> At the marriage in Canaan
> King Negus and his mother was there.[12]

Alternating the title 'King Negus', the Ethiopian word for 'king' or 'ruler', with 'King Jesus' and 'King Rasta', Ras Michael weaves an identity between Jesus and Selassie I into the mind of the hearer, as he interchanges the phrases through the end of the piece.

Such a practice is followed regularly in Rastafarian reggae and can be seen everywhere. For example, Christ and Haile Selassie are so closely identified by the mystical Rasta Ijahman Levi that he weds the two names together in his hymn 'Jesus Selassie I Keepeth My Soul'.[13] In 'Give I Grace' Israel Vibration tells us that, though Yesus Christ was crucified, he is revealed as King Tafari now, the conquering Lion.[14]

Another common practice is to take the words of or about Jesus and apply them to Haile Selassie. So, Peter Tosh adapts John 1.1 in the beginning of his song 'Creation', telling us that the Word that existed in the beginning was 'Jah'.[15] Bunny Wailer in 'Blackheart Man' echoes the old Shepherd / Allen hymn when he asks if 'Jah' should bear the cross alone, Babylon having no place for this new wine, or the cornerstones that the builders refused.[16] The Itals adapt John 3.16 in 'Rastafari Chariot', telling us 'Jah' sent 'I and I' his son.[17] Who is 'Jah'? The enigmatic Junior Byles in 'Jordan' tells us Jah, the 'Field Marshall of the Universe', is the one who lights the world, before whom sun, moon, stars bow down.[18] Jah is even made to declare, 'I A Field Marshall', in Peter Broggs' song of that name.[19] Therefore, Broggs follows with the chant, 'Ethiopia, We're Coming Home'. 'Field Marshall' is one translation of the title 'Ras' that Makonnen Tafari earned before he was crowned emperor. In 'Every Knee Shall Bow', Johnny Clarke transfers the apocalyptic promises of Isaiah 45.23, Romans 14.11 and Philippians 2.10–11 to Jah.[20]

That David 'Ziggy' Marley intentionally ascribes Jesus' words to Jah / Selassie I becomes clear when he interpreted his song 'Pains of Life' to me. I had asked him, 'In "Pains of Life" you quote Jesus' words (in Matthew 18.3, Mark 10.15, Luke 18.17) ... The way you put it is, "Jah said if you ain't like a child you can't enter Zion".[21] I was wondering, are you suggesting there that Jesus is Jah, since they're Jesus' words, but you say Jah said this?' Ziggy Marley replied, 'Yeah. Jah and Yesus, yeah.' Does this mean he believes Jesus and Jah were the same? He agreed. Does he also believe that Jah and Haile Selassie were the same? He does, seeing a basis for his belief in the New Testament:

> Well, in Revelations it tell you that the Father will come, you know? And he'll be crowned 'King of Kings and Lords of Lords.' So, Haile Selassie is the only man who has been crowned 'Kings of Kings and Lords of Lords' in the whole world. So, if you believe in the Bible, then you have to believe. You can't believe in some things and disbelieve others. You believe in the Bible, you have to believe that the Kings of Kings and Lords of Lords – you know? So, that's what I believe.

For him Jesus and Selassie are distinguished in their flesh, not in their spirit: 'Same spirit, but not physical in the same dress'.

Again, in a similar view to Ras Michael's, Ziggy Marley sees the same spirit returning in Selassie I that was in Jesus Christ, but this time in a Fatherly aspect. His view will be explored more fully further on in our examination.

The significance of this position is far-reaching and apocalyptic. If God has indeed come to dwell among people, then the age of the Apocalypse is at hand. What these Rastafarians are positing is that the prophecy envisioned by John the Apostle in Revelation 21.2–3 has come with the advent of Haile Selassie. In that vision, John, exiled by the hostile Roman emperor Domitian to the rocky, volcanic hills of the island of Patmos *c*. CE 95, saw a new city of Jerusalem descend from the sky to the earth. With it he heard a voice cry out, 'Observe! the tabernacle of God [will be] with people, and [God] will dwell with them; and they will be his people, and God himself will be with them (their God)' (Revelation 21.3). If Haile Selassie is God come to earth to dwell with people, then Ethiopia is that prophesied 'new Jerusalem', where in the presence of Haile Selassie John's prophecies in Revelation of the immanent reign of God are being daily fulfilled.

Further, when the apostle John sought an analogy to describe the advent of Jesus in the prologue to his Gospel in John 1.14, he was inspired with the image of a tent. Jesus came and pitched the tent of his body among people, just as God had ordered a tabernacle or meeting tent to travel among the wandering Israelites, a dwelling where God could come and meet with them. The advent of Haile Selassie to Ethiopia is interpreted by Rastas as God again pitching a bodily 'tent' among people. But this time God seeks to fulfil the promises in Revelation. With the advent of Selassie I, God has re-established a new Zion in Africa, where God will dwell forever with the faithful on this earth.[22] Therefore, a new dispensation has dawned and the relationship between Jesus and Selassie I is understood in light of this changing of the age. As Christianity superseded or fulfilled Judaism, so, Rastas argue, does Rastafari supersede or fulfil Christianity. 'You have to understand Jesus in the old dispensation', Rasta journalist Barbara Blake Hannah told me, 'in order to understand Haile Selassie in the new.' What in essence these Rastas propose is a new covenant, a third testament, one now for the Blacks. This is what many Rastas believe the Bible has been prophesying. It is the core of traditional Rasta teaching and, if the current was reggae, it provided the power source for Bob Marley's electrifying message.

'Could you explain to people exactly what it means being a Rastafarian?' Neville Willoughby asked Bob Marley in 1973. Bob Marley replied:

> I would say to the people, man, be still and know that His Imperial Majesty Emperor Haile Selassie I of Ethiopia is the Almighty. For the Bible says so. Babylon newspaper says so. And I and I, the children, say so. You know? So, I don't see what, what kind a need more reveal? Our people want more of God for reveal to them? What them want? Them want a white God? Well, God come black.[23]

In the new dispensation, God comes black. But what did this new black God think himself? Did he unequivocally accept his own divinity? Or even his own blackness?

DID HAILE SELASSIE CONSIDER HIMSELF BLACK AND DIVINE?

When Haile Selassie I returned unopened Marcus Garvey's invitation to attend his international conference of black leaders, Garvey was understandably annoyed. The great freedom fighter interpreted the emperor's action as motivated by shame for being black and he took Selassie I to task for idolizing Whites, placing Italians rather than Ethiopians in many powerful positions in his government and for turning to 'white' nations for help during Mussolini's invasion of Ethiopia. Astutely, Garvey included in his attack Haile Selassie's Semitic claims, urging, 'We hope the Emperor will forget that he is from Solomon and realize that the world looks upon him as a Negro, and it was because he was a Negro why they treated him as they did.'[24]

Garvey's interest here was two-fold. First, he was no unequivocal admirer of Jewish people. And, second, he wished to make an example of the need for black solidarity out of the Ethiopian situation. Garvey's anti-Semitism is evident in such articles from *The Blackman* as 'The Jews in Palestine' (July / August, 1936) and 'The Jews' (1937). In these, Garvey went to the extent of blaming the Jews for their own persecution. In Garvey's skewed perception, Jewish persecution 'has been brought on by themselves, in that their particular method of living is inconsistent with the broader human principles that go to make all people homogeneous', What mode of life did he consider wrong? 'The Jews like money. They have always been after money. They want nothing else but money, and this disposition of theirs has caused resentment everywhere, because they have made money.'[25] While Garvey praised the solidarity of the Jews in other parts of these two articles, this anti-Semitic strain clashed against Ethiopia's historic stance of pride in its claimed Jewish heritage. From the Beta-Israel (as they call themselves) or 'Falasha' (or 'exiles', as others term them), the mysterious black Jews of Ethiopia, frozen in the Torah by being cut off from rabbinic tradition by the rise of Islam, to the heavy Judaic spirit in the Ethiopian Orthodox Church, Ethiopia has looked to Israel for the spiritual roots of its cultural identity.

When Marcus Garvey was castigating Selassie for emphasizing these roots over his 'Negro' heritage, Garvey was assuming that the emperor agreed he was a 'Negro head of state'. But Selassie was himself a scholar and keenly aware of the lively intellectual discussion of the Bible going on in the first half of the twentieth century. In light of the discussions, he may have been ambivalent about how much he actually considered himself a black person.

Selassie may have found proclaiming to his mixed population that he was the heir of a Semitic Solomon and a Hamitic Sheba politically expedient to ensure the loyalty of all elements of his so-termed one third Semitic, two thirds Hamitic people. But such a scholar as Selassie, who had himself presided over the translation of the Bible into Amharic, could not have been unaware of the debate over the origins of Sheba. While some scholars claimed her as a black queen, descended from the line of Ham (Genesis 10.7), progenitor of nations considered by tradition to be black,[26] other scholars place Sheba in the line of Seth (Genesis 10.28) and, therefore, another Semite like Solomon.[27] The Bible itself makes no comment on her colour and neither do many of the legends. While folklore considered her empire to be the Nubian empire, represented by the Ethiopian eunuch of Acts 6, many historians have considered it rather to be a Yemenite kingdom on the far end of the Yemen peninsula, just across the Red Sea strait from Ethiopia.[28] Those Yemenite Semites crossed the Red Sea and founded the Axum empire, precursor to present day Ethiopia.

The key to understanding Selassie's racial consciousness is to ascertain within which line he placed the Queen of Sheba, the famous ancestor claimed for him. If he believed she descended from Ham, then Marcus Garvey was right, Selassie I was in flight from one half of his heritage. But if he privately chose the second interpretation, then he simply returned Garvey's invitation unopened because he considered it did not apply to him. He was not, in his own regard, a black monarch.[29]

Theologian Robert Hood in his excellent study *Must God Remain Greek?: Afro Cultures and God-talk* notes, 'Ironically, when Selassie fled to London to escape Italian occupation of Ethiopia, he let it be known that he wished no contact with "Negroes".'[30] Not really ironic, of course, if Selassie, who had non-negroid features, considered himself fully Semitic and not 'negro'. Then, perhaps, he was attempting, in his own mind, to avoid what he considered a constant misunderstanding. Not seeing himself as black, he may have felt he had no real answer for Garvey and his followers.

In the same way Haile Selassie I appears to have resisted Marcus Garvey's assumption that he was a black monarch, so did he gently resist the Rasta assumption that he was divine. In fact, that the emperor arrived in Jamaica not considering himself God is abundantly clear in his speeches. On 19 September 1938, lamenting the death of Blatengeta Heruye Wolde Selassie, an Ethiopian intellectual who died abroad, the emperor mourned, 'Now, however, it has become your fate to obey the order of the great and merciful Lord, a lot that befalls each and everyone of us in our turn.' Recognizing his own mortal limitations as common with all humanity's, he did not say 'everyone of you' but 'everyone of us' and continued by distinguishing his own activity from that of 'God the Almighty': 'Dear Heruye! As God the Almighty has permitted Us to lay to rest your bones, while your spirit joins with those of your forefathers, We bid you goodbye in this hospitable land (the United Kingdom) to which we came as guests.'[31] Selassie I could bury, but could not make alive. This fact was so obvious to all observers that it resulted in the theory about the limitation of his miraculous abilities espoused earlier by Ras Siam.

Other Rastas, however, have not been able to conceive of a non-miraculous incarnation of God or Christ. Consequently, legends of miraculous feats by Selassie I abound in Rasta circles. Michael Rose related some of these to me:

> When His Imperial Majesty used to go to school in England he cut an apple in 32 pieces – he threw it up and cut it in 32 pieces – King George cut an apple in four first and Selassie cut the apple in 32 pieces and he went home back to the palace and tell them that, 'I met God today.' ... And when he used to go to school, Selassie used to walk and King George used to pass in his Rolls Royce. And like he used to stop to give him a ride. And he'd say, 'No, I'm fine.' And when he gets there, he's there before him in school.

In addition, he noted, 'And he was the only one who speaks over so many languages. That no one, no one ever spoke on earth ever speak so many.'

Ras Michael also told me of a story he had heard of a marvellous gift given by evangelist Billy Graham to honour Haile Selassie:

> When Billy Graham came and him said, well, he was looking for a righteous king. And him say, well, him look out over the whole universe. The only king him see that him could go to is His Imperial Majesty, and him give him this big book which four men had to carry – I don't know if you read about this? Four men had to carry, one on each end of the book, one here, one there, one here, one there. And His Majesty was the only one that opened that book. It's written, you know.

The Billy Graham Evangelistic Association, graciously responding to the inquiry Ras Michael asked me to make about this account, 'found nothing which would support what Ras Michael Henry has indicated to you':

> To be more specific, Mr. Graham did not make the comment listed in point number one, that Haile Selassie is 'the only righteous King.' Number two, Mr. Graham has not given a book which only four men could carry to Mr. Selassie.[32]

The legends are marvellous, but the facts about Haile Selassie are much more human and in that sense impressive, for, in fact, his true achievement as emperor was in overcoming by ceaseless human effort the continual blows of international, national and personal adversity thrust upon him.

One staggering buffet came in the death of his son Prince Makonnen, Duke of Harar, a death he was unable to prevent. Moved by the weeping of students as he followed his son's casket at the funeral, Haile Selassie's brief remarks three days after his son's interment on 18 May 1957 were poignantly personal, filled with reflections and personal anecdotes. His inability to save his son by any extraordinary power became evident when he said:

> We had hoped that we might precede him, but unexpectedly this tragic loss has deprived us of him. Even if we comply fully with God's commands and take care of his wife and children, can this to us be a substitute for Makonnen? However, Makonnen cannot be to us more than the whole Ethiopian people who are our sons and daughters.
>
> Mortality is man's inevitable course. We must patiently accept God's resolution in giving us Makonnen the one whom He gave us to be the ornament of our life and recalling him.
>
> Today is the third day since we have laid him to rest, and we must go to him since he cannot come to us ... let us return to our duties.[33]

Haile Selassie wept at the graveside of his son as Jesus is recorded to have wept at that of Lazarus, but he could not raise Makonnen back into life in the model of Jesus raising Lazarus, as recorded in John 11.

A similar loss was experienced when Empress Menen, whom the Rastas call Queen Omega, died. Selassie issued a similar expression of helpless, though devout, submission to 'the Almighty'. Speaking at his queen's death on 15 February 1962, Haile Selassie said:

> She was devoutly religious and did not lose her faith even in the time of hardship. During the memorable days of Our companionship We never had differences that needed the intervention of others. As Sarah was to Abraham, so was she obedient to me. Our wishes were mutual until we were separated by the Almighty ... We are thankful to the Almighty for having vouchsafed to us that long and uninterrupted union which is not very common in the world today: There could be no more profound prayer for me to utter.
>
> In spite of Our utmost efforts to save her life in her time of illness, she was overtaken by the fate of Adam and passed away.

We cannot fly in the face of the Almighty ... May these tears We shed be accepted by God as price for peace in Ethiopia and in the world.[34]

This is not the voice of God, or a god, or one who thinks he is God. This is the voice of a loving husband, a concerned ruler, a human doing his 'utmost efforts', suffering but heroically carrying on because duty to others is of greater concern to him than his own grief. This is the voice of a great man, a man pleading with his Creator to accept his tears as sufficient suffering and give comfort to the world. But this man asking God to accept his tears clearly does not consider himself God.

Throughout his speeches, Selassie presents himself as humbly obedient to the 'Almighty', counting himself among the 'followers of Christ', 'Our Saviour'.[35] Religiously tolerant, he commended religion to everyone, pursuing a remarkably gracious policy toward Moslems, who fought loyally on his behalf against the Italian invasion. Yet he was not universalistic in his views. He praised, for example, the Ethiopian Saint Tekle Haimanot for championing Christianity 'when Ethiopia was gravely threatened with heathenish and Islamic engulfing'.[36] Thereby, he showed his distinct preference for Christianity and against Islam and the traditional religion of the non-Semitic majority of the population.

He highly valued the Bible, commenting:

All the ancient Scriptures were written for Our instruction, in order that through the encouragement they give Us, we may maintain Our hope with fortitude. Because We desire that the light which comes from the Scriptures may shine to all, this [Amharic] Bible by Our command and will has been revised and printed in the Thirty-First year of Our reign.[37]

He did not perform a similar service for the Koran. For these and other reasons, on 21 January 1965, Selassie was formally declared 'Defender of the Faith' by a conference of Oriental Orthodox churches. That same year he hosted an All-Africa conference of Lutheran churches.

On 4 November 1966, at evangelist Billy Graham's invitation, he opened the World Congress On Evangelism in Berlin with a stirring address he entitled 'Building an Enduring Tower'. While, perhaps, on the one hand, not being certain of his blackness, he refused Marcus Garvey's invitation, on the other hand, being certain of his Christianity, he accepted Billy Graham's.

His address was a powerful support of global Christianity, tracing the 'great struggles to preserve Ethiopia as an island of Christianity' against being 'overrun by and succumbed under a power opposed to the Christian faith'. He urged the gathering, 'Therefore, O Christians, let us arise and, with the spiritual zeal and earnestness which characterized the Apostles and the early Christians, let us labor to lead our brothers and sisters to our Savior Jesus Christ who only can give life in its fullest sense.'[38]

What he did not say or do is of equal significance. He did not imitate the actions of Jesus that Saturday morning, *c.* CE 26 in Nazareth, when after a period of teaching and healing in the area surrounding the Sea of Galilee,

Jesus entered the town in which he had been reared and stood up in the synagogue to speak. Handed the scroll of Isaiah's prophecy, Jesus turned to what has now been numbered chapter 61.1–2 and read:

> The Lord's Spirit is upon me, which for this reason he has anointed me to preach good news to the poverty stricken, he has sent me to preach to the captives release and to the blind restoration of sight, to send the oppressed into freedom, to preach the year of the Lord's favour. (Luke 4.18–19)

When Jesus sat down in rabbinic fashion to teach, all watched him. Then he said, 'Today this Scripture has been fulfilled in your hearing' (Luke 4.21). The assemblage was thunderstruck. They seized him and forced him out of the city, trying unsuccessfully to throw him off a cliff, for he had not only challenged their sincerity but also declared himself the Messiah, God's appointed one.

But some nineteen centuries and forty years later, facing a representation of global Christendom, Selassie did not make a similar announcement. Choosing as his text Matthew 18.20, 'Jesus Christ has said: "Where two or three are gathered together in my name, there am I in the midst of them"', he did not rise and announce, 'Well, here I am again – returned in a new incarnation – as Conquering Lion of the Tribe of Judah.' Instead, the emperor simply gave his 'expressed hope' that God would let these words come true for the assembly. Instead of declaring himself the Christ, he identified himself as a follower of Christ and reminded the gathering:

> It should be our prime duty to preach the Gospel of Grace to all our fellow men and women. The love shown in Christ by our God to mankind should constrain all of us who are followers and disciples of Christ to do all in our power to see to it that the Message of Salvation is carried to those of our fellows for whom Christ our Savior was sacrificed but who have not had the benefit of hearing the Good News.[39]

Rather than the Christ, he counted himself as among the 'followers and disciples' of Christ and saw his role as evangelist as the calling of the monarch of the 'Christian island' of North Africa.

Finally, when travelling by train across Canada in April 1967, he publicly answered a point blank question about his reputed divinity posed by the news programme *Project 67*, while interviewing for an episode it subsequently broadcast in June 1967, entitled: 'The Conquering Lion of Judah: A Profile Study of His Imperial Majesty, Haile Selassie I, Emperor of Ethiopia'. The interviewer commented:

> There are millions of Christians throughout the world, Your Imperial Majesty, who regard you as the reincarnation of Jesus Christ.

Haile Selassie I replied firmly:

> I have heard of that idea. I also met certain Rastafarians. I told them clearly that I am a man. That I am mortal. And that I will be replaced by the on-coming

generation. And that they should never make a mistake in assuming or pretending that the human being is emanated from a deity.[40]

A year and a half later, in December 1968, back in his own palace in Addis Ababa, Selassie I elaborated on his commitment to Jesus Christ as his Lord and his own need for Jesus as saviour in his life to Dr Oswald Hoffmann for a special Lutheran Laymen's League presentation of the programme, *Bringing Christ to the Nations*, on the celebration of Christmas in Ethiopia:

> When Jesus Christ was born from virgin Mary, from that time on he lived an exemplary life, a life which men everywhere would emulate. His life and the faith that he has proffered assures us of salvation, assures us also of harmony and a good life upon earth. Because of the exemplary character of the life of Jesus Christ, it is necessary that all men do their maximum in their human efforts to see to it that they approximate as much as they can the root example that has been set by him. It's quite true that there is no perfection in humanity. From time to time we make mistakes. We do commit sins, but even as we do that, deep in our heart as Christians we know we have a chance of forgiveness from the Almighty. He tells us that all men are equal regardless of sex, their national origin and type. And he also taught us all who seek him shall find him. To live in this healthy life, a Christian life, is what makes me follow Jesus Christ.

Acknowledging 'we make mistakes. We do commit sins', but 'we know we have a chance of forgiveness from the Almighty', he underscored his own distinction from divine perfection and his union with imperfect, sinful humanity.

In addition, he indicated that his knowledge of God's nature was based on speculation, not certitude, when he announced: 'I think God commiserates with us that find themself in misfortune'. He did not say, I know.

Further, he used his own example as a fallen, but redeemed, human as an opportunity to send a message of the need for repentance of sin and submission to the Lordship of Christ to the programme's worldwide audience. He announced:

> I would tell a person that's considering the claims of Christ, that for the first time, that it is necessary to have faith in the Almighty. That it's necessary to have love. And that it's necessary to conduct oneself in a manner that we have been taught to do in the Bible. I would advise him to read and to study the Bible. I would also advise him to seek particular knowledge, for the more one knows, the more he realizes the need for a Prime Mover, the need for a Creator, a Creator who is good, and who ordained for salvation and also for faithful life upon earth. I'll also tell him to learn and to think for himself the ways he would serve the Lord. In these thoughts and in this undertaking of his, he will inevitably find the way of serving his fellow man. For, his faith would then be manifested by his conduct. If Christians behave in this way, if we dedicate ourself to this fundamental task, then we will have a peaceful work and we'll be assured of what God's grace is, a gift, that we'll learn the commandments of God.

Explaining that his own faith was what sustained him in 'those crises in my life', he revealed:

> In particular, when my country Ethiopia was invaded by enemy forces, several years ago, I was sustained in that period by my faith in God and in the abiding belief that justice, however it may take time, would ultimately prevail. If I did not have faith in the Almighty, his righteousness, and that justice inevitably prevails, then I would have lost hope. Then and thus, the interest of my country would have been blocked (vid?). Because I have attempted to maintain my faith in it and because all Ethiopians maintain their faith in the ultimate goodness of the world and then the design, grand design, that the Almighty has for all men in the world, we were able to victoriously reenter our country and rid ourselves of evil – evil forces. If I did not have in my heart the love of God, I don't think I would have conquered in the manner that I did. The love of God means a sense of courageous in a human being, gives him comfort for the future and assurance that right causes will ultimately prevail.

For Haile Selassie:

> Without love all of our human efforts in the sight of God can be useless. He loved us and on our behalf he was given as a ransom and it was because of love and his love for us that he accomplished the act of love ... After our blameless Creator was sent to this world by his Father, then the hearts of all believers became the temple of God. The love of Christ cannot be fathomed by a series of questions and answers and man's soul cannot experience deeper enrichment as a result. We believe that man at all times can be bound by his love and grace.

How deep his submission to letting Christ's gracious love work through him was evidenced by his refusal to allow retaliation against enemy captives. At 76 years of age at the time of the Lutheran interview, he was still praying an hour each day, sleeping three, and working twenty. Near the close of the broadcast, he charged his listeners to heed 'the New Testament in which our Lord himself gives the command to go into all the world and to preach.'[41]

Such calls to fulfil Christ's great commission to evangelize that he gave these Lutheran listeners and the attenders of the Berlin evangelism conference were not empty words for the emperor, or hypocritical charges made to others he did not himself fulfil. When in April 1966 he found himself confronted with an opportunity to bear the 'Message of Salvation', when he visited Jamaica and received a tumultuous welcome from men and women whose beliefs appeared to him to be in error, since he found them worshipping himself as God, he responded in a radical manner. He went to the root of the issue and gave these Jamaicans a church to correct them.

Selassie I as Ambassador for Jesus

The welcome in Jamaica obviously affected the emperor as powerfully as it did his acclaimers. Some report that he wept at the sight of the straining throngs. Profoundly moved by the spiritual yearning of the Rastafarians, the emperor commissioned the young Laike M. Mandefro to go to Jamaica and establish as a gift to the country a branch of the Ethiopian Orthodox Church. The young churchman was not enthusiastic. In an interview with Rasta journalist Barbara Blake Hannah he reflected:

> I didn't want to go. But the emperor said, 'I want you to help these people. My heart is broken because of the situation of these people. Help them find the true God. Teach them.' It was the emperor's order and I could not refuse.[42]

Having arrived from his initial see as head of the Ethiopian Orthodox Church in the United States, Archimandrite Laike M. Mandefro, now renamed Archbishop Yesehaq, the Abuna, was encouraged by his welcome. 'Hundreds of enthusiastic people waving Ethiopian flags and banners gathered at the Palisadoes Airport to welcome us', he reports in a book he wrote in 1989.[43] But that welcome soon turned sour. At a registration meeting at the Ebenezer Church on Spanish Town Road, Rastafarians demanded to be baptized in the name of the emperor. When the archbishop refused, the meeting ended in an uproar. Like his emperor's before him, the abuna's own heart was broken. He recalls:

> It was an extremely sorrowful and unforgettable moment for me at the registration meeting at Ebenezer Church, especially when some Rastafarians angrily demanded to know 'Who is Christ?' However, in spite of the fact that I had not yet learned the deep motive for their misunderstanding and their various philosophies, I understood their discontent and frustration. Here were a people searching for their identity, which was lost in Western civilization – a scattered and rejected people. I thought there must be some institution from their motherland to which they could constantly reach out, to link them to themselves and to God.[44]

The abuna determined that the Ethiopian Orthodox Church would be that institution. But the way to reach out to the Rastafarians was not easy. He found himself confronting the legacy of alienation and suspicion inherited from slavery.

In assessing Jamaica's history, he himself could clearly see that Western 'Evangelical Protestant missions played an important role in bringing the Gospel to the slaves in the process of their liberation and education', after the Moravians were invited to 'come over and help' by a West Indian slave in 1754. Indeed, he discovered leaders like the Baptist William Knibb 'played an important role in the final stage of the abolition movement',[45] but misuse of Christ's name by slavers had robbed many of the view of Jesus as a liberator. He realized:

> Beyond almost every action lies a deep-seated motive for reaction, and from my observation of Rastafarians and according to what I have learned from them, there existed a serious motive beyond the fact that some do not identify with Jesus Christ. They believed that Christianity had been used by the Western world to

create slavery, so many passed away without accepting any baptism from Western churches.

Rastafarians developed a militant nature as a result of their concept of an 'oppressive system' and therefore will not as much as listen to any mention of church, much less baptism. Some condemn the idea of slavery to such a point that they hold the 'slave master' responsible for indoctrinating them with church, Christianity, and Jesus Christ. Their question is, How can people inflict oppression upon another group of people and at the same time preach Jesus Christ, His love for mankind, and Christianity?[46]

His answer involved taking time to understand the depth of Rastafarian concern and to hold up as a corrective an Eastern approach to Christianity as represented by the Ethiopian Orthodox Church.

Immediately, he discovered that not one monolithic Rastafrian theology confronted him, instead, 'I must say, however, at the meeting we found some true followers of Christ among holders of many different philosophical ideas.' These he baptized, excusing the riotous behaviour of the others, admonishing, 'Rastafarians should not be ridiculed or condemned ... they must be brought gradually to Jesus Christ. I also emphasized that the emperor was a deeply religious man and would give his life for the Church of Christ.'[47]

Despite his gentle approach, the abuna encountered resistance: 'Many thought the church was not genuine and did not have their interest and general welfare at heart. Therefore, they were cautious when they learned that the Ethiopian Orthodox church proclaimed Jesus Christ and baptism for the remission of sins.' Rasta antipathy to organized religion had extended even to the church of their 'divinity'. With these the abuna hit an impasse: 'Some were willing to be baptized – but not in the name of Jesus Christ. I made it clear to them that I could baptize in no other name than that of Jesus Christ.'[48] Soon those two reactions would deepen further.

Those Rastafarians who were primarily afrocentric in their interests easily fit in with the Ethiopian Orthodox Church's African definition of Christianity. The abuna was delighted to note that 'Rastafarians who have accepted the Church and have come to be known as Orthodox do not seem to have any problem identifying with Jesus Christ.'[49] But, for the second group, caution soon turned to dismay when these Rastas discovered that the Ethiopian Orthodox Church was holding joint services with the 'whore of Babylon', the Roman Catholic Church itself. Appalled, they railed on the church. And even the first supportive group was shaken. The new abuna had not reckoned the depth of their anti-papal exclusivity. He was saddened to see that 'hundreds of angry baptized members in Jamaica ran away from the Ethiopian church when they learned that the church had an ecumenical prayer service with the Roman Catholic, Anglican, and other denominations, not only here in Jamaica but also in Addis Ababa. As a result, the newly established Saint Peter's Church was closed down. The dissenting Jamaican members shouted, "Ethiopian Church should never pray together with these Western churches!"'[50] The exclusive concern of such Rastafarians was so strong and focused that even the wish of the emperor, their object of worship, was not able to turn them to follow his own ecumenical example.

As the abuna explored the philosophies of the Rastafari more deeply, he came to realize the true depth of their theological departure from the tenets of the Ethiopian Orthodox Church. Many of the Rastas he encountered had been reared in Christian churches.[51] But their Christian orthodoxy, the abuna discovered, had given way to a view wherein 'the Rastafarians link the power of the Godhead with the emperor as the Christ – the fullness of the Godhead bodily. Before he acquired flesh from woman, this powerful Godhead rested within the habitation of the Holy of Holies as the Second Advent came closer.'[52] Now, he understood the tumultuous welcome at the emperor's 1966 visit. It was akin to Christ's long-awaited second coming: 'The emperor's visit to Jamaica in April 1966 was a great fulfillment for the Rastafarians. It was observed as an event never before recorded in the history of Jamaica. Rastas robed in white, holding palm leaves, gathered in thousands shouting, "Hosannah – blessed is He that cometh in the name of the Lord – Rastafari!"'[53]

The abuna tried to explain Ethiopia's different perspective on the emperor. But he soon found himself, instead, throwing up more barriers. In particular, another uproar greeted his dismissal of ganja as a sacrament and a means of divine revelation:

> The herb used for smoking, not only by Rastafarians but used widely by non-Rastafarians, is illegal and contrary to the Ethiopian culture. The emperor was not God to the Ethiopian people and other nations. He was a religious man who was elected king of Ethiopia. While one can appreciate the respect, love, and devotion given to him as a clergyman, it is my duty to speak the truth and to strongly advise my brethren and sisters, young and old, to be aware of the commandment of God: 'Thou shall have no other gods before me – for I am a jealous God. And they must turn their hearts and walk in the right direction, which is the Lord Christ, without whom salvation is impossible.'[54]

While some Rastafarians rejected this message, the abuna found enough variety among the Christological leanings of others to be able to move them along the road of an Afro-expressed orthodoxy:

> In regard to the divinity of the Emperor, all Rastafarians do not have the same view. There are some who directly address the emperor as Almighty God or Christ, while others do not regard him as God but rather see Christ through the person of the emperor. For them he is the Bible, the handbook and effective instrument through which they can learn about Christ. There are still others who say that Haile Selassie could not be the returned Messiah since the second advent will be seen by everyone at the last and final judgment of mankind.[55]

This variety of views encouraged the abuna to see Rastas of the latter categories as two thirds world Christians of a non-Western persuasion. He concluded that Rastafarians were sincere believers struggling to find a Christianity not polluted by Western slave-holding theology. Adopting a pastoral approach toward Rastas, following his policy of not permitting them to be ridiculed or anathematized, he emphasized his own African origin as he gently explained the differences between the Ethiopian Orthodox Church and the Western churches, while still acknowledging both proclaimed Christ. 'Nevertheless,' he concludes, 'as I had come from Ethiopia I was welcomed to teach the right doctrine of Christ and thousands accepted the faith.'[56] This wise programme of kind, caring, sympathetic instruction proved successful. Writing in 1989, after two decades of ministry in the West, the abuna could report that the sixteen-year-old Jamaican church had by that date over fifteen thousand baptized members and many candidates for baptism seeking instruction.

But the puzzle of those Rastafarians who refused to accept the Ethiopian Orthodox Church, despite the fact that it was the emperor's gift for their instruction, continued to plague both the abuna and the emperor. Why worship a god who refuses to accept his apotheosis and gives his allegiance to another? Why worship a reluctant deity who sends emissaries at his own expense to terminate his worship? Some leading Rastas took the emperor's disavowal seriously. Rasta stateswoman Barbara Makeda Lee (Blake Hannah) in her book *Rastafari: The New Creation* noted, 'Despite the hero-worship accorded him on his visit, the Emperor continually repeated: "Do not worship me: I am not God."'[57] As a result, she concluded, 'However, since Rastafari compels one to search the Scriptures, it will be found that there is no condemnation to those who hold fast the name of CHRIST AS THE ONLY NAME IN WHICH SALVATION AND ETERNAL LIFE WILL BE GRANTED, and THROUGH WHOM PRAYER TO GOD MUST COME. Selassie cannot be an end, but a means to an end – CHRIST, and God–JAH.'[58] But she also observed, 'This did not stop Rastafari from revering him, and in fact as a result of his visit, the movement increased in number.'[59]

What did stop many and shock all, however, is the report in 1975 that their God had died in Zion.

4 Haile Selassie as a Crucified Christ

WOULD GOD DIE TWICE?

When Joseph Owens was researching his book *Dread* in the early 1970s, Rastas could point decisively to 'the fact that Selassie is already well into his ninth decade and has outlived every other ruler of his time' to prove him 'the definitive presence of the Immortal God among men', imparting 'a share in his "ever-living life" to all those who live in righteousness'. 'That man cannot dead, you know', one Rasta explained to him. 'He came to do something. It's not like the first time when he came and got disappointed.'[1] But even while Father Owens' book was being completed events were moving swiftly in Ethiopia.

The year between 12 September 1974 and 27 August 1975 was one of high anxiety for the people of Ethiopia and the Rastas living at Shashamane in Ethiopia and in Jamaica. On the first date, a Marxist revolution deposed the emperor and on the second the new government announced he had died of natural causes.

In Kingston the Rastafarian Movement Association announced, 'We Rastafarians stand firm and know that God remains the Almighty, one forever that can never die and will never die.'[2] Bob Marley responded with a beautiful song 'Jah Live', that was later featured on the 1982 soundtrack of the film *Countryman* and recorded as recently as 1991 by Judy Mowatt. Explaining the song to *Esquire* contributing editor Jon Bradshaw, Marley said:

> Check me now, many people, dey scoffers, many people say to me, 'Backside, your God he dead.' How can he be dead? How can God die, mon? Dese people dey don't tink too clear, y'know, dey have de devil in 'em and dat devil he some trick devil. He smart de eyes and vex de brain. Dat's why me wrote 'Jah Lives.'[3]

Others, however, did not respond with such certainty. One former Twelve Tribes' Rasta and current evangelical Christian, who asked to remain anonymous as he still maintains his friendships with his former community members, told the present author:

> What I found recently is that there is a tendency now, there's a hopelessness that is creeping in. Yes, a hopelessness in some of them that is creeping in. For example, I'll tell you what. This article – I'm just looking at the headline [picks up a copy of *Reggae Report*, (8 : 9(1990)29), E. Lee Johnson, 'H.I.M. Haile Selassie I: The Man Who Lived to Be Emperor (Part 2)'] – where it says Haile Selassie 'disappeared.' Somehow they can't understand what really is happening in terms of what the Old Testament talks about the second coming. And since they've already greeted Jesus

or the Messiah as Haile Selassie, then some things should be falling in place. And it's not. Those things are not happening today. And so they still see Babylon as in charge. And that sort of sends a hopelessness along their way. So, they're not as verbose, not as vocal as they once were.

Death for Rastas has traditionally been seen as a sign of sin. Researcher William A. Blake reported in November 1961, 'When a member of the cult dies, his brethren believe this to be the result of sin. They move away from the scene, leaving his body to be burried by non-Ras Tafarians.'[4] The Abuna, Archbishop Yesehaq, notes, 'Many Rastafarians do not go near a dead body, even of a person related to them.'[5] Peter Tosh never attended the funeral of his former band mate Bob Marley, explaining, 'He had no time for "generals and funerals."'[6] Attending no funerals is the mark of a Rastaman in Pablo Moses' 1990 descriptive song, 'I Am A Rastaman.'[7] In fact, when Bob Marley was dying, Frederick 'Toots' 'the Maytal' Hibbert expressed his concern to noted reggae historian Stephen Davis, 'I really want to know something about Bob, I want to know if he feelin alright cos I wanna give my message to Bob dat he could feel alright – my bredrin, yuknow? So I always say special psalms dat he could uplift.' 'You keep him in your prayers?' Stephen Davis asked. 'Yeah', Toots Hibbert replied, 'Cos is really not the death of a sinner, but the sinner to repent, so therefore when one of the bredrin ill we all feel it, yuknow? So therefore, we say psalms of redemption for him dat he could be uplift.' Reciting Psalm 121 and 19.14, Toots Hibbert closed, 'Amen. That was for Bob.'[8]

Reflecting on this statement fifteen years later in a 1997 interview with me, the Maytal was careful to clarify his position, maintaining the Rasta view that sin brings about death, while demurring from the logically drawn conclusion that in Rasta cosmology personal sin caused Bob Marley's death. Alluding to his previous statement, I asked, 'Did you feel that, if he [Bob Marley] had repented, he wouldn't have died?' Toots Hibbert replied:

> I wouldn't say so. I don't know what his situation would have been from. I don't know. I wouldn't say that. I wouldn't use that word. I'd say, when serious called illness come your way, is not the God, is not Christ, who is to be blamed, you know? It's just the things of the world come on you to maybe is to suffer your body so you have to die. Can't think of anything particularly I think he should have died from.

Does he believe people could live on and on and on if they do not sin? He does, but with a limit:

> You could live for a long, long time. Not forever anymore, because you have to eat bad food, drink bad water. You have to deal with the bad things: too much difficulties. But, you cannot eat a lot of salt or eat a lot of too much things, you know? Eat the real good food like first time to make people live until the end of time. If it wasn't for that you would. I would believe that. Too much chicken. Too much meat. Too much beef. Fertilizer, you know? Too much poison in the air.

In these responses, this thinking Rasta moves to another theological stage. In the infancy of a new sect (and consequently when one is fairly recent in a separatist faith) finger pointing seems necessary to separate the faithful from the fallen, to establish a movement's identity. But the 'us and them' attitude can only last for so long. It hits a number of roadblocks that stop it in its tracks and force a thorough re-evaluation. For example, when the next generation comes along, children do not always follow the paths of their parents. They do not always adhere to the ideology and, when they do, often it is hybridized with views from the larger church and the larger culture. 'Come ye out from among them' works well once for each generation. By the third generation, 'us and them' can be indistinguishable unless a communal 'incubator' is achieved to the proportions the Amish or Hutterites have created one. But even their success rates are sometimes limited with the young.

While Rastas historically attempted such an 'incubator' in the Pinnacle Hill commune and still maintain certain enclaves like that at the late Prince Edward Emmanuel's camp at this writing, most are in the world, distinguished only by locks, ital food, and/or ideological attitude. The culture, coworkers, playfellows for the children, dedicated fans of other ethnic origins and religious persuasions for musicians and other factors can exercise an incalculable impact on separatist attitudes. The continual Rasta plea to 'walk in my shoes' calls both ways. Rastas are themselves empathetic people, having themselves suffered. And they are thinking people.

For a high level, creative genius like Frederick Hibbert, whose mind is alive and whose thought progression can be traced through the lyrics of his songs over a four decade career, adherence to Rasta 'orthodoxy' is tempered by his own perceptions. 'Sinners die from their sins' is a Rasta tenet of faith, but Bob Marley, a man he knew intimately, was not that different ethically from many other successful musicians he knew. In fifteen years of reflection, his thought processes were guided to a similar conclusion to the one Jesus wanted his hearers to reach when he pointed out that the people killed in the fall of the tower of Siloam were no more sinful than themselves (Luke 13.4). Taking the shift reflected in Toots Hibbert's thinking, passing from a simplistic theodicy, or view of suffering and death, to a more sophisticated one, became a challenge facing all Rastas, when Bob Marley died, yes, but even more so when the Emperor Haile Selassie himself was reported to have succumbed in Zion.

When Bob Marley died, the Rasta community was saddened, but those who witnessed the effect of both the deaths of Marley and Selassie noticed a dramatic difference. Richard Custerbeck, serving as a nurse near a Rasta enclave with whose members he had formed friendships, noted this difference in degree. When asked, 'Did you notice much reaction or change when Haile Selassie or Bob Marley died?' he replied:

Not with Marley, no. He wasn't that much of a hero, really. Not like the press said. He was just like one of the people, you know? That's all. Now, with Haile Selassie, though, that was different. It was a shock. They were all in shock. But they kept going. They just kept on. It was a cultural thing.

Theologically, the death of Selassie I made no sense. Many Rastas had accepted the theology of Jesus as the one in the ancient dispensation to die for sins, Haile Selassie as the one in the new dispensation to rule in God's kingly quality manifested on earth. How could God then die twice? Three options lay open: to deny that Selassie I had died; to reinterpret belief in him; to abandon belief in him as divine. The latter two options demanded change. The first did not. Sincere Rastas have gone for all three, while still remaining Rastas.

Haile Selassie Did Not Die

When Bob Marley was confronted with reports that Haile Selassie had died, Stephen Davis recounts, he and his comrades shocked the reporter by a counter inquiry. Allan 'Skill(y)' Cole, Marley's athletic trainer and personal manager, challenged, 'Do you have personal knowledge of this?' And Bob Marley explained, 'Selassie I, you can check him so. 'Cause if him eighty-three today, tomorrow you see him and he twenty-eight. And next mornin' him a baby, and today him a bird. Yeah man! Jah Live! Ya cyaan kill God!'[9]

That denial of Selassie I's death has continued through the change of millennia bordering both sides of the present writer's conversations with Rastas. In 1979 the first Rastafarian I interviewed, a young St Lucian who had immigrated to Louisville, Kentucky, to find work, challenged with eyes flashing, 'People say he dead. Everywhere say he dead. What I want to know – where he buried? In Ethiopia? In Jamaica? In States? Where?' Fourteen years later, in 1993, Garth Dennis of Black Uhuru still assured me Selassie I was alive:

> The Conquering Lion he came, the one they couldn't kill the second time. So what them say? Selassie I dead now? Say, well, him now no let them do what to do like what them been trying the first time: destroy the flesh! So, Jah just disappear from them one more time. But we know, say, 'Jah live within I and I and ever live from that time until this time.' Whatever would want on with Jesus?

What form does Selassie I now assume? For the members of Black Uhuru he has not changed. He is not in a spiritual form now. For Black Uhuru, he is 'still fleshly, still fleshly'. When I noted, 'But, he's not in the news. We don't see him', Derrick Simpson replied, 'We don't eat with spirits. Huh? Do you still see Christ? So, why you questioning Selassie I in this time?' My asking, 'So, you feel he's still in the flesh?' brought a storm of response. 'Feel???' challenged Garth Dennis. 'No, no, no, we don't "feel"!' explained Derrick Simpson, 'When you "feel," you doubt.' 'Jah live, man!' Garth Dennis declared.

For these Rastas, Haile Selassie cannot have died, because his task in the new dispensation was predicated on his identity as the 'Conquering Lion'.

His mission was to rule earth, he must be present to rule still. The task of Jesus to be slaughtered as the sacrificial lamb had already been completed in history, as Derrick Simpson explained: 'He wasn't going to be crucified like Jesus. So there was mystery around his death and his disappearance. To prove what he want to prove.'

For Don Carlos, the lack of a final ceremony was suspicious: 'But, first of all, you know, he died and then like they have a public funeral? And them never even have a funeral?'. Derrick Simpson agreed, 'There's no person on the face of the earth who can point to Selassie I grave.' Don Carlos finished the defence: 'Such an important statesman all over the world for so much years must have a couple of friends who should like that, but it's no like. You understand?'

Rasta reasoning understands all too clearly that 'Babylon newspaper' spreads its 'bone lies' about the truth. As Duckie Simpson assured me, 'We know what the press can do. You understand? We knows what the press can do!'

For others, this idea of the inability of God to die extends back to the previous dispensation, to the sacrificial lamb as well! Michael Rose made this point clear after identifying Haile Selassie as Jesus returned. Previously 'The Lamb to Slaughter', 'he returns now as "The Conquering Lion"'. When I asked for clarification, 'What was the point of him dying first as a lamb?', he surprised me by responding, 'He didn't die.' 'Jesus?' I asked. 'Yeah, he didn't die', Michael Rose replied. 'He didn't?' I said. 'No'. 'Oh,' I asked, 'Who did?' 'Then, Okay,' explained Michael Rose, 'remember why they claimed they killed him? Didn't they go to the tomb and no one was there? So, what is it? That sort of thing! You know what I'm saying? It's like you have to remember these things.' 'So,' I reasoned, 'you think that it's similar to Haile Selassie dying, but not being able to find his body? Or, disappearing?' 'Yeah', agreed Michael Rose, 'these people, they don't know what to tell the public, so they say he's dead. See what I'm saying?'

Mihlawhdh Faristzaddi in 'the second itation' of his illustrated series of meditations *Itations of Jamaica and I Rastafari* even depicts for us what that disappearance was like:

> Emperor Haile Selassie I does not need this throne right now because he has already fulfilled all the necessary prophesies related to this and He has now gone to prepare for the history breaking World War III Revelations. It is said that the Military on the personal request of the Emperor took HIM to Chapel to worship one morning; he returned on the first two mornings, but he never returned on the third day. When the soldiers went to investigate he was no where to be found and there was no door seen where he might have escaped through. In deep trouble they concocted the story that he had died under mysterious circumstances and buried in an unmarked grave without even a funeral. This was on July 24th, 1975.[10]

Similarly, in the Koran Jesus does not die on the cross, but, through a trick of the Almighty, someone else (some legends say Judas) is catapulted onto the cross and given the visage of Jesus, while the true Jesus is taken up by God to heaven.[11] As the Black Muslim movement adopted this tenet of Islam, so do these Rastas incorporate a similar view in Rastafari.

These are sincere and ongoing beliefs. When the present writer after just such a conversation would refer again to the 'death' of Jesus, he would be regularly corrected with a curt, 'Didn't I tell you he don't dead?'

But not all Rastas are prepared to deny the death of Haile Selassie so categorically. Some like the African Rastas accept it completely. Some like Ras Michael believe Selassie I has changed to a spiritual state. But all have had to reinterpret their theology to some extent to account for the emperor's obvious suffering.

THE PASSION OF SELASSIE I

Perhaps no Rastafarian has done more to publicize the plight of the 'Sufferer' in reggae than Joseph Hill of the group Culture. Beginning to record in the wake of Haile Selassie's deposing and disappearance in 1976 in song after song he has brought before the public consciousness those who have suffered from slavery, those who are still suffering in poverty and the plight of women and inmates. In his song 'Sufferer' he also laments the suffering of Jesus Christ.[12]

In interpreting that song to me, he drew a parallel between the passion of Jesus and that of Selassie I, seeing Jesus and Jah as the same and Haile Selassie and Jesus as 'one family.' How would Joseph Hill understand Jesus and Selassie to be the same person? He explained, 'Between one and one and three: Father, Son and Holy One. Three in one and one in three.' For him, Haile Selassie is Jesus returned, 'and being persecuted once more. Because the transgression of man is not over. It is presumptuously stirring up all the time. So, because of that, their own will never be well. They were bleeding all the time.' In his song, 'Sufferer,' he chants that nobody else knows the 'pain' he feels inside for sufferers, at one point specifying Jesus Christ. Believing the suffering Jesus is within him, he feels moved by Christ's compassion to care about the pain of others:

> 'For the sufferers them.' Yes, for the sufferers. The sufferers. You know, people whose justice are miscarriaging, for the rest of that in prison, you understand, before nothing, you know what I mean? Those things are really unjust, you know, and if we take care of one another and we believe it to take care of the feeling of Jesus I Jah, who is dwelling, who is living inside. But, if you have no interest of taking care of your brother, as much as you do it unto one of those, you do it unto me.

Joseph Hill's contemplation on the suffering of Selassie suggests to him parallels with the suffering of Jesus and ends in the charge of Jesus in Matthew 25 to treat all with the care one would extend to and receive from a suffering Messiah.

But was the suffering of Selassie I self-induced? When a prolonged drought began to cause thousands of deaths in Ethiopia's northern provinces in 1973, resentment of Selassie I's jet-setting lifestyle and reports that he had huge sums of money hidden in foreign banks were presented as evidence by Marxist revolutionaries under the leadership of Colonel Mengistu Haile Mariam that the emperor had become physically and emotionally unfit to continue in office. These charges led to the people supporting his deposing.

Such allegations have become a sore point with Rastas. Different Rastas have dealt with them in different ways.

Some like Mihlawhdh Faristzaddi see them as a ruse of the malcontents, the 'Judases', so to say, to Selassie's 'Jesus'. He writes:

> So as not to provoke any civil war, the army worked carefully on the mind of the masses whoes reverence for His Imperial Majesty was renouned and God like. They used the television media as a means for a well orchestrated propaganda campain to denigrate the Emperor in whom they had found no fault. They also did very well in making the gullible believe that it was Haile Selassie who was responsible for creating the then famine in the provinces of Wollo and Tigre that swept away the lives of hundreds of thousands. Indeed this was the incident that was propitiously used by the world as an aliby to imply that His Imperial Majesty was a wicked autocrat. This is why the Rastaman says that the record breaking famine in the Ethiopia during the mid eighties was a deliberate act of God to embarass Ethiopia in particular, and the world in general for upbrading HIM when he was Emperor of Ethiopia.[13]

Duckie Simpson of Black Uhuru echoed this view when he ruled, 'Man, they're against people who praise Selassie in Africa, man! You see all those sufferation going on down there? Yeah-h-h, they blaspheme. They gotta pay the penalty. In this modern time people are suffering like that? Something's wrong. We was telling them men. But they say they kill the emperor and they get Mengistu. Well, you have to live with that!' With the same kind of scorn, he dismisses the charges that Selassie I stole money from the people of Ethiopia: 'See that 30 million they say the Emperor Selassie I stole? The 30 million? Oh, we got it, spend it. Rasta been spending it. We used to live in caves one time? Now we living in mansions.'

Other Rastas deny knowledge of any 30 million dollar theft and point to an international conspiracy behind the emperor's deposing.

The Meditations are among the few Rastafarians who have dealt with the emperor's situation in their reggae. When I asked Anguillan Rasta Bankie Banx why reggae singers addressed so many songs to white oppression of Blacks in South Africa, but only a few, like Andrew Tosh and Majek Fashek, dealt with black oppression of Blacks in Ethiopia, he replied, 'I think it is too painful. Definitely.' But the Meditations faced that pain on their 1985 *Wake Up!* album when they sang about not wanting 'no money lover' in 'Ethiopia', 'our homeland', where 'they sell out Our Father for gold and silver'.[14]

For the Meditations the 'money lover' was responsible for the deposing of the emperor, but that 'money lover' was not the emperor himself. To the

Meditations, the 'money lover' was the English. In response to the allegation that Haile Selassie had a lot of money in the bank when he died, Ansel Cridland replied:

> Hold on now! God didn't mention it. I didn't get an answer for that. So, there is no comment to that, seen? All the millions that we have on earth here, it's lent. It's lent. All belongs to the Most High. Because we all have to believe HIM. It just lent to us for our material term, for mankind's life is like the tree. Your life is like the tree. When He give him, say, life everlasting, you see, it's the earth seeds. You see, when does the world come to an end.

In his perspective, the people of Ethiopia did not put the emperor out of power, the British did! According to Ansel Cridland,

> Is not them themselves, you know, real into that, you know. It's the over it, see? Because it was better beneficial to the peace of England. It was a blueing wash thing, you know, that them were on with them, because them want to control, them want to control. Them want to control this whole world in them hand, seen?

In his view, the English brainwashed the Ethiopian people. As he explains:

> Yeah, it was just like the firing staff [squad] like what will them picket in South Africa now, seen? I won't listen much in one of those report news. And they know say Africa belongs to the black man. Them know that. Them no hide it and things. Them know that it belongs to. And them was interviewing a white man how, ask the white man, what him think about giving the land to the black people. Him said no, him wouldn't give up the land. Him would kill every black man work first than let them have the land.

How does this Rastafarian idea of blaming Whites for a black insurrection make sense? Why blame the United Kingdom for a revolt by Ethiopian Marxists against Ethiopian Imperialists? For Rastas like Ras Seymour McLean of Ras International Consultants of Wandsworth, London, the answer dates to the Napier Expedition against the Ethiopian Emperor Theodore. Annoyed that Queen Victoria did not respond to a letter he sent her, Theodore imprisoned some British officials at Magdala. Victoria's reply to what she considered a provocation was to dispatch a military force under Robert Napier to free the British diplomats. The subsequent war left the Ethiopians defeated, Theodore dead by suicide, and the British withdrawing in victory, but not before soldiers in search of loot sacked Ethiopia's churches. For Rastas like Ras Seymour, the British looting of the Ethiopian Church on 13 April 1868 is as infamous and definitive as the Pope's blessing of Mussolini's forces. According to Ras Seymour:

> Concerning the judgement of Babylon. Revelation 17–19. The Queen of England and the British Commonwealth. Queen Elizabeth 2nd is the Queen of Babylon. Set fire to her ministers, this judgement is sure ... The story of the Ethiopian loot. Addis Tribune Ethiopia. Documents form core beliefs of Ras Tafari movement.[15]

This looting, so significant to Britain's Rastafarians because it seized documents articulating their 'core beliefs', involved not only the taking of sacred manuscripts and sacred representations of the ark of the covenant, but in addition to plundering royal regalia, a deceased abuna was exhumed and his crown, chalice and rings were stolen.[16] Through the efforts of Ras Seymour and other British-based Rastafarians, Prince Lij Mulugeta Asseratte, cousin of Haile Selassie, chaired a Rasta-sponsored inquiry to determine where in the museum system of England the Ethiopian artifacts were being held and demanded their return.[17] This unresolved incident, though over one hundred years old, augments the continuing Rastafarian rage at Great Britain for its role in the slave trade. Because of the United Kingdom's active role in peopling the West Indies with African slaves and allowing the looting of sacred relics in Ethiopia, contemporary England becomes suspect in Rastafarian eyes in any international incident that smacks of intrigue.

Other Rastas take a more spiritual reading. Selassie I, like Jesus in the resurrection, has transcended his hateful opposition, whether it be Ethiopian or foreign, and, having completed his work in the flesh, has assumed a higher form – a spiritual one. In this new spiritual state he gives assurance to these faithful that his work continues. Ras Michael Henry, for example, sees the betrayal of Selassie as similar to that of Christ, because like Christ he tried to help a recalcitrant people:

> Africa is a continent where there are so different nations and type of people, and languages and diverse. And he came and he did set up the first constitution and that mean he's dealing with a building program for his people – constitution, literally, where a man can know. It deal with university education, hospitals and all them things. And tell that and him send some of his people to different countries, that them can at least have an idea of the different form of cultures round and about and to come forward. But, same way like how you had Christ and the disciples them. And one of them betray him. So, you see him way it went with His Majesty with certain things?

For Ras Michael, his people did betray him: 'They people start get greedy and lustful and start disobey. Certain trend.'

But as Jesus conquered death, so did Selassie I for such Rastafarian believers. And as Jesus proved his resurrection with appearances, so Ras Michael is convinced that he received just such an assurance that Selassie I lives in a vision, a vision intended by Selassie I a few months after his disappearance to confirm Rasta biblical interpretations about him:

> We the Rastafarians say, well, His Majesty is a representative of the Almighty God according to his all that was fulfill in him through the Bible, and then he say it can be interpreted that way undoubtedly. You understand, see, God is great. You know, he manifests in such a way. I vision, see His Majesty when they say he died, all them kill him, martyred him, this and that. And when I vision His Majesty, I was at the river and he just came down in his white colored cape and he came down and he said – and I get down and say, and bow down – and him said to me,

say, 'They say I'm dead. But, I'm not dead. I'm just floating through the passage of time.'

For the sceptical who know about the Rasta use of marijuana for revelations, Ras Michael is quick to point out that this vision was not chemically induced. To my question, 'Was that with ganja or was that just by yourself?' he assured me, 'Just inna myself on my bed. Jah Jah's put me for rest, I'm adjusted to that.'

But all Rastas have not adjusted to that faith-shattering event of losing the Christ again and this time no tomb to stand empty and no resurrection appearances but to the isolated few. For these the disappearance has become prolonged and it demands an adjustment of faith. The most common reaction seems to have become a pantheistic response, moving farther into what the Mansinghs consider the more 'Eastern' perspective in Rastafari.

GOD AS MAN, MAN AS GOD: SELASSIE WAS JUST A HUMAN

Cognitive dissonance is a fascinating concept in the literature of psychology. One of the demonstrative studies was published by Professors Festinger, Riecken and Schachter in 1956. Though it came at the mid-twentieth century, their study has an eerie applicability to the time of my writing in the 1990s, some forty years later. Currently, global popular culture is undergoing a kind of apocalyptic mania.[18] Amidst shootouts with the Branch Davidians in Texas, germ warfare by Utopians in Japan, Solar Temple cult murders in Switzerland, Canada, and elsewhere, Satanic sacrifices in Greece and Brazil, and mass suicide by the Heaven's Gate community expecting to translate in some sort of post mortem soul migration to a spaceship supposedly hiding behind a comet, this is indeed a bizarre if fascinating time to survey the landscape of popular theology.

Millennial dreams are nothing new, of course, for either the United Kingdom with its Darbyite prophetic heritage or the United States with its Millerite adventism. Neither are they new for Africa with its rich mystical traditions, nor for Jamaica, where Prophet Bedward, as we saw, was but one in a long line of apocalyptic figures.[19] But what dissonance theory attempts to do is to examine and explain what happens when millennial dreams are frustrated, when believers come back off the hills, shivering in their thin white robes in the grey; bleak, revealing stab of dawn or finally tire of watching potential anti-Christs parade by into oblivion as earth's ages continue relentlessly to roll. And dissonance theory may shed light on the reactions of many contemporary Rastas to the growing realization that Earth's Rightful Ruler is no longer apparent on his throne in Zion.

In the Festinger, Riecken and Schachter study the researchers infiltrated a group of utopians convinced that, like Prophet Bedward, they were about to ascend, this time in an extra-terrestrial saucer while the world was engulfed by a flood. Armed with their 'passports' (instead of the photographs and tickets Leonard Howell and Claudius Henry sold to adherents), these well-educated, middle class people were given only a blank page and stamped envelope. They also had a password ('I left my hat at home'). And each got an assigned seat on the spaceship. A last minute panic removing all metal (like zippers) off their clothing heightened their sense of expectancy. In silence, forbidden to approach the windows, the group huddled on the prophesied night as their leader received telepathic messages from 'the Guardians', who were even then circling overhead, zeroing in to rescue them. The time of departure, midnight, struck, and then it passed. So did the time of the proposed flood. As the hours piled up on the shoulders of the faithful an increasingly ponderous weight of dissonance between what they believed and what obviously was true – that no rescuing saucer and no demolishing flood were coming now or ever – an explanation finally presented itself that relieved the dissonance's unbearable pressure: God had delivered the world because of the faith of these believers. As a result, they began to proclaim the message of earth's deliverance in the mass media to enlighten everyone else.[20]

The attempt to apply dissonance theory to religious experience is common among those who reject the validity of the experience itself. Common too has been the attempt to apply it to Christianity, particularly to the resurrection accounts of Jesus. One such example, more interesting than most since it purports to come from inside the camp of faith, was proposed by a Harvard University Divinity School professor of theology, Gordon Kaufman, an ordained Mennonite minister. In Kaufman's view:

> The erstwhile despair of the disciples was transformed into a powerful hope . . . these alleged appearances were in fact a series of hallucinations produced by the wishful thinking of Jesus' former disciples who had so strongly hoped and believed 'that he was the one to redeem Israel' (Luke 24.21).[21]

The New Testament evidence combats such application of dissonance theory to Jesus' resurrection. 'This was not done in a corner', the imprisoned Paul reminded his examiner King Agrippa. 'Indeed, the king knows about these things, and to him I speak freely, for I am certain that none of these things has escaped his notice' (Acts 26.26, NRSV). What Paul was referencing was that, from the moment of the resurrection, when the guards fled the confounding tomb site, Jesus made a multitude of appearances to a variety of witnesses: former believers (like the faithful women), onlookers and bystanders (like those on the road to Emmaus), even sceptics (like Thomas, with his 'show me' attitude). Appearing both to individuals but as well to large groups all at once (one comprised of over 500 eyewitnesses (1 Corinthians 15.6)), Jesus' appearances provided tangible, empirical proof of his resurrection. John could write confidently, 'We declare to you what was from the beginning, what we have heard, what we have seen with our eyes, what we have looked at and touched with our hands' (1 John 1.1, NRSV). Whether being hugged by Mary to the extent he had to tell her gently to let him go (John 20.17), hosting a fish fry on the beach for his startled disciples to prove to them they were not seeing a ghost (John 21.9–22), or inviting the abashed

Thomas to go ahead and handle his wounds for concrete proof (John 20.27), Jesus provided a physically perceptible demonstration of his return to life that provided the basis for the defence of the validity of the resurrection. The acceptance or rejection of Christianity rests upon whether one accepts or rejects the eyewitness accounts that this one who was dead has conquered death, returned to life, and ascended to his proper sphere in the Godhead, transfigured eternally (1 Corinthians 15.14–23).

The problem for post-1975 Rastafarians is that Haile Selassie has made no such unequivocally empirical resurrection appearances. A dream like Ras Michael's, as detailed in the previous chapter, may be dismissed by hearers as wishful thinking, for it is a solitary experience, achieved with no direct correspondence to the waking state of sense experience. Sceptics were none too gentle in pointing out such a conclusion to Bob Marley, as we saw in his report to Jon Bradsaw ('Many people say to me, "Backside, your God he dead"'[22]).

Many thoughtful Rastas find themselves driven back to re-examine their belief system and, if they are to maintain their faith, discover another role for Selassie I or another mode for Jah to work through him.

However, contrary to what one might expect, not every Rasta came to the traumatic period of 1974–75 with a firm belief in the divinity or transcendence of Haile Selassie I. The fact is that, even before the reports of Selassie's death, some Rastas were taking his disavowals of his own deity very seriously.

Karlene Faith had been working as an administrator for the US Peace Corps in Ethiopia when she learned about the Rastafarians' devotion to Ethiopia and the emperor. Fascinated, she travelled to Jamaica on her return and lived for a number of months with Rastafari in the countryside. In 1969 she wrote up her field findings, then reworked them for publication in the collection *Cargo Cults and Millenarian Movements* which appeared in 1990. Ably researched, her essay sheds fascinating light on many aspects of rural Rastafari, particularly illuminating the self-understanding of Claudius Henry, whom she knew personally.

Arriving with the two usual assumptions often automatically made about Rastafari, namely 'Haile Selassie is a Living God, and those who worship him seek repatriation to Ethiopia',[23] she was shocked to find that the first Rasta compound she encountered in Montego Bay denied both. As she approached 'in a voice that barely betrayed the intimidation I felt so keenly' a 'man whose long, twisted locks stood from his head in every direction' who 'emerged from one of the small buildings', she reports:

> I introduced myself by explaining that my experience of living in Ethiopia as a first-hand witness of Haile Selassie in relation to the Ethiopian people had given me a great curiosity about the Ras Tafarians, who were said to worship 'His Imperial Majesty' as the 'Living God.' And with that he spoke – slowly and deliberately, and piercing my vision with his: 'Haile Selassie – he's nothing to me.' (At which he spat upon the ground). He's a man, same as me. A man. No more.[24]

Soon she was to discover more Rastafarian camps holding the same humanized viewpoint on Haile Selassie. As she summarizes their beliefs: 'They explain that "God is all men but no man is God" and "Worshippers of Haile Selassie are members of a temporal organization – they do not have substantial wisdom."' While these dreadlocks did 'acknowledge Haile Selassie as the figure who inspired the movement toward Ras Tafarianism', they looked beyond H.I.M. to 'the object of their worship, whom they call God and the Lord interchangeably', but which 'is not a tangible personal figure in their lives, but rather an all-encompassing world force'. What is interesting is that these encounters took place when Haile Selassie was at the ascendancy of his Jamaican reputation, following close upon his triumphal visit and still years before his deposition.

While at the time Karlene Faith encountered them these Rasta camps regarded 'their own approach as an offshoot of that movement', since 'they do not consider him to be God' and 'they do not seek repatriation to Ethiopia',[25] once Haile Selassie removed from the scene a major moving began shifting the majority more toward their view.

5 The 'Eastern' Christ of Rastafari

SELASSIE AS ARCHETYPE

Dennis Forsythe was an intellectual whose work was pivotal for Rastafari in the rethinking period immediately post-Selassie. Born on 25 July 1946 in Islington, St Mary, Jamaica, he joined the West Indian migration to England in 1962, eventually graduating from the London School of Economics. Taking another degee at McGill University, he became a lecturer, roaming around the academic landscape from Canada to Jamaica, teaching at Sir George Williams University, Howard University, Federal City College, and the University of the West Indies. Interspersed with his teaching, he produced a constant flow of articles and two books, *Black Alienation, Black Rebellion* (1975) and *Racism in Canada* (1972). Working out of the sociology department at the Mona campus of the University of the West Indies, he found himself trying to make sense of the elimination of the supposed Black Messiah, having himself embraced Rastafari. In 1979 he produced a mimeographed paper, titled 'West Indian Culture through the Prism of Rastafarianism', which was later reprinted in the *Caribbean Quarterly* monograph on Rastafari (1985) and was to become the basis for his book *Rastafari: For the Healing of the Nation* (1983). In it he articulated in print the new wave of accommodationist thinking that was seeking to reinterpret Selassie I's removal from the physical scene, working with the parameters of the Bible on one hand and inherited Rasta thought on the other. Launching his discussion off the African concept of the 'ananci', the trickster spider, he expanded upon the Rasta theology that Jah shared his spirit between Jesus and Selassie and individual Rastas to place the emphasis on other potential recipients. Forsythe's contribution was to attach such a clear grappling hook between Rastafarian theology and Eastern religious thought that the connection has since been a point of contention for many and a new way to understand Rastafari for others.

Forsythe accomplished this task by centring his focus of attention on Rastafari as 'the most dynamic and powerful expression of the African pulsation in the Caribbean today. It is the voice of Africa crying out in the Caribbean.' For him 'Rastafarianism is the re-surgence of African revivalism and spiritualism, and hence qualifies as an authentic mass African Renaissance movement',[1] 'a Black Power movement that is struggling to assert itself'.[2]

By reminding his readers that 'above all, Rastas are Africans. And it is in the light of the African cultural background and subsequent historical experiences that Rastafarianism is best understood', Forsythe explained that 'our forefathers' were animists and 'natural forces' 'were part of their being':

> Their religious beliefs at this time reflected this organic relationship to the world around, and included (a) belief in Animism (b) belief in a God-head and (c) a belief in the power of the rational mind.[3]

'Lion', he reminded his readers, is but one 'tribal totem' in which 'Africans tell how they saw themselves and what they aspired to be'.[4] While the Lion 'stood for power and dignity, and was a complimentary title for a chief',[5] the spider was a survivor who was an ideal image for the common people since 'Africans realised that since they were relatively weak physically, they could only prevail against the strong and mighty forces not through use of force but through mental alertness.'[6]

Thrust suddenly into the Caribbean through slavery, Africans found their 'condition was worsened ... by the White God-father image which Christianity injected in their minds. For, just as the "Massa" of the plantations resided in his Great House, so also was there a "Big Massa" (or "Puppa Jesus") reigning in the sky, who controlled the activities of the elements such as Thunder and Lightening, as well as the fate of human beings'.[7]

So, born to be lions, Jamaicans 'quickly moulded into Anancis by a cultural tradition which systematically down pressed Black manhood – and Black womanhood'.[8]

Enter Rastafari. Re-emphasizing the 'lion' imagery, rescuing Jesus by positing 'Ganja' as 'the mysterical body and blood of "Jesus" – the burnt offering unto God made by fire which allows a member to see and know the "living God," or the "God-in Man"',[9] redeveloping the 'I' in popular consciousness,[10] Rasta, for Forsythe, shifted the diasporan African away from a Selassian and back to an afrocentric frame of reference.

In his schema, rather than scrapping Moses and Jesus as detrimental myths, these became for Forsythe archetypal African tokers (smokers of marijuana), Moses experiencing a 'high' from his 'burning bush', which was actually cannabis, and Jesus getting 'high' on 'mount Sinai'.[11] One thinks here of the Bob Marley interview several years earlier in the September 1976 issue of *High Times*, titled 'This Man Is Seeing God and God Says He Smokes Only the Best. This Man is Bob Marley and He Smokes with God'. When asked if cannabis would ever be legalized, Marley answered, 'I don't know if dis government will, but I know Christ's government will.'[12] For Dennis Forsythe that sentiment becomes part of an overall afrocentric context involving slavery, the Bible, ganja, and anancyism that he employs to set the emperor's current situation into perspective.

At this juncture, Forsythe introduces a spiritual continental shift. His suggestion was certainly not unknown to Rastas, as we saw earlier in Karlene Faith's encounters, but its timing was important. At the specific moment of faith-crisis aftermath, when the first panicked denials had faded and the Rasta brethren were recoiling from the loss of their almighty God as a living man-among-us, a recognized intellectual in the movement, in a source that was soon reprinted and developed into a major statement, was reminding his fellow Rastas that Selassie was, after all, only one of many African 'lions'. He wrote:

> Rasta heroes are all power totemers – Haille Selassie, Mau Mau, Marcus Garvey, Patrice Lumumba, – Stokely Carmichael, Nkrumah, the Maroons, Paul Bogle and many others.[13]

Although deapotheosizing His Imperial Majesty, Forsythe positions Selassie in the primary place of honour among all the 'lions' of Black Power. But now the lion concept, not necessarily any particular lion, not even the man crowned with the title 'Lion of Judah', is presented as what one should follow:

> The Lion in general is an international symbol of some of the more 'ancient' qualities which man has always cherished. He is the Emperor by Universal (popular) consensus, the universal specimen of nature's compact wholeness and power, used by rich and poor alike, black and white.[14]

Lest anyone misunderstand the magnitude of what he is saying, Forsythe drives this point home in a pivotal statement that opens the way for a post-Selassian Rastafari, even underlining his key points:

> Lionism transcends even Haille Selassie who merely came in the name of the Lion – as 'The Conquering Lion of Judah' or as the 'man-lion from Mount Zion.' The face, features and presence of the Lion have become more firmly implanted on the consciousness of Rastas than the face of H.I.M. – it is coming more and more openly acknowledged as representing the ideals and essence of the Rasta movement. Even the non-Rasta Jamaican population now associates lions immediately with Rastas. Since the fall of the Emperor from his Ethiopian throne by the military junta on September 13, 1974. The Lion totem (by itself) has become even more prominent.[15]

Having laid all this groundwork, Forsythe proceeds to demythologize the figure of the fallen emperor:

> Haille Selassie, in his person and at phases in his life exhibited some of the qualities which made him a clear-cut example of a Rasta Lion. Haille Selassie himself saw the African Lion as embodying a spiritual force higher than himself, and symbolising both abstractly and concretely his ideals of African manhood. Haille Selassie tried, therefore, to fuse his power and spirit with that of The Lion ...
>
> In light of the importance of this lion-image to Rasta, we must view Haille Selassie I, as part of this larger and more universal philosophy of lionism, as a servant to the spiritual force of the lion, and in his concrete individual form, embodying some of this spirit.[16]

Forsythe's approach is brilliant, setting up the poles of 'lionism' and 'anancyism' and then locating the emperor within that larger schema. But such language as he uses for the emperor marks a dramatic departure for most Ethiopianist Rastas. Now the emperor only exhibits 'some' of the power qualities. H.I.M. 'tried' to add them to his spirit, but realized they proceeded from a 'spiritual force higher than himself'. Effectively, as we noted, Forsythe separates Rasta afrocentrism from Selassian-centrism. With his emphasis on an animating spiritual force beyond Selassie that animates all things, he frees Caribbean Rastafari from disappearing along with the emperor. The emperor was a hero, certainly, and expected to do his part, but then should have been expected to step from the stage as did all the heroes before him like Marcus Garvey, Paul Bogle, the Maroons. The important thing on which to focus was the higher animating spiritual force with which the emperor aligned himself – that force, symbolized by the lion, is the true heart of Rastafari.

Given that perspective, every 'kingman' in Rastafari can be similar to Selassie – he can attempt to embody the force of the lion. Each one can become a 'Rasta Lion'. The remainder of Forsythe's paper and the subsequent book that followed elaborated on implementing the characteristics of 'lionism' and achieving Rasta's true ideal: 'Lions are those who know God in the form of the unfolding power of the "I",[17] not, we note, through the person of the emperor. The popularity and influence of Dennis Forsythe's work among Rastas cannot be overestimated. His articles are cited everywhere and copies of his book abound. Forsythe did not create a new demythologized figure of the emperor *ex nihilo*. What he did was apply his knowledge of Afro-Caribbean thought and culture to highlight an aspect already latent in Rastafari: the sharing of Jah's spirit among more than one human. If Jah's spirit could illuminate both Jesus and Selassie, then, according to his reasoning, it can illuminate the rest of us. Rastas had always believed this. They just had not generally believed it without Selassie.

Forsythe's work, of course, was never intended to debase Selassie, but to salvage the Rastafarian ideal. As an academician, he drew out and highlighted one aspect that served to 'liberalize' Rastafarian doctrine into a more durable post-Selassie form than was achieved by simply denying the emperor was dead and gone.

What Forsythe does with Rastafari is what scholars like Gordon Kaufman, quoted above, wish to do with Christianity. He attempts to 'demythologize' it. Attacking Rasta reliance on the Bible as having 'left us feeling that our redemption had to come from mystical forces outside of ourselves',[18] he debunks the miracles associated with Haile Selassie such as 'reports of changes in weather conditions when H.I.M. disembarked from the plane'.[19] For Forsythe:

> All of this heavy reliance on the Bible must lead to mystic interpretations as the Bible beseeches man to turn his back from reality. The Rasta brethren who are up in the hills trying to control lightening and thunder remain fastened also to this Bible mysticism. No wonder orthodox Rastas like Brother Mac and Uncle Harry ignore the real concrete history of the Emperor, and irrespective of the facts paint H.I.M. Haille Selassie as the 'highest moral authority in the world.'[20]

Had Professor Forsythe written such flagrantly seditious statements five years prior, he might have been scorned and shunned by his brethren. But by 1979, hearing the accusations of Ethiopian brethren against the human failings of the emperor and seeing no clear evidence of a divine conquering of death, many Rastas found themselves considering Dennis Forsythe's arguments seriously. After all, he was placing the blame for all this misinterpretation of the true place of the emperor on the effects of economic 'cultural imperialism', not on themselves. And he was providing a solution by promoting an 'emerging Lion consciousness among the Brotherhood of Rastaman'.[21] Since the beginning Rasta had been a movement of decentralized power. Neither Howell, nor Hibbert, nor Henry had been able to capture the entire body. Now Forsythe was offering a spiritual decentralization of power past the emperor himself. Every Rastaman could become a lion, or as Big Youth chose to put it in his hit song: 'Every Nigger is a Star'.[22] Odd phrasing to those outside the Caribbean community, perhaps, but the former Twelve Tribes' member, quoted earlier, who wished to remain anonymous, explained to me the significance of just such a sentiment:

> When I left school, because of my family's socio-economic situation, I had to work. And at that time, you know, if you had locks, you were nuts. There's a song at that time that said, 'Long hair people – pickney – need not apply./Don't want an old nigga or Rastafari.' So all us knew that persons with dreadlocks were considered as 'old nigga,' which is an early, degrading name in Jamaica.

Now the outcast, the downpressed, the marginalized locksman, shunted aside and discarded as 'old nigga', was being placed upon the same plane as the emperor himself, if only he would develop the lion qualities within him, as the emperor had done before him. That was Forsythe's message, and it was a heady message, indeed. The emperor was merely an archetype to follow. And the path down which this archetype pointed was boundless.

After all, ever since Haile Selassie had been crowned 'Lion of Judah', his potent leonine African image had fascinated Rastas. One of the earliest gospel songs appropriated by Rastas proclaimed: 'The Lion of Judah shall break every chain/And give us the victory again and again.'[23] This phrase is weaved through many Rastafarian songs, just as the image of the lion is ubiquitous throughout Rasta artwork, eventually finding its way into craftwork, carvings, paintings, and on to album covers. The imperial symbol of lion and sceptre can be seen adapted, for example, on Third World's artwork for *Committed*, reproduced as the Ras Records emblem, and is especially prevalent on the Marley Family's Tuff Gong albums (e.g. Rita Marley's *Who Feels It Knows It*). I-Roy, on his *Heart of a Lion* album, sports a huge lion's head that fills the entire cover. The group Jah Lion have a roaring lion depicted as emerging from their beards and dreadlocks on *Columbia Colly*, while Bunny Wailer has a lion embossed like a fresco on the forehead of a Rastaman on the cover of his *Blackheart Man*, while a small sketch of the emperor with globe, sceptre, and glowing cat's eyes emerges from his locks. One of the most striking adaptations adorns the cover of Ras John Moodie's book *Hath ... the Lion Prevailed ...?* It features a sketch of the Ethiopian

Imperial Lion, sceptre in paw, sporting the head of a dreadlocked Rasta whose facial features are reminiscent of the emperor's. As the depiction of the lion appears everywhere throughout Rastafari, so does the traditional hymn applied to Haile Selassie echo in the Morwells' 'Jah Lion', gathered on their *Best of the Morwells,* in the Mystic Revealers' 'Conquering Lion' on *Young Revolutionaries,* in Judy Mowatt's beautiful 'Get Up Chant' on *Love Is Overdue.* The 'Conquering Lion' is also extolled in Yabby You's song of that name on *One Love One Heart.* The lion imagery is also used in developing other Rasta themes. For example, repatriation is the concept when Joseph Hill and Culture, on their apocalyptic *Two Sevens Clash,* chant 'Get Ready To Ride the Lion to Zion', a song followed immediately by their tribute to Marcus Garvey's attempt, 'Black Starliner Must Come'. (Hill later chose 'Lion Rock' as the title track of his solo album.) 'Don't Wake the Lion' warn the Itals in a song that dramatically impacted the public and is collected on their Nighthawk album *Early Recordings 1971–1979.* The song's lyrics refer ominously to the 'Lion of Judah' 'eating to the edge of the bone'. What exactly does that strange phrasing mean? I asked composer and lead singer Alvin 'Keith' Porter to clarify: Was that a cryptic response to Selassie I's disappearance, or something composed beforehand? According to Keith Porter:

> Well, it was written after that time. Yeah. Because of a lot of things that happened, a lot of stupidity that goes on with people. You know, to me sometimes he can get angry with the behavior of people because there's one thing he ask: just to praise him.

But the reference, he noted, was not necessarily simply to Haile Selassie: 'It was a universal reference'. This generalizing of the 'Lion Heart' that can get stirred to anger by evil, whether it be the emperor's or a greater universal Jah's or an individual Rasta's heart, is the response of Rastas to the leonine aspect of the emperor. As 'Sampson' and 'Moses' before Selassie, the Rasta can be a 'Black Lion', as Jah Lion sing. Rastas have a 'lion heart' intones Carl Dawkins on his *Nonstop to River Jordon* 12 inch 1983 Sydcal title track. The 'Rastaman' is the 'Roaring lion' chant Albert Griffiths and the Gladiators on their *Symbol of Reality* title song, for, as the Roots Radics explain on their *Forward Ever, Backwards Never* collection, Rasta is 'Strong like a Lion'. Perhaps the best summary of the implications of identifying with the emperor can be found on Winston 'Burning Spear' Rodney's 1991 *Jah Kingdom,* a logical follow through of his 1976 plea to spare the African symbol '(Don't kill the) Lion'. In *Jah Kingdom* all types of Rastas, Twelve Tribes, Bobo Dreads, Nyabinghi, are considered to be lions in the reign of Jah. Clearly, when Dennis Forsythe centred on the image of the lion, he had pierced to the central core of what it meant to be Rasta.

But the question remained, if an individual Rastafarian had himself become the lion, who now were Haile Selassie and the Jesus who came before him?

Who, essentially, for example, was Jesus for Dennis Forsythe? In his book *Rastafari: for the Healing of the Nation,* under the subheading in chapter 2,

'Christ as Mystic', Forsythe notes that he turns for enlightenment to A. (sic) Spencer Lewis, whom he identifies as a 'notable Bible scholar'.[24]

A former Methodist, H. (for Harve) Spencer Lewis in 1909–1915 founded the Ancient Mystical Order Rosae Crucis (AMORC), a secret fraternal society that draws both from the eclectic doctrines of the Masons, whom we touched on earlier, as well as from ideas of the Rosicrucian Order. Rosicrucians are noted for their belief in alchemy (with claims that some members have been able to create gold), their religious syncretism (amalgamating all religions with occult ideas), and odd theories of human origins (Blacks, rather than the primal race from which leprous Whites develop, as many Rastas believe, are presented as a later human development from the lost continent of Mu, Whites (Aryans) are a still later evolved human strain from Atlantis). Such an odd approach to human origins emerges in Lewis' view of Jesus. In order to posit Jesus as a reincarnation of Zoroaster, Lewis contends Jesus was neither Jewish nor Semitic!

> Just about the time of the birth of Jesus the great library and archivist records maintained at Heliopolis were transferred to Mount Carmel, and the Essenes Brotherhood in Palestine together with other branches of the Great White Brotherhood were preparing for the coming of the great Avatar who was to be the reincarnation of Zoroaster, one of the famous Avatars of the Brotherhood in centuries past.
>
> The birth of Jesus in the family of Gentiles living in the Essenes community at Galilee fulfilled the expectations of the Brotherhood, and from this time on the outer and inner activities of the Brotherhood became centered around the ministry of the great Master Jesus.[25]

Although 'sponsored by the Great White Brotherhood', the resulting 'Christene Church', established by 'the original Apostles', who were 'chosen from the Essenes Gentile community at Galilee', 'gradually evolved into a more or less independent public organization' since the Brotherhood 'was interested in the work of all religious movements in all lands, and did not become a part of any of them'.[26]

Instead of affirming the Bible's proclamation of the uniqueness of Christ as the salvific God-Among-Us, Rosicrucians imbibe a heavy draught of gnostic influence and posit a Christ spirit as one of the seven spirits before the throne in Revelation 1.4. Created by the Father, the Word, or Cosmic Christ Spirit, illuminated Jesus, as it did Buddha and many others, to inspire humanity to strive for evolutionary advancement, not through a need for redemption in one lifetime, but an upward progression through many incarnations. How pantheistic its doctrine is can be underscored by its application of the term 'humanity' to God the Father and 'divinity' to human beings. As Spencer Lewis himself explains:

> The Divinity in man is the only real part of his existence, and all else is but a servant unto it. The world is the footstool for this Divine Being, and everything in the universe is enslaved by the omnipotent intelligence of this highest expression

of creation. This Divine Self of man knows neither disease nor death, failure, nor discouragement. Its trend of activity is always upward and progressive ... There comes an influx of Cosmic consciousness and Cosmic Attunement, and in this man finds a power and a strength that is beyond any power or energy of the material world ... The laws of Karma and of Cosmic Compensation reveal to him that he cannot do an injustice to another ... He must let the God Consciousness of his soul control and direct the health and activities of the physical self so that it may truly be the servant unto him, and not a master whipping him into submission and earthly servility. In this way will man rise to power and glory and attain the highest degree of success and happiness ...[27]

Following Lewis' lead, Forsythe theorizes that Jesus emerged from a 'Gnostic' 'Mystery Tradition', possessing 'some rare secret, divine or spiritual knowledge' that is 'revealed only to those few illumed wise men or prophets who have been "initiated"'.[28] Thus, Forsythe reaches into apocryphal literature like *The Gospel of Thomas* and other Gnostic literature to construct a 'Christ' from books 'deemed "Heretical"' by the early church fathers.[29]

The source of these so-called 'hidden' books of wisdom, Gnosticism, named after the Greek word for 'knowledge', *gnosis*, was a syncretistic mixture of neo-pagan Platonic philosophy with Christianity that occurred after the New Testament times. While incipient Gnosticism may be discerned as being combatted in the prologue to John's Gospel and in his first epistle as well as in the Pastoral Epistles (1 and 2 Timothy and Titus), Gnosticism proper did not flourish until the second century. Gnostic books departed significantly from the teaching of Jesus and his disciples by adopting the Platonic idea that matter was evil and in it was imprisoned an immortal, divine soul. Positing a number of celestial way-stations between earth and the fixed stars where a soul aspired to go after death to enjoy the perfect harmony of the music of the spheres of life which endlessly revolve around the Still Point, God, the Gnostics offered (for a price) to enlighten those capable of receiving heavenly knowledge with spiritual secrets so that one might pass through each of these evaluations and achieve bliss in immortality contemplating the Deity after death. In Lewis and Forsythe's schema, Jesus would be one of these ancient teachers, enlightened by the 'Christ' spirit sharing the secret knowledge of ascent to God.

Such a position in his book of 1983 represented a major shift from Forsythe's 1979 paper in which he adjured Rastas to free themselves from being '"locked up" in religion', a trap he saw Marcus Garvey occupying by simply 'painting' God 'black'.[30] Now he was promoting the relevance of Christ:

Neither Christ nor the Prophetic tradition which has gone on for thousands of years can be easily pushed aside as mere mythical folk superstitions. On the contrary they are solid historical happenings. Christ lived(s) and our historical social sciences cannot ignore this historical reality, nor the message and 'meanings' of this Man–God reality.[31]

Refusing to pause at an afrocentric animist solution, Forsythe forged on to arrive at a position regarding the Christ not as simply an archetypal concept or example of nurturing the lion attributes within oneself, but to posit 'Christ' as a '"Man–God" reality' 'inseparably linked to African traditions':

> Our Western tradition has caused us to frown on the Mystery tradition and has created a great divide between us and it. Black Nationalists, Marxists and other political ideologies, however, who seriously quest after Africa for their 'roots' and for their 'culture' (in the search of 'finding themselves') must sooner or later come to terms with the 'Mystery Tradition' and with the works of Christ and with the other 'Teachers of Righteousness' as these 'Prophets' constitute the highest traditions of our past.[32]

As for Lewis and the Gnostics before him, for Forsythe now Jesus could once again 'save' 'mankind' – but through sharing knowledge:

> Many wise men and scholars travelled from all over the world to study under Egyptian priests – including Christ, Plato, Moses and Pythorgoras. The calibre and fame of the official priesthood of Egypt was in fact legendary ... Christ was unique because he <u>perfected</u> this spiritual prophetic tradition to the point where he had a Divine university in his head and he undertook a divine mission which no other God-man had attempted before – to <u>save all mankind</u> – by revealing to them the 'secrets' or the 'way' to immortality, of the all-important 'spirit' in man.[33]

Made 'conscious' by an increased 'usage of Herbs' which, he claims, aids one 'to explore one's self and to find God',[34] Dennis Forsythe found a number of perspectives converging to form a new post-Selassian approach. The Spencer Lewis theology he adopted was similar to that popularized by J. M. Robertson (in *Pagan Christs*), Morton Smith and others. It speculated about Jesus travelling to Egypt to become a magician. It saw him as having developed the Christ consciousness within him. Jesus, if not uniquely divine, had become, like many 'God-men' before him, an individual whose learning had enlightened him to the secret knowledge (gnosis) of the universe. He had so surpassed others that he could even 'save all mankind', not by dying for sins that separated humanity from God in this schema, but by revealing '"great truths" for the use of all humanity'.[35] By this study and development, Christ had become someone perfected to manifest divinity, an enlightened, ascended master: a 'God-man'. That idea, the border over which animism moves into pantheism had been incipient in Forsythe's earlier work, for, to him, even 'Ananci's saving grace is that he has lurking deep within him the idea of his own divinity and power'.[36] Therefore, to Forsythe, Christ had manifested, within an afrocentric context, the means by which divinity could be midwifed out of one and could raise the 'lions' of Rasta to divinely inspired status. And whether that status had limits, as the alleged self-deifications of Leonard Howell, Claudius Henry, Prince Emmanuel Edwards revealed, was an intriguing point. But the way to it, for Forsythe and those who followed him, had been blazed by the enlightened Christ. Clearly, as the seven 'chakras' he proceeds to explore in his book reveal, the way he was recommending to comprehend it was through adapted Eastern forms.

JESUS AS AN ENLIGHTENED TEACHER

In Hinduism, and its off-shoot Buddhism, an enlightened teacher and an avatar are not exactly the same thing. An enlightened teacher (Bodhisattva) is a seeker who has attained the illumination of truth and now seeks to share that enlightenment with others. An avatar (or Avatāra) is an incarnation of Krishna (Kṛṣṇa), who is the original or supreme personality of the Godhead, through Krishna's expansion in three Vishnus, according to the interpretation of proponents of Krishna consciousness.[37]

Earlier, when distinguishing between the perspectives of Leonard Howell and Joseph Hibbert, I cited a much disputed article, published in the *Caribbean Quarterly* issue on Rastafari in 1985. Titled 'Hindu Influences on Rastafarianism' and written by the well published East Indian scholars, Ajai Mansingh, a senior lecturer in the Department of Zoology at the Mona campus of the University of the West Indies, and Laxmi Mansingh, librarian at the Medical Library at the same campus, this article sought a Hindu basis for many key aspects of early Rastafari.

Objections were fervent. Barry Chevannes, author of the splendid *Rastafari: Roots and Ideology*, objected to the Mansinghs' claim that dreadlocks originated with East Indians. Their basis was a photograph circa 1910 at the National Library of Jamaica of an East Indian on a Jamaican plantation in what appears to be locks.[38] Chevannes himself 'traced the origin of the dreadlocks hairstyle to an organization known as the Youth Black Faith'. Therefore he dispensed with the Mansinghs' interpretation of the common belief that locks originated with the followers of Leonard Howell in their mid-twentieth century sojourn at Pinnacle as having been adapted from East Indians with the dismissal: 'Pursuing the Howell angle, Mansingh and Mansingh (1985) speculate on the plausibility of an Indian sadhu source, but without any evidence, oral historiographical or otherwise.'[39] My friend and colleague professor N. Samuel Murrell goes even further in the literature review chapter of our *Chanting Down Babylon: The Rastafari Reader*, when he writes, 'Ajai Mansingh and Laxmi Mansingh's "Hindu Influences on Rastafarianism" (1985) exaggerates the influence of Hindu tradition on aspects of Rastafarian rituals.'[40] But, while battles may rage over the degree of East Indian influence on specific aspects of Rastafarian style and practice, where the Mansinghs make their most intriguing contribution is in their reading of the Hindu religious influence on the thought of founders Howell and Hibbert. Their insistence that Rasta theology bears parallels to and is influenced by Eastern religion has become undeniable, particularly as the movement evolves.

While the beleagured Mansinghs built their case by attempting to trace origins of Rasta customs to the East Indian indentured workers who arrived in the 1840s, an intriguing, though possibly overlooked, precursor, who may have set a context for interpreting biblical material in Eastern modes, seems to have been no one less than the great Marcus Garvey. Despite his orthodox Christian stance, unquestionably, a certain pantheistic flavour comes down from Garvey into Rastafari.

In his 'God helps those who help themselves', thoroughly free-will oriented, nearly deistic view, Garvey saw God as creating and saving humans, then leaving them to progress and to achieve for themselves. If people choose to bow down before others, that is their choice. God will not liberate them. That is their own job. Further, Garvey saw God's spirit dwelling within each person, and only willing good. If that person does choose to bow down before another human, such obeisance is blasphemous to the spirit of God within her or him. This precursory view to the more pantheistic wing of Rastafarian thought is nowhere more in evidence than in Garvey's assessment of Father Divine:

> I don't want to go into the Father Divine stuff but there is something about this Father Divine. He is intelligent enough to know that there is a God in man and not in Father Divine particularly. That God is what that scamp doesn't tell the people. He is part of God and that is how that man is fooling those who are too foolish to understand the relationship between God and man. Added to that spirit is the soul, a free soul, which the spirit of God always tries to direct. The spirit of God is always good. That spirit never dies and when you bow down that spirit before men you are debasing the spirit in you that is God because man was never intended to worship man but God. I haven't time to develop these theories, to set you thinking and realizing your importance. Every man is God walking on two feet.[41]

The Rastafarians who followed him did have time to develop these theories and 'Every man is God walking on two feet' became a central pivotal thought to some Rastafarians.

Garvey's intention here, of course, was pedagogical, for he added immediately:

> There is no man more so than the other. There is no man who can be so bad but he has the spirit of God in him. Do not cringe before other men because God will be vexed with you. I am not telling you in your limited intelligence to start being arrogant. Get intelligence. See that no man is more intelligent than you. So long as one man is more intelligent than you he will be your superior. Until you can produce what the white man has produced you will not be his equal. When you have built your cities, your cathedrals and know that you did it on your own initiative no man will turn his back on you. That is the philosophy taught in a nutshell by the UNIA.[42]

Clearly, Garvey is not making a theological statement as much as an inspirational one. His point is to show his listeners that no one has higher standing by creation or favour with the Deity than they do. His doctrinal shorthand is hyperbolic, used, as any good speaker uses such technique, for effect. He jolts his hearers awake with a bold statement, then educates them with an explanation before they sink back into somnambulation. However, read these statements as anything more than rhetorical affirmations of the essential quality of humanity as reflecting God's image, for example read them as theological statements, and they do take on an Eastern concept of either avatarism, as we shall see in the next section, or divinely enlightened pedagogy. Today in post-physical-presence-of-Selassie Rastafari some have opted for a divinely-inspired, enlightened teacher role for Christ.

Clement 'Bankie Banx' Banks is an Anguillan poet, songwriter, performer who holds superstar status in the Caribbean from tireless performing and the impact of such albums as his 1978 *Bankie Banx and his Roots & Herbs*, which featured his first hit 'Prince of Darkness', 1982's *Soothe Your Soul*, which presented his tribute to Bob Marley 'Remember Bob', to which we shall return shortly, 1989's hit and accompanying album *Terrestrial Spirits*, 1991's *Island Boy*, followed shortly by the live Moonsplash '92 recording. An entrepreneur who owns 'The Dune,' a restaurant that looks out over Rendezvous Bay in Anguilla, he has also appeared on television in Fox Network's *Key West*. His approach to Jesus, and, as we will soon see, to Bob Marley, falls under the category of 'enlightened teacher'. He senses God within himself and separates this 'Presence' from any who have an equal sense of God within them:

> In the Caribbean we were always looking and searching for something for real. Do you know what I mean? So, definitely, I'm conscious of God and truth of the Bible that was invented, you know. But I don't place God in any names, so I don't put a name to God. You know, I see 'Jah' means 'God.' No, I don't say 'Jesus.' I don't say 'Selassie I,' [though] yes, these are the same persons, yes. I see God comes in different forms, in different places, in different times.

Does that equation of Jesus and Selassie mean that he holds a traditional Rastafarian view? Not exactly:

> My idea is that the Bible has been translated, written and rewritten so many times so that you need to feel God, the Spirit of God, within yourself, because the birds and the beetles born but into God, and the other ones, you know? Nobody taught them about God. That's my philosophy: that you know God. You're born; you know God. You can find God.

Jesus, for him, was just such a person who found God:

> Jesus was a great man who lived somewhere in the great continent of Africa in the creative time. And he was just another man like me and anybody else. That's what I feel. I'd rather say he was just another man. I mean, he was inspired. He was given a mission. You know, because God is in everybody, in everyone. Some people get powers to do other things, you know? God was in Bob Marley, you know?

With this remark, Bankie Banx sheds light on a most interesting phenomenon that has been occurring since the death of Bob Marley on 11 May 1981: a movement that can almost be called 'the apotheosis of Bob Marley.' It fits in the category of someone becoming so enlightened that that one's status, spiritually speaking, begins to rise. If one looks at this phenomenon in the Eastern sense, one sees Bob Marley as becoming an 'ascended master' to the point in certain quarters of being worshipped. A momentary survey of his spiritual rise might be instructive as a tool in assessing the significance of the divine claims attributed to Selassie or Jesus in Rastas shaped by Eastern religious ideas.

When Bob Marley succumbed to cancer at the age of 36 he had already helped propel reggae into international consciousness. A bridge figure, half black, half white in parentage, intense, creative, intelligent, generous, unaffected, a charismatic performer with a sexual appeal that had beauty pageant winners throwing themselves at him, Marley was the consummate artist. But his appeal was not simply showmanship, high songwriting ability, and personal charisma. He had managed to find a way to convert the economic poverty and hardship of his early years into a social message that put a reformist nutrition into his lyrics. These he sang with utter conviction, whether he was blasting organized religion, calling for justice, or proposition-ing someone other than his wife. Suddenly, he was gone and, as with the unexpected death of any celebrity, still young, vibrant, and actively engaged in a momentum gaining movement, his popularity hyperspaced, so to say, into legend status. The United Kingdom's Princess Diana, the United States' John F. Kennedy, Argentina's Eva Perón are but three examples of this phenomenon. Though Jamaica had produced an impressive array of musical talent from the great Irving Burgie (Lord Burgess) on, Bob Marley was its true global superstar. Immediately, reggae filled with tributes. His colleagues and family led the way. The 1981 Reggae Sunsplash was dedicated to Bob Marley. Rita Marley and the I-Three, Bob's backup singers, presented some of his songs as did bands like the United Kingdom's Steel Pulse. At the next year's Sunsplash, the great Toots Hibbert kept the momentum alive with his '(Marley's Gone . . .) His Songs Live on'. In 1983 Judy Mowatt released 'Joseph', a tribute to Bob Marley by his chosen Hebrew 'tribal' name, a common practice by Twelve Tribes' Rastas who pick a name of a biblical patriarch by the month they are born.

In a most poignant tribute, his son Ziggy Marley sang about a vision of Bob coming to exhort him while he was 'Lying in Bed', convincing him of the truth of Rastafari. And again he lists 'my daddy' along with 'garvey', 'emperor haile', 'yesus kristos' as having warned about the rise of the 'rastaman' and defeat of the 'wicked' in 'Unuh Nuh Listen Yet', and lists him again with Malcolm X, Martin Luther King and Garvey in 'This One'. Black Uhuru pays tribute in 'Emotional Slaughter', while songs with the title 'Tribute to Bob Marley' were released by Brigadier Jerry, Papa Finnigan and Junior Ranking. Mikey Dread placed him 'In Memory' with Marcus Garvey and Jacob Miller of Inner Circle, who died in a car accident. Carlene Davis also saluted 'Brother Bob'. By 1986, Rita and the I-Three had expanded the scope of their tribute to the song 'He Is A Legend', while his mother, a fine gospel singer in her own right, recalled his last words to her, 'Mother Don't Cry', and confirmed eternally: 'He's a Rastaman'. Monty Montgomery picked up on the spiritual dimension in Ziggy's 'Lying in Bed' by proclaiming Bob's spirit lives on in 'Irie', which credits Bob with exhorting the words of the prophets. And Joseph Hill of Culture contributed both a 'Double Tribute to the O.M.' (Bob was awarded Jamaica's Order of Merit, its third highest honour, a month before he died) and by 1989 a 'Psalm of Bob Marley'.[43]

But what for most of these were handsome tributes had become for others of Bob's circle something much more literal. According to Stephen Davis:

After his death, many of Bob's friends began to think of him as a Christ figure.

Tyrone Downie: 'Bob was a little like Christ for me. Christ wasn't perfect. Christ fucked women. He swore. He did what we all did. He was studying the laws of nature, the laws of the universe. He wasn't trying to teach us to be good, 'cause life is not about being good. Life is about being yourself, being free. How could he know so much about society if he wasn't part of it. Look at Mary Magdalene. So Bob . . . when he was alive I wasn't sure. Since he died, my perspective is that he is really *the* prophet. Because I was right there with him, I never considered him as Bob the prophet. I considered him as Bob my friend.'

Diane Jobson: 'Bob must be seen as a Christ figure, and his songs as a new book of psalms. There will be no more prophets, so his message *had* to reach the ends of the earth. Even Japan, even Italy, where Rome is. "This could be the first trumpet, might as well be the last."'[44]

Amy Wachtel, noted reggae disc jockey on WNWK FM in New York City (whose stage name 'Night Nurse' is taken from Gregory Isaacs' 1982 reggae chart topper), depicts Bob as a 'Messiah':

Selassie, in Amharic, means 'the power of the Trinity.' Bob's Ethiopian name, Berhane Selassie, means 'light of the Trinity.' In many ways, he's an elder brother who encourages us by saying 'come on, you can do it!' In the same way, Bob is the father, too. He loves all equally and unconditionally. We are his children. Still, he's the son. As he said in the *Time Will Tell* video, 'I am the child of life' . . . In support of any Messiah, there are at least 12 apostles. In the case of Bob Marley, there is an undisclosed number of disciples whom he chose to send forth and preach the (Reggae) gospel in this time. In addition to members of his Wailers band and the I-Threes, he left behind a family full of messengers.[45]

Roger Steffens, Marley musicologist, historian, and archivist, told me he has encountered an enclave of Californian 'Marleyite Rastas' who centre their beliefs in Rastafari on Bob's songs and sayings. But beliefs about him are not confined to Rastafari. Native Americans have embraced Bob Marley. The Hopi and Havasupai Amerindians consider him a prophet and one of their own.[46] Sanjay Dev of Katmandu, Nepal, even reports:

Nepal, where deities mingle with mortals, is still beset with many problems, chief of which is rural poverty. Hunger, premature death and inadequate housing are rampant. Music is a main artery of Nepal .'. . Nepalese people embraced Bob into their souls through his music and Rasta beliefs: after all, 'rasta' in Hindi means a path, a roadway, mostly of the spiritual journey. To this day Bob is worshipped in Nepal as an ascetic, as a holy man, as an incarnation of Vishnu. His music will live forever.[47]

Prophet? Messiah? Incarnation of Vishnu? How far will the deifying of Bob Marley go? Are we talking here about a 'First Presleyterian Church of Elvis the Divine', a tongue in cheek joke that is apparently for some turning serious, or a Reformed Druids of America, which began as a satirical college protest against mandatory chapel and today is a full fledged religion in Wicca?[48] Not exactly. There is humorous dimension to the adulation of Bob Marley. His generous spirit touched countless people and articulated for the voiceless a cry that begged to be put into apocalyptic words. His portentous message dignified what many dismissed as a lowly struggle to a mythic battle between Zion and Babylon. He raised the struggle of the diasporan heirs of slavery and all those who identifed with them into an Armageddon clash of biblical proportions and in this he became for many Mosaic or messianic. But how far will his family let such adulation go without a check?

His mother, Cedella Booker, believes he had a special calling:

> You know Jah ordained him to be who he is and what he is and then nothing can ever change that. The stone that the builder refuse in the morning, in the evening it become the head cornerstone – and that's Bob's work now and what it's doing.[49]

But she does not extend to him messianic claims.

When I was interviewing Ziggy Marley, I asked about the vision described in 'Lying in Bed', was it a real vision or imaginary, a fiction made up for the song? Ziggy assured me it was quite real to him, 'I was in bed and there was this force of my father, you know?' But when I asked about 'Reggae Is Now',[50] a song which talks about 'the line of King Marley' 'running through the roots of Africa', and about whether he saw his father like King David or Selassie I or Yesus, he chuckled, 'No, not really, no, not so. I saw my father as a real man who was inspired by the Almighty and another high spiritual man. So a high spiritual man: what we all should be, but not necessarily like Selassie I or Yesus.' When I asked his opinion of all the tribute songs, like Bankie Banx's beautiful 'Remember Bob', which envisions Bob sitting at the right hand of God, and asked him, 'I just wondered how far you were going to let this go. You want him honoured as a man, not made into some kind of deity?,' he replied:

> Well, you know, is a thing where – the same thing with Yesus Kristos. Yesus Kristos come teach us by example, but people follow him, put this on and turn it into something else, where even though the whole church is sin, is corrupted. And the whole praising of the Father is in a corruptive way, the way the system set it now. To me, when my father come, him come natural, normal, with the power, with a natural power. And it not make no sense if you try to put it any higher than that, because you'll get corrupted.

Bankie Banx himself, in interpreting 'Remember Bob' to me, explained its significance in Garveyian terms: 'God was in Bob Marley. God is in everybody, you know?' But the impact of Bob Marley was such that it triggered in people who watched him perform thoughts of something higher.

Betty Wright, a minister and performer well known for songs like 'Cleanup Woman' and 'Tonight Is the Night', detailed this impact:

> Bob Marley is Bob Marley. He is a legend. A reggae legend . . . I had never seen the power of a prophet mystify people and make them pass out. I stood by the [sound] speaker and he would point some kind of way with his finger and throw his head back and folks would faint . . . I think that anytime God puts that kind of a spirit in a man, it's not 'mere mortal,' it's the divine working through the mortal. It is the divine talking, touching the mind, and him taking what God gave him and being able to touch people. No more mortal like just the average man, except they're touched and anointed by God, could stand there and make people faint.[51]

As Danny Sims, record producer and manager of singer Johnny Nash, told Stephen Davis, 'I think Bob was a very mythical character. He was like Jesus Christ. Not to say that he *was*, but he was a saintly kind of figure.'[52]

For his family members and friends like Bankie Banx, Betty Wright, Danny Sims, he was an enlightened teacher and this enlightenment touched others.

In incipient Buddhism, Gautama, the Buddha, the enlightened one, was a teacher who gained insight and wished to enlighten others with it. In these family and friends' view Bob Marley was similar. For many Rastas like these who view through a parallel vision to early Hinduism or its early Buddhist development, first Jesus, then Selassie, then Bob Marley become enlightened.

But as centuries passed, the figure of Buddha was elevated until he was seen as an avatar, the ninth and latest manifestation or incarnation of Vishnu, that is, more a 'descended' than an ascended master.

For Rastas who look with a perspective similar to these later developments, such religious figures are thought to reveal themselves to be appearances of God. In Rastafari, the adaptation of such a perspective may explain what has been a most baffling, even aberrant tendency among some of its most prominent leaders: the pushing aside of Haile Selassie and declaring themselves God.

SELASSIE, JESUS, HOWELL, AND HENRY AS 'GODS'

At the Festival of Dedication, while walking in the Temple, Jesus suddenly found himself surrounded. 'How long will you keep us in suspense? If you are the Christ, tell us openly', cried the devout (John 10.24). Jesus was exasperated, 'I have told you and you do not believe. The actions which I myself do in the name of my Father witness for me' (v. 25). And then in the fury of his reply he makes a momentous statement, 'I and the Father are one' (v. 30). The crowd is enraged. This is clearly blasphemy, for Jesus is making himself equal with God. They run to snatch up stones, for this carpenter from the alleys of Nazareth is blaspheming right in the portico of Solomon, their wisest ancestor, by 'making' himself 'God' (v. 33). But Jesus' time to die has not yet come, so he unleashes his wit and tangles them into helpless confusion, 'Is it not written in your law that "I said, you are gods?" If those were called gods to whom the word of God came, and the Scripture is not able to be destroyed, the one the Father sanctified and sent into the world you would say he blasphemes, because I said, the son of God I am?' (vv. 34–36). Then reminding them of the great good he is doing among them he challenges them to arrest him if indeed he is doing any harm, but to believe him if he is doing good. He finally confounds them by explaining that he is doing all these healings and miracles among them so that they will know and understand that 'in me (is) the Father and I (am) in the Father' (v. 38). Apparently the crowd falls out over leaving Jesus in peace because of his good works or arresting him in spite of them and he escapes.

Hard pressed by his opponents, what he has done in this interchange is to reach back into Psalm 82.6, '[And God said] "I said: Ye are godlike beings, And all of you sons of the Most High"' (Masoretic text). So, Jesus' strategy was to block their murderous onslaught by pointing out they were children of God. Where the double-edged sword of spiritual truth cuts through them in this verse that Jesus cites is in what the rest of the psalm says (and which they would well know): 'Nevertheless, even though you're god-like beings, you're going to die like mere humans' (v. 7, my paraphrase). Why will this happen? Because, verse 2 tells us, they 'judge unjustly, And respect the persons of the wicked' (Masoretic text). Jesus, by reminding them of their favoured status and then holding up his own good deeds as a foil against which to test their injustice and sycophantic opportunism, confounds them, just as true tradition tells us he confounded those who would stone the woman caught in adultery in John 7.53–8.11, by holding her up as a mirror in which her accusers' own conditions should be assessed. While this was clearly Jesus' strategy, given the particular psalm he chose, for the Rastas seeking a new definition of Selassie and Jesus after the former's departure, the psalm opened up interesting Eastern dimensions. Manley 'Big Youth' Buchanan seized on it as a part of his message, 'I then tell the people them so them must know them god, you understand, and don't pray to the idols that they gave us.' Instead, should one look to the God of Ethiopia? 'Right, the God of lords and God of all gods. 'Cause there's a lot of gods and you know you are god. Of course, man a god-man.'

The great burra drummer Ras Michael Henry captured the thrust of the reference to Psalm 82 when he observed to me:

Remember, we are all chosen of God. We are all! I remember when once they asked Jesus, they said, 'Christian?' And he said, 'Ye are all gods and children of the Most High,' so to you who seek Him, reformers say that the things that you seek of him and really mean it from your heart, he will make you do even greater. So, is not this so well, then, you are the greatest, but you becomes great through your humility to him.

Expounding further on this passage in a later interview with me, he explained:

> He brought it up to them that they could have an understanding, 'So, well, okay, you're jealous because I say I'm the Son of God, but, you see, that's the truth.' They were jealous because they were not. They didn't have that light burning in them that they could see themselves to be the son of God. So, when he said that he's the Son of God and Son that, it created a jealousy in them, part of satan, and saying – being a man – and saying he's God, you know what I mean? He had to say, 'You're all gods, children of the Most High, but ye die like men. Likewise, you'll die. You judge unjustly and you rob the poor and the needy,' you know what I mean? That's what. But anybody wants to show in themself in the positive vibes, they hold on to the right vibes.

But, to at least one founder of Rastafari, this message may have personally gone even deeper.

Previously, we noted the controversial work of Ajai and Laxmi Mansingh and the furore over their positing Hindu bases for the doctrines, rituals and distinctive trappings of Rastafari. While battles wage over whether or not locks, ganja use, vegetarianism, philosophy, theology – even the characteristic salute 'Jah Rastafari!' which punctuates all Rastafarian discourse and introduces and ends many songs – can be traced to Hinduism, the Mansinghs pile up some of their most interesting evidence in their reading of the Hindu influence on founders Leonard Howell and Joseph Hibbert.

Particularly in their dealing with Hibbert, the Mansinghs do attempt to provide the 'oral historiographical' evidence that Barry Chevannes demanded of their bold thesis, because they had the opportunity to interview Joseph Hibbert himself in 1982. During that interview they learned that:

> When Joseph Hibbert, the co-founder of Rastafarianism, first heard of the Indian God-incarnates in 1918, he acquired books to learn more about them, discussed their divinity with friends, and conceived the idea of an African God-incarnate, similar to Rama, Krishna and Buddha. He was convinced that 'every nation have their Gods; whiteman have Christ, Indians have their Gods, and African too have ours except that we don't know him.'[53]

Earlier, we quoted Marcus Garvey's famous statement published in 1923, 'If the white man has the idea of a white God, let him worship his God as he desires. If the yellow man's God is of his race, let him worship his God as he sees fit. We, as Negroes, have found a new ideal.'[54] That this saying passed down as a legacy from Garvey is common knowledge, but what may not be observed so readily is that in Garvey's hearers the message subtly altered. No one less than Garvey's own son, Marcus Garvey, Jr, who was a teacher who influenced Mutabaruka, among others,[55] appears to have shifted the focus of this message theologically. As Marcus Garvey, Jr, who headed up his own Black Power organization, framed this thought, 'If Jesus is God born as a Jew, and the Buddha is God born as an Indian, why cannot Jah (God) appear as a Black Man.'[56]

Between the two Garveys' statements is a theological continental shift. Marcus Garvey, Senior, is saying clearly that God has no colour, but since other races choose to see God through the spectacles of their own colour, Blacks may as well follow the same practice. Marcus Garvey, Junior, is saying, if God appeared as a Jew (Jesus), and an East Indian (Buddha), then God appeared as a Black as well. For Garvey, Sr, the focus is God's nature and its relation to all humans. He is not talking about God incarnating. When he deals with the incarnation, he focuses on Jesus as a great reformer.[57] His reason, as we will soon see, is that he affirmed Christianity. But his son, Garvey, Jr, is not focusing on God's true nature, but on God's incarnation, suggesting that God incarnated many times, not just exclusively in Jesus. Therein is the shift away from Christian orthodoxy to Eastern religion.

In Christian orthodoxy, the incarnation of Jesus was a unique event: once and for all God became human. In Eastern religions God incarnates many times. As Barbara Blake Hannah explained to me when I asked her, 'Who do you think Jesus was?' 'He was God. Yes. He revealed God to us. So was Mahatma Ghandi and Martin Luther King and so many others. Whatever you call Him – Allah, Buddha – but we all refer to one God.' 'But Mahatma Gandhi and Martin Luther King co-existed', I observed, 'so you must believe that these are all emanations from God?' 'Yes', she replied, 'all showing us God'. 'So this is Eastern thought, the avatar or atman who reveals God?' I asked. 'Call it what you will', she said. As we saw earlier, in her written discussion about the uniqueness of Christ, that only in Christ's name can one be saved and not in the emperor's, she seeks to adapt Christian orthodoxy. Only Christ came to save us, the emperor came to rule us in a kingly way, though, as we saw, her reflections on information about the emperor's lifestyle have caused her to bracket dealing with that problem until eternity. But for those who step more definitively over the borders of Eastern religion, the implications of such speculations as Barbara Blake Hannah's serve to move religious figures from being enlightened teachers who reveal God to us to being actual appearances of God. In other words, they shift from Garvey, Senior's, to Garvey, Junior's position. Now, to me, the Mansinghs have made their most penetrating point in tracing this tendency to Howell and Hibbert, two founders of the movement.

Hibbert, adding data to the argument that Marcus Garvey, Senior, never made a prophecy about Haile Selassie coming as God to earth, explained to the Mansinghs that though he never heard him prophesy about the emperor when he followed Garvey, Hibbert himself centred on Haile Selassie because of the titles with which the emperor was crowned. From these titles, Hibbert decided the emperor was Jesus returned, while Howell identified him as God the Father. As the Mansinghs explain Leonard Howell's position:

The confusion about the exact status of Haile Selassie – a God-incarnate, or Jesus-incarnate – reflects the depth of Hindu influence on the two concepts. Those with deeper knowledge of Hinduism and a more independent approach (Howell et al) regarded Haile Selassie as the manifestation of God Himself, more like Lord Rama who is regarded by the Hindus as the first human manifestation of Lord Vishnu; Lord Krishna and Buddha are regarded as the second and third reincarnations of Vishnu. This concept refuses to share Haile Selassie's 'divine soul' with any one, least with the Europeans' Christ. Indeed, Howell's followers are more Hindu in philosophy, rituals and codes, than Hibbert's.[58]

This explains to them why Howell, for one thing, tried to adopt a Hindu nom de plume for his work and ended up with the corrupted Hindi title G. G. (Gangunju (or Gangungu), which, they believe, misspells Gyangunji) Maragh.[59] He was an Eastern influenced teacher, attempting to found his teaching on Eastern thought. Hibbert, though also influenced, was more Bible based:

> Hibbert and his followers, with more knowledge of the Bible, regard Haile Selassie as a re-incarnation of Jesus Christ, just as Krishna and Buddha are the reincarnations of Rama. This concept is in line with that of several non-conformist churches such as Unity Church, which regard Krishna, Buddha and Jesus as the reincarnations of the same divine soul.[60]

If the Mansinghs are right (though Rastas like John Moodie or Byron Antonio Beckford, whom we shall meet in the next chapter, who claim Jesus is both the Son *and* the Father befuddle such neat categorizations!), their schema might put into perspective many of the views we have seen so far.

What they may also do is shed some possible light on why leaders like Leonard Howell and Claudius Henry and even Prince Emmanual Edwards of the Bobo Dreads claim entrance into the Trinity.

In 1941, the police invaded the Pinnacle plantation for a number of alleged infractions: growing and selling ganja, raiding their neighbours and assaulting them if they tried to get back their property. Howell became a fugitive, but he and 70 of his followers were soon arrested and hauled into court. When the depositions were read, many were shocked to hear them reporting Howell as having declared, 'I will give you ninety-six lashes, I will beat you and let you know to pay no taxes. I am Haile Sellassie, neither you nor the Government have any lands here.'[61]

Howell, who was living like a potentate with thirteen wives and concubines, presiding over a community of some 600 followers, had appeared to have declared himself Haile Selassie. Further, Karlene Faith, whose work I noted earlier, reports that the followers of the Rev Claudius Henry also were elevating his role in the divine plan and bestowing an 'adulation' that 'approaches idolatry, and he is regularly likened to Jesus Christ, Moses, Marcus Garvey, and even Haile Selassie'.[62] Barry Chevannes, reviewing pamphlets of Henry's, concludes:

> The reader is told that Jesus is the morning star, hence he can infer that Henry regarded himself as Jesus. And indeed so did his followers ... All converts to Henry's church, then, believed in his divinity and in his special role in the designs of God, that is Emperor Selassie, for his people. As Jesus was to his Father, so is Henry to Selassie.[63]

Prince Emmanuel Edwards, who presided over the Bobo Dreads, was also regarded as a member of the Trinity.

Are all of these men mad? Do they all think they are Haile Selassie or Jah? The courts definitely thought so, for both Leonard Howell and Claudius Henry were committed to insane asylums. But, by declaring 'God is Man', 'You're a god-man', 'Almighty God is a living man', the Rastas have opened up their theology to the possibility of personal apotheosis.

The first Rasta I ever interviewed in 1979 was a young St Lucian dreadlocks. When I asked him, 'What do you think of Jesus?', he replied, 'Jesus? I am Jesus'. 'You wouldn't see Jah as outside?' I asked. 'You would see yourself as Jah?' 'That's right', he explained, 'I am Jah. Jah is inside.' At what point did this Eastern-oriented theology cross over the line of madness for Howell, so that he was lording it over people, threatening to whip them, and declaring he was the emperor? Or did he just 'do a Father Divine' on them, as Garvey saw it, a move permitted by his theology that God was in all humanity and he, as opposed to his followers, was aware of the fact?

Whatever the explanation of Howell's state of sanity, or of Claudius Henry's, or of the others', personal apotheosis, as we saw in the case of Bob Marley, is a potential follow through of this brand of Rasta thought. And when it is applied to Jesus, it posits Jesus as god. Not as God in the exclusive, or one might say 'Big G' – God – sense, but in the 'small g' sense, as in the idea that we are all 'gods'.

Andrew Tosh adapted this view when he explained to me, 'I praise Moses, David, Joshua, all earthly prophets, but I worship only the Almighty.' When I asked if Haile Selassie was the Almighty, he replied, 'Haile Selassie is the son of the Almighty.' Is Jesus the Almighty, then? 'Jesus is the son of the Almighty and Haile Selassie is the son of the Almighty', he explained, and pointing to me, 'You are the son of the Almighty', and pointing to our mutual friend, the Marcus Garvey expert Kevin Aylmer, he went on, 'And Kevin here is a son of the Almighty. Rastafari is the real creator – Jah Rastafari. Jesus Christ is his son and you've got to learn to worship the Almighty.'

Jamaican-Canadian Junior Taylor is a college graduate who has served as a computer programmer, director of a college student centre and manager for several music groups. He sees himself as representing the new wave of young, college-educated Rastas who gravitate toward the Twelve Tribes. Son of a Catholic mother and an Anglican father who forbade the speaking of patois in his home, he was attracted to Rastafari because 'society looked down with great extremes on Rastafari, the culture, its belief, dreadlock, the music – it was all sub-culture, anti-conformatory, belittling, ghettoish, backward ... it was the forbidden thing. You couldn't talk about it nor people like Bob Marley'. 'The more you were told you shouldn't be like this, it's the more you wanted to know why and studied.' Low key ('I'm not a – for lack of a better word a "testimonial person." I don't go out and preach ... stand on the streetcorner and tell you, you know, you've got to believe'), he too looks for an Almighty above all religions:

Whether you are Muslim, Hindu, Christian, Rastafarian, you know, Hebrew, you believe and as long as you believe that there is a Supreme Being, a Father, then you have faith. And as long as you don't neglect that faith and allow that faith to become you, you know, like your life, you'll feel better.

What makes Junior Taylor 'feel better' is consciously infusing his Rastafari with the teachings of Krishnamurti and practising the 'Bij Mantra'. As representative of the new, liberalized Rastas, who find themselves driven back to re-examine the belief system and, if they are to maintain their faith, find another role for Selassie I and another mode for Jah to work through him, he separates belief in Jesus from belief in Haile Selassie, whom he looks beyond:

> Who is the father of the movement? It is not Selassie, because when he came to Jamaica in '66 or '65, he was amazed at the reponse of the people. He was thrown back. You know he was — I can't say scared. He was a tad terrified, a little overwhelmed that he was being called God. So, we're not talking about someone who proclaimed to be God, or the reincarnation thereof.

Yet, for Junior Taylor, 'he may be the closest thing we've had to Christ and to a second coming'. But, was he Jesus returned? 'No':

> Jesus Christ was the son of God. That I will say. Selassie, direct descendant of David and the Queen of Sheba, is in the same line, but not the same person. A direct descendant does not make God. His heart and his head was in the right place and he was in the right place, talking about being in the right place at the right time with the right view. Because, there's Howell, there's Selassie. One man trying to make you believe that this man is the Man. And this man doesn't accept it and he tells you, well, it's not really him, it's me! You have no choice but to disbelieve this statement and return to your other. You and I stand in the room. You've preached to everybody in the room that I am God. And when I am introduced, my first reaction is, 'But I am not.' And then you say, 'Well, actually, it's not Junior, it's me.' I, the person in the crowd, would banish you and then go back to what I was believing all before, because that was what it was based on. Howell's teaching was that this man was God. So, he had all these people believing that and then tried to make them believe something else ... And that's what happened to the sect. I can't call it a religion. And people ask if that's my religion. It's my faith ... And my true feeling — and this might be the essence of all this stuff I said on this tape — is that Rastafarianism is Howell's interpretation of the Bible.

Empowered by his education, Junior Taylor has examined the roots of Rastafari and discerned it as an invention of Leonard Howell on a reluctant Messiah. This he takes into perspective: 'There's nothing wrong with Howell when Howell's beliefs are true and committed. But, I've seen where he has said he was god. In the end it was nothing but a power struggle for him. He lost his way.' Therefore, Taylor rejects the 'exclusive' approach to Rastafari. He jettisons such favoured teachings as that Jah is 'the hidden name, the secret name of God' 'when it's actually there in the book. Someone who knows the book will tell you. What are we going to call our God? Call him, Jah. It's in the book. It's hardly referred to. It's hidden.' Yet, he affirms himself as a Rasta, even to practising the dietary laws. Like Andrew Tosh, his is a Rastafari that looks to the Almighty and affirms Jesus as the son of God. But, in contrast, his version goes one step further. His Rastafari relegates Ras Tafari himself to the lesser teacher role.

Is he then Christian rather than Rasta? Not in his mind. He is a Rasta who consciously melds Rastafari in with Hindu thought, looking through it to find the Almighty. His syncretism with Hinduism opens him to respect other faiths. As he explained to me, 'Bill, I don't want to take away from Christianity. I don't want to take away from Jewish, Hindu, Muslim, but each one interprets their book their way to suit themselves.'

An even more intense attempt to syncretize Rastafari and view it as sharing a common source with other religions is by 'Aakhun' George W. Singleton, BA, DH, who bills himself as the 'Scribal Messenger of the Eternal Light'. In 1997, he issued a complex book entitled *Esoteric Atannuology, Egyptology and Rastafariology: The Defalsification of Ancient Predynastic and Dynastic Egyptian History, Chronology, Culture and Spirituality*, Volume I. Professor Singleton's goal is to produce a work of comparative religion that looks behind Christianity, Islam, Mahayana Buddhism to discover their source in an ancient Annu/Egyptian faith, whose scriptures 'were copied originally from the now missing Text Books of Hermes (Tchuti/Seth) of the Annu Mystery School esoterically the "Schools of Annukhet", the Shabd. "Creative Word", "Inner Lighted Sound" Currents'. These primary texts were stolen and sold by a 'corrupt Theban priesthood', who proceeded to cover their perfidy by 'a systematic coverup and falsification of history and its artifacts'.[64] Within such a framework, Rasta, for him, becomes 'eoterically the Astral or first spiritual plane; and esoterically the Rasta/"Rastau" plane in the ancient Egyptian terminology'.[65] As he explains in 'Poem 8', a section identified as 'Esoteric Rastafari: It's Meaning and Significance (*Rastafariology*)':

> King Haile Selassie of Ethiopia was named 'Rasta Fari,' Given by his parents on the birth day he arrived; this name traces back to more than three thousand years, when Israel and Sheba were united and much feared; by those nations who were aligned with the 'Magog,' who exploited the planet and on the weak trod. Yet 'Rasta Fari' goes back beyond Israel, when black Annu tribes ruled the river of the Nile; whose mystery school taught the 'Path of the Aten,' and graduated 'Sun People' who were purged of sins; 'Rasta Fari' is a mystic hieroglyphic term, denoting one who had deification earned; notice that 'Ra-sta' rearranged spells 'Ast-ra,' where 'Ra' generically means the 7 inner sun gods; and 'Ast' means the heavens which are these gods' abode, 'Rasta' the first mystic (astral) plane initiates go.[66]

Singleton goes on to transliterate 'Fari' to 'Peraa' for Pharoah, interpreting the term to mean an enlightened one who has ascended to divinity only to discover that that one is already part of 'God's light'. Gnostic in its concept of 'rising above the body' ['to escape the "body tomb bind"'] to the astral plane of 'Rastau', and Eastern in its picture of 'the "path of Rastafari"' as 'using "inner lighted sound" meditation' to 'learn to "while alive leave the body and die"', it interprets dreadlocks as a sign showing 'surrender, to God's will'. Samson, Samuel, Daniel, John the Baptist are all called 'dreadlocked Rasta spiritualists'. Proof that 'the Rastafari was Nile valley high priests' is summoned from ancient Egyptian paintings showing dreadlocked priests leading processions. Finally, 'true "Rastas"' are adjured to be vegetarian, monogamous, agrarian, egalitarian, non-technical, artistic, 'at peace with other people', as 'true Rastafari strives to be human gods'.[67]

Speculation such as Singleton's may very well be fuelled by the prevalence of cognates of the word 'Ras' in Afro-Asiatic languages. 'Head' is indicated in Arabic by *ra's*, in Hebrew by *rosh*, in Aramaic by *re'sh*, in Akkadian by *rishu*. In Yoruba, the 'rs' component is built into *orisa*, which has come to mean 'gods'. So 'Ras' in Afro-Asiatic terminology denotes 'head' and connotes 'god'.

Against such a framework, Rasta songs like Peter Tosh's 'I Am That I Am', where he alludes to himself as the 'I Am', 'the Son of David', the 'son of God',[68] appear to fit right in with this Eastern slant.

Another inclusive take on Rastafari is *The Living Testament of Rasta-For-I* by Ras J. Tesfa, a gifted artist, actor, composer and performer. His liberalized vision of Rastafari has him affirming 'Children of all Beliefs' in the lead off song of his 1985 Meadowlark album *The Voice of the Rastaman*. The artwork on the back cover comprises the symbols of many faiths: the Rasta royal Ethiopian lion, the crescent and star of Islam, the yin-yang, the ankh, Kali, David's star, sphinx, a traditional African mask, pyramid. In his book he exhorts, 'Young lion of JAH, pleaded the elder; let not your locks be a blockade in the avenue of brotherly love between thyself and the Unlocked, least you be swept up in the wave of confusion from which the Father brought you.'[69] For him, the 'message of The Brethren' is 'man in God, and God in man by which all are equal under the sun'.[70] A careful scholar, he attributes Garvey's alleged prophecy about Selassie to 'legends', calling Garvey a 'missionary, preaching the gospel of "Blackness"'.[71]

Well intentioned accommodationist views like these attempt to include a place for all beliefs from a basic standpoint of Rastafari. But not all Rastas, even with an Eastern slant, affirm all faiths.

Ansel Cridland of the Meditations agreed, 'God made a lot of appearances', and is comfortable with calling God Jah or Allah, since 'is only one God upon earth, heaven upon earth'. But he disagrees with certain kinds of worship:

> See, can't be no two, Man. One on heaven and earth. In this world we have a lot of religions, in my name you will have a lot of people say they are God. These people pray to stone, people's spirit. People worship melted bull and worship bull as God. They tack up things and say they is god. No, them things are not right. What kind of print-up stone you put out kind of thing upon people about them things like that — that not right.

He sees a conspiracy of 'white people' to 'print up' and send out things for people to 'believe' and thus to 'control a person's mind'. But for him:

You must believe in the Most High. Some people because them rich and have so
much money them just seem that that's their God. But remember, if them go try it
about them to the person that still have God – Jesus you see, man?

For him the rich are 'carrying that kingdom within your bag of riches' like an
idol worshipper carries his god. Readers might recall the ironic scene in
Melville's *Moby Dick* (1851) where Queequagh carries his god in his pocket,
producing it to praise when things go right and blame when things go wrong.
This kind of reduction of deity the thoughtful Ansel Cridland wants to avoid.

In similar fashion other Rastas also draw back from positing God as
correctly worshipped by all faiths. Further, certain Rastas have re-evaluated
Haile Selassie to human status, elevated their view of Jesus back to being
God, and, while maintaining their identification as Rastas and allegiance to
the principles of Rastafari, have begun to grope back toward Christian
orthodoxy. But the orthodoxy they are seeking is markedly freed from an
oppressive, slave master type, Euro-western definition.

6 God as Man

THE HUMANITY OF GOD

A shift from seeing the emblem of one's faith demoted from universal God to mere human may seem vast, but, in the case of the Rastafari, enough precedent had already been established in the movement to make the step for some a surprisingly easy one. As early as the first preachers, the emphasis had been on humanity not divinity. One can trace this focus to a source as seminal as Leonard Howell himself, who shaped his theological language with a kind of patriarchally inverted incarnationalism. By that phrasing I mean it was patriarchal in that it was masculo-centric, 'man' being a defining term even for woman (Queen Omega, for example, he calls the 'womanhood of man'.[1]) It was inverted in that it began not so much emphasizing pre-existent deity, as proclaiming Haile Selassie as the presence of the 'living God' being crowned on earth.[2] And it was incarnational, revealing a human as possessing the fullness of God, then moving backwards from that declaration to affirm 'His Majesty Ras Tafari is the head over all man for he is the Supreme God. His body is the fullnes of him that filleth all in all'[3] (a reference to Ephesians 1.23). From there Howell went on to posit Haile Selassie and his queen in retrospect to be the Creators:

> King Alpha and Queen Omega said that they are Black Arch Sovreign of most Holy Times, and perfect Virginity, and Supreme Crown Head of Holy Times. The Pay Master and keeper of the Perfect Tree of Life and are Creators of Creation, Dynasties and Kingdoms, Holy Genealogy and Holy Theocracy, and Celestial in Terrestial Mediator if you wish to know their profession.[4]

'Celestial in Terrestial' aptly summarizes Howell's seminal proclamation. The emphasis is not on God becoming human, but on a human being God. From that adaptation of the incarnational theme predicates all the this-worldly interpretations of Rastafari: God is a living human, heaven is on earth in Africa, the apocalypse is now and its Anti-Christ is Rome; its deliverer the reigning monarch of Ethiopia.

Because it is built in a Christian culture on a foundation of Christian tools and concepts – including the Bible, doctrines like the incarnation, salvation, divine justice, destruction of the wicked, pre-millennial eschatology – Rastafari also seeks a place for Jesus. In some cases, but by no means all, as we shall see, Jesus shares the changing fortunes of Selassie I. While Selassie was reigning and thriving he was thought to share the same divine spirit that Jesus had. But for those who have begun to reassess the position of

Haile Selassie, a question arises about what fate Jesus will share. Do both figures devalue in regards to deity? Do they split off and receive different spiritual assignments? Are they re-examined against biblical revelation and personal experience? Each of these avenues, as we will see, is being explored by Rastafarians.

But many Rastas I have met, no matter what views they hold on the figures of Jesus or of Haile Selassie, will define God as 'a man', remaining true to this seminal tradition. For example, dancehall's voice of consciousness Tony Rebel terms God 'the Man' with 'the plan' in his song 'Creator':

> Omnipotent omnipresent omniscient character
> The I am that I am Alpha and Omega
> The ever-living ever-truthful faithful forever ...
>
> Because ah God ah the man who have the plan
> Whe the whole world have fi go call upon
> Mi bawl out God ah the man wha have the plan
> Him have the big wide world inna him hand ...
>
> Me say the way the man good and great
> We shoulda give thanks and shouldn't really wait
> Him can destroy and Him can create
> Shut and unlock the gate ...
>
> Him ah the ruler of all ruler
> Him ah the king of all kings
> Him ah the morning and evening
> Ending and the beginning
> He's the one that take care
> And the one you should fear
> Him ah the natural mystic that is flowing through the air
> Ah beg unnu seek wisdom and try understand
>
> Jah Jah made us because him have an excellent plan
> Created us in his image and oh just so we tan
> Say him no want us to represent no other man ...
> Because ah God ah the man who have the plan ...[5]

When I asked the significance of terming the Deity 'the Man', he replied, 'He is "the Man" because it's obvious that He is a man.' Why is it obvious to him that God is a 'man'? He explains, 'We're like Him. Because He made us in His own image ... We was with God. Because if he made us, all of that ingredients that he used to make us was with Him. And he was from the beginning, so we was from the beginning with Him ... Here's what I'm saying: He made us out of Him. Because He reproduce himself and He made us.' Such a view takes literally the concept that humans are made in the image of God. In a literal rendering this suggests to him that since humans mirror their Creator, therefore, God must be a human. This is not simply to say that God is being anthropomorphized and presented in human terms so that this spiritual reality called 'God' can be grasped by the finite, material mind. This is to say that God is essentially a human being!

Part of the goal of this book is to articulate the various positions on Jesus in the multi-faceted movement labelled 'Rastafari'. Another part is to locate the various theologies or Christologies, when applicable, within any previous religious views. This one is analogous to classic Mormon theology, where God is also considered a human. In the traditional Mormon view, God was voted by a divine council to be the Supreme Being and therefore Creator of the world. As founder Joseph Smith put it, 'In the beginnning the head of the Gods called a council of the Gods and they came together and concocted a plan to create the world and people it.'[6] Popular Mormon theology pictures each universe being ruled by a creature who was such a success in another universe that he was given his own universe to create and rule. The way Smith explained it, 'God himself was once as we are now and is an exalted man.'[7] Further, in his collection *Doctrines and Covenants*, he taught, 'The Father has a body of flesh and bone as tangible as man's; the Son also, but the Holy Ghost has not a body of flesh and bones but is a personage of spirit.'[8]

Mormonism, like Rastafari, is a heterodoxy. That is to say, it is a diverging set of doctrines, drawn out of Christianity, employing Christian tools such as the Bible, Christian figures and objects of worship, and even adapting its doctrines and some of its terminology, but reaches heretical conclusions. Therefore, concepts like the Trinity remain, but they are infused with newly altered meanings.

Earlier we noted another parallel to Rastafari, a linkup to the Masonic movement traced to founders like Joseph Hibbert and Archibald Dunkley. Masons, we noted, also acknowledge the Trinity, but as 'Juh-buh-lon': Jah, Baal or Bel, and On or Osiris. As those searching for the origin of use of the name 'Jah' for God in incipient Rastafari are certainly given pause by this potential source, particularly in light of such provocative language as the reference to the 'Black Arch Sovreign' in the earlier quotation from co-founder Howell, so are others given pause to wonder at the exact content of a Masons-influenced Triune God-head, accompanying the 'Jah' of 'Juh-buh-lon'.

While such a configuration like 'Juh-buh-lon', as a composite of divine names, would fit within sections on Eastern or even Rosicrucian parallels to Rastafarian theologies, a this-worldly 'God is man' theory is less Masonic and more reminiscent of the view of the Church of Jesus Christ of Latter-Day Saints. In the nineteenth-century milieu Mormonism was as notorious as Rastafari was in the twentieth. Holding a similar Ethno-Israelite view to the Rastafarian idea that diasporan Blacks are the lost tribes of Israel, or the Anglo-Israelism of Herbert W. Armstrong, which adopted the idea of Richard Brothers (1757–1824) that the Anglo-Saxons were the lost tribes of Israel, the Mormons posited the American Indians, among others, as the descendants of a wandering group of Israelites who arrived in the Americas in two emigrations in prehistory.

Mormon scandal, however, was caused less by this popular nineteenth-century theory than by its polygamous views, Smith's despotic rule, the silencing of his opposition by his ordering the destruction of its printing press, and the resultant murderous reactions such views and actions elicited from the surrounding culture.

When Joseph Smith was shot to death by a mob, Brigham Young took over and sought to explicate Smith's doctrines further. On the 'God is man' issue Young now expanded:

> When our father Adam came into the Garden of Eden, he came into it with a celestial body and brought Eve, one of his celestial wives with him ... He is our father and our God and the only God with whom we have to do.[9]

If Adam was a human similar to each of us and passed through life so successfully and progressively from accomplishment to accomplishment that he was assigned to be our God, the implication lies open that anyone of us can, with a little pluck and courage, achieve divinity. We should keep that view in mind when assessing the divine claims such leaders as Leonard Howell and Claudius Henry eventually put forward for themselves.

Yet, to note the striking similarity between Rastafarian and Mormon language is not to suggest that what Rastas and Mormons mean is synonymous. They may be reminiscent of each other, but for the Rasta, the genesis of the affirmation is not nineteenth-century progressivism, but the elevation of the downpressed black diasporan male. For God to be revealed as a black male is to place an exorbitant value upon one who has been stolen, subjected, despised and – now dramatically – reasserted. The concept may seem to be blasphemous, but it comes from the depths of a psyche whose identity was supposedly irretrievably taken and had substituted in its place a 'Quashie' mentality of self-loathing servility. Rather than irretrievable, the true identity of diasporan black males is seen to have been safe in God's keeping.

As a thoughtful and creative Rastafarian thinker, Ansel Cridland of the Meditations, told me, 'I've just always seen that God is a black man, you know?' Bob Marley and Peter Tosh declare in their famous piece 'Get Up, Stand Up' that 'almighty God' is 'a living man'.[10] With the Wailers, many Rastas are comfortable stopping with a completely immanent this-worldly figure of God. When I asked Ansel Cridland, 'So, is there a supernatural being we call God?', he replied, 'Supernatural? No.' God is inextricably involved with God's creation.

But this is not to say that either Ansel Cridland or Tony Rebel simply hold an africanized Mormonic view. For Ansel Cridland, Jah = Jesus = Selassie I. These share the same person. As a result, despite what the press claims happened in 1975, he believes, 'God can't dead, Man. God can't dead. If God dead, the world crash.' When I asked, 'What do you think happened to Haile Selassie?,' he replied, 'Well, you see, so he's in the spirit, like a spirit form. Here and everywhere. Jah can't dead, man! Anytime Jah dead, them whole world crash.' So, Selassie I may have assumed a spiritual form, but to call him 'supernatural' is to suggest he goes out of the realm of nature, and Jah never abandons his world. This interpretation is similar to the one proffered by the Rastafarian Joel Lawson of Reality Publishers of the Pitfour Nyahbinhgi Centre of Montego Bay in his major article 'From Jesus Christ to Rastafari' in the Rastafarian journal *Rasta Vibrations*. According to Ras Joel, believers should have expected the emperor to suffer removal:

> He was deposed; His monarchy was abolished. In fact, all these inglorious things prophecied in Psalms 89.35–45, precisely happened to Haile Selassie.
>
> Therefore, when all these ugly things were happening to Haile Selassie in 1974, the Rastaman who knows his bible well, only marvelled to himself and acknowledged another fulfillment of a major prophecy. On the other hand, those who professed Rastafari, but did not know the prophecies, were very disappointed.[11]

Why were these Rastas 'disappointed'? For the same reason that Christians have not accepted Haile Selassie as Christ's new advent, according to Lawson, because 'their view of God is so remote that there is no way they can fathom Him (God) in the framework of human flesh'. He equates this lapse with the warning given by the Apostle John in 1 John 4.3 ('And every spirit that confesseth not that Jesus Christ is come in the flesh is not of God: and this is that spirit of antichrist, whereof ye have heard that it should come; and even now already is it in the world'), 'That is why many denied Jesus in the flesh as well.'[12] But all this humanity does not mean for Ras Joel that Haile Selassie necessarily died, anymore than it does for believers like Ras Ansel Cridland. Lawson points to the usual Rasta proofs, 'There was no funeral, no grave – nothing that would indicate that a dignitary had died.' So what happened to H.I.M.? Joel Lawson gives a careful explanation, unusual for a Rasta who adheres to the disappearance theory in that he allows for a possible death scenario if it is coupled with a resurrection and a future revelation component:

> While in one of his ostentatious moods, Menghistu remarked that he buried Haile Selassie I under his throne so that he would not raise after three days. (This throne was said to be a toilet in the Imperial Palace.) This means that even Menghistu is aware of the God-like powers of His Imperial Majesty Haile Selassie I.

While pointing out that 'no bones' have been exhibited, despite claims of exhumation for official burial by a royalist group and the report of the smothering of the emperor by a soldier as cause of death, Lawson equates such a possible fate with that of Jesus:

> One may reflect on the fact that history says that the heathen beat Jesus Christ to death, nailed him to a cross and buried Him in a sepulchre. But after three days, He was nowhere to be found in there.

Citing a Reuter News Agency story from June 1992, Ras Joel points out that Haile Selassie's tomb is also empty and he equates that fact with what he sees as a prophecy about Selassie in Revelation 1.18 ('I am he that liveth, and was dead; and, behold, I am alive for evermore, Amen; and have the keys of hell and of death'). Lawson admits, 'Of course, the Christians can say that this is

Jesus as well', but he is undaunted by that: 'But the Rastafarians have no qualm with this'. For him the issue is simple: 'Speculation is: when His Imperial Majesty will officially reveal Himself?' The appeal of this position to a people who have historically, in effect, been crushed and left for dead and have arisen in power and glory is undeniable. As Jesus' resurrection appealed so potently to New World slaves as a chance for rebirth and another opportunity for life, so does Selassie I's fate represent that of oppressed black humanity, crushed – perhaps even killed – but ready to reappear and 'make His personal revelation and intervention'.[13]

In ways similar to these, a number of Rastas have continued to explore the idea of positing Jesus as well as Haile Selassie as having been only a man.

DREAD JESUS AS ONLY A MAN

Somala is an artist and poet who thinks constantly about spiritual matters. A dreadlocked Rasta from Dominica, he maintains the equation between Jesus and Selassie I as he attempts to work out the way God has worked through them. As he explains:

> According to what the Bible says, Jesus is not really Jah, but is thus come through Jah to bring Jah. He bring Jah, so, technically, he is Jah. You know, because in order for Jah to set example for man he have to come with a man as man to set principles.

For Rastas like Somala, the deapotheosizing (or dedeifying) of Selassie I entails a deapotheosizing of Jesus, since for him 'Haile Selassie and Jesus is the same man . . . that just come in different forms'. The effect is to emphasize his oneness with the rest of humanity:

> He talk about 'our Father.' So different is like which is the dress of all of we – so, he just like one of we still. Just like a man. You know? Because he's a man. Because all of we is one, so he talk about 'our Father.' So, he's part of we. He's one of we. But, where he comes Jah now is because he knew Jah before we, you know? Because he comes direct from Jah to we.

While this view moves toward the concept of Jesus as an enlightened teacher, Somala chooses to retain Christian theological language to describe Jesus:

> So, then, there in this form we consider Jesus Christ is Jah, you know? It's like he know where the Maker and he come down. So, you know, it's Father, Son, and Spirit in Trinity's strength and courage. It's the I-Threes all the time, you know?

Since Haile Selassie's name means 'Might of the Holy Trinity', Rastas have built into their theology the understanding that somehow God is a Trinity. Those like Somala, who are engaged in reinterpreting Christ to parallel a reinterpretation of Selassie, must find a way to express that concern in trinitarian terms.

This idea of God being 'One of Us' was a popular twentieth-century fashion, particularly expressed in United States music from the 'Partners With the Lord' ramblings of cowboy singers like the great Stuart Hamblen to Joan Osborne's rendition of Eric Bazilian's (of The Hooters) song 'One of Us', which depicts God as a lonely human catching a late night bus.[14] Such reductionist views fit the United States' egalitarian ideal perhaps more comfortably than they do Jamaica's or the United Kingdom's more monarchical traditions.

Among Rastafarian groups that have emphasized the humanity of Jesus in reggae music is Jamaica's Wailing Souls. From the beginning, the Wailing Souls have filled their material full of biblical allusions, as in their Studio One song 'Mr. Fire Coal Man', which adapts Jesus' warning to Peter in Gethsemane when Peter attempted to thwart Christ's arrest (Matthew 26.52). The Souls substitute 'gun' for 'sword', proclaiming that those who live by the gun die by the gun. 'Got to be Cool' is built on the teaching of Psalm 1.3 that those who trust in God will be like a tree planted by an inexhaustible river of life. 'Run My People' identifies Rastas in the place of Israel as the chosen ones of God (Deuteronomy 7.6) who will overcome wicked adversity some day. Throughout the following twenty years of their recording history they continued to build songs from the Bible. 'War', for example, includes Jesus' warning in Matthew 24.6 and Mark 13.7, 'And you shall hear of wars and rumours of wars'. 'Old Broom' uses a biblical image favoured by the Wailers, who shared with the Wailing Souls the same Kingston kitchens in which hopeful harmony groups would cram as many people as would fit to sing day into night. These felt like the stone that the builders refused, this time quoting Jesus' adaptation of Psalm 118.22 in Matthew 21.42, Mark 12.10, and Luke 20.17, echoed in Acts 4.11, Ephesians 2.20, 1 Peter 2.6, 7. 'Jah is love', their Rastafarian adaptation of 1 John 4.16, surfaces in 'Stickey Stay', a song about God helping the faithful to survive.[15] When I asked founding member Winston 'Pipe' Matthews how he regarded Jesus, given his constant quoting of him from 'Mr. Fire Coal Man' through 'War' and 'Old Broom', he replied:

I see him as a man for all, for each and every one. You know, a man with no partiality – a man with love and understanding for everyone, a man of no race, creed, or class.

When I asked if he saw Jesus as Jah, he explained:

His image is in that. There is no other is man but Jah. You know what I mean? There's no other is man but Jah. There's no other is man. I no care where you are or go or say out there. Whatsoever a guy may call him, you know. Is the same man every man I preach to.

When I questioned, 'So Haile Selassie and Jesus, would they be the same?', he fitted his reply into the received Rasta language, but maintained his human-oriented perspective:

Well, coming down through the lineage, all right? From the holy days of creation until this time. He was the only holy man until this time. He was the holiest man on earth until this time, all right? Well, I want to tell you that God is with us every day. I don't have anything else to say to you about that. But I going to tell you say God is with us everyday. As you seek him and find him and you know who him is.

One of the most astute of contemporary Rastas who holds the position of Jesus as simply a man and consciously inculcates much of what we have reviewed thus far into a position she terms 'Revisionist Rasta' is Imani Tafari-Ama. Her views serve as a kind of internal summary of the Eastern-oriented contemporary appropriation of past Rasta reasoning on Jesus. An educator and filmmaker who has thoroughly versed herself in historical Rasta thought, she begins, as most Rastas do, recognizing the need to depart from the 'extremely oppressive' manner in which the 'concept of Jesus' 'has operated in our history':

> Missionaries come with the concept of Jesus, which is a white, blue-eyed, blond-haired representation of Michaelangelo's uncle. So, when you think 'Jesus,' you think of that image that people have upon their walls and they blind us, which is a part of our internalized oppression. All right? So, until we would have reproduced that notion of Jesus with something in our own image, Allah, Haile Selassie, then we wouldn't have then relinquished the chains that have kept us in mental slavery by the Christian theology. So, it's a subliminal that is oppressing us to this day.

Seeing 'Jesus' as 'a concept' used by the 'slave machinery' set in motion by Columbus and continued by 'a lot of the slave trading vessels [which] were called "Jesus," the S.S. Jesus,' she seeks a new paradigm. For her the extreme 'internalized oppression' must be counteracted by just as extreme an internalized liberation: that humanity see itself as circling in value a full 180°, as far as from slave to god, while still remaining humans:

> I think as well all of us have that possibility that we are the Christ, because that Christ can manifest in each and every one. It's to the extent that you accept this divinity within your persona.

Referring to Dennis Forsythe among others, and incorporating from him the Rosicrucian conception of the 'Christ consciousness' available to the enlightened, she recognizes her view as a departure from the early tenets of Rastafari:

> We evolved. We don't have a static ideological conceptualization as Rasta. In fact, we obviously borrow from a lot of different sources in trying to formulate our self-concept and in rejecting a lot of things that have been fed, in a sense, a synthesizing and a sifting through as we go along. So what might have applied 10 years ago, as people have reevaluated and rethought, then you get different dimensions. It is not that we will be saying what Rastas used to think 10 years ago is invalid, but it is along a continuum of time.

Such a perspective has the advantage of preserving Haile Selassie:

Mind you, we don't see Haile Selassie as being lost. We maintain that image as a concept ... And we have to contextualize this so-called disappearance of Selassie, as we would Enoch's. 'And Enoch walked with God and he was not, for God took him.' That's from Genesis. And that is talking about: you don't have to see that in the physical to then see the other part of life. You know? So then, Enoch was one of the examples. Elijah was another example of that soul that did not see death, but was translated.

But what is lost is the uniqueness of Christ. When I asked if Jesus as the only way to God would fit in her theology, Imani Tafari-Ama replied:

No, because in fact it would contradict where we're coming from in seeing Haile Selassie as a reproduction of the concept of the Christ ... Yeshua is what the Hebrew people call this man. And then what we say, as a concept the Christ appears in every dispensation. And so, this Hebrew man was not this blond-haired, blue-eyed representation that we have been fed, but was an actual person who existed in that historical time who did these wonderful works and who reproduced the concept of Christ in his time ... We make the claim that His Majesty is the Christ in this time. I mean, it's probably only mind-blowing to the extent that it's black people who come up with this thing and decide that we love ourselves to the extent that we will reject this notion of white supremacy and see ourselves in our own image. And that liberation of our minds allows us to see ourselves as gods and goddesses in our own right. And that, I think, is a major breakthrough in terms of the internalized racism and the internalized oppression that is a part of our culture, so that we can then even mentally break the chains that would prevent us from that self realization that is so important to Christedness.

Even Haile Selassie's own fervent self-identification as a Christian, espousing Jesus as his Lord and denying that he himself was the Christ, does not dissuade her. Her view handles Haile Selassie's denial of divinity not by following his pointing to Jesus Christ, but by including Selassie with Jesus as a human:

It's an oxymoron, because he says, during his lifetime, he has explained to the Rastas his correct stand by emphasizing that he's a human being and should therefore not be worshipped as God. But, the Jesus that people have represented over time – the man that them call Jesus – wasn't that a human being? Wasn't that the human being that showed man the possibility of divinity?

In that way, despite Selassie's denial, she does not see his adherence to Jesus and her adherence to him 'as being a contradiction in terms that we would see this one as being the Christ, that one in our time', because her position can accommodate many representations of Christ:

It is fine for Jesus to be white in the blond-haired, blue-eyed conception ... Mind you, it was historically convenient for them to contrive this image, because if you couldn't conceive of the Almighty in your own image, then you could never conceive of yourself as being thoroughly human or potentially divine. You know? And therein lies. Because, even now, if you ask most people, when you hear the name 'Jesus,' what do you think immediately? What's the first image that comes to you? Shut your eye as Muta[baruka] would say and think of Jesus – as a famous example.

Imani Tafari-Ama's eclecticism is so open it even leads her to include in Rasta the kind of power religion elements firmly rejected by most of the founders of the movement:

> Mind you, it's a value judgment calling it neo-pagan, because it's what our ancestors used to do which was absolutely rejected as paganism and bad when the missionaries came to christianize us, you know? So, when we recollect these traditions and reproduce them in our daily living, we don't celebrate them as neo-pagan, we see them as being recognition of – yes – sacred rituals that had meaning and still do. Because, for example, this architect says to me, 'I will never build a house unless there's some shedding of blood, because these are the experiences that I've had where bad things have happened.' So, when somebody's going to build a house, you have to kill a chicken. You have to mix some blood that day, because the ancestors and the spirits need that kind of gratification. Yes? And no matter what your belief system is, there's some kind of genetic memory, let us say. Because, maybe we're carrying the DNA in our genes that will impell you along with the popular culture to say, 'Do that for protection.' Yeah? But you more find it in churches – that what they call the Pocomania churches. People would subscribe to that kind of belief system than in Christian church, because people reject it as being pagan. Yeah, because again it's so widespread and so subliminal and so complete, the factoring in of rejection of things African.

Joseph Hibbert, inspiring his group to break up a Revivalist meeting, as we will see in the next section, or Leonard Howell, who despite being labelled a 'samfie (obeah) man' himself, for healings he performed,[16] declared, 'No admittance for Fortune tellers witch and old hige. No admittance for obeah dogs none whatever'[17] to his Balm Yard, might be scandalized at a contemporary Rasta countenancing such a practice as blood sacrifice. But Imani Tafari-Ama sees such magical elements as provided not only by Africa, but also by Jesus:

> This person went to Egypt and was initiated into the holy rituals and rights and became a holy man in his own right which was different from the jump from 12 to 31 or whatever that the Christian story tells you. What happened in the intervening period, then, if you were to interrogate that representation of the Christ? You know? . . . But, then, even coming back to the nativity story, some of us do interrogate. I'm not new in this type of thinking in questioning this whole immaculate conception and which then begs the question that you elevate Mary to a deity . . . It's another aberation, right? But, up to this day, well, where's the historical evidence that she was actually impregnated by the Holy Spirit and not by her husband or by a man, you know what I'm saying, sir? The mystification of Jĕsus's origins like placing him in the supernatural realm and not in the natural birth realm as we know it, I think it's also a contrivance of whoever it was interpreting that story, because we have no historical evidence to say this thing happened outside of the mythicized or the supernaturalization of the man . . . The

notion of resurrection is, again, a historical aberration ... Mind you, some people, just to play angel's advocate now, see the whole crucifixion thing as a contrivance of the Catholic, the Roman system. To them, they find Jesus as a means of absolving themselves from having murdered this man, so that when they turn around and say, the same one that they endorsed to be killed, to be crucified. Yeah? Because you follow the Bible story is Pilate's facilitation of the crucifixion that allowed it to happen, right? And then it's the same Catholic church that turn around and make the crucifix a holy thing. So, that, you said to yourself, by some sleight of hand here what happened?

In her paradigm, in place of the doctrine of God coming in Christ once to redeem humanity, she sees many comings for enlightenment:

On the other hand, if you believe that transmigration of souls is another part of our reality, people reproduce it. Matter cannot be created or destroyed, that's how it happens spiritually too. So that, the concept that we have of the Christ is that reproduction concept. And the Christ can manifest in different ones in different generations, because it is not a personality thing that is you particularly that got on in that world, therefore is you going up into the air. There is you personally same one that to come back and save us from this destruction in the world. I mean, if you see it as being a historically ongoing process, like how they go – eastern people – see it, that new die and that soul got into a new baby a come forward and therefore your spirit never will see death as such, because it is a holy thing.

Thus, the Bible's proclamation of Jesus coming once she recognizes as antithetical to her perspective:

That would defeat the purpose in my view. Because, if Jesus Christ or Yeshua was the perfect example, the reason for having that perfect example would starve away in front of us. But, it's the representation of the possibility each one of us has, because that is why this flesh is the temple. And in this temple dwells that ever living Spirit.

Therefore, she focuses her efforts on developing the 'possibility' of herself to become a 'temple' of the 'ever living Spirit', having invested 'fourteen years of me forward recreating myself in my own image':

When I changed my name fourteen years ago, I didn't have locks. And I have a university degree and I couldn't get work.
Faith: Imani means actually. So, because that had meaning and it had real meaning because my mother had sent my father to get the midwife and before they came back she had me. And then she thought, 'Oh, I'm all alone!' Then she said, 'No, God is with me,' so she called me 'Faith.' It's a wonderful story, and all the symbolism. So, then when I discovered that it means 'Imani' in Swahili and in Arabic and in Amharic as well. And I said, well you know, I'm going to change, so I might change it. So, then the flack came down. Because, first of all my family was outraged because internalized oppression works as close as that.

But she persisted in working on her syncretistic Revisionist Rasta perspective, drawing even from the Seventh Day Adventism in which she had been reared, and in which her family remains:

> Yeah, man, they still are Seventh Day Adventist. Of course, I turn around and tell them that I'm grateful for having been raised Seventh Day Adventist, because of the theological basis of Rasta is very similar in terms of the recognition of the Pope as the antichrist and the food culture, you know? I didn't grow up eating pork and shell fish and all this thing. So that the Seventh Day Adventist food social practices are very Judaic in a lot of ways.

Such a programme of recreating one's past she recommends to Christians too:

> Any message I want to give to Christians? Oh. Recreate history is the synopsis how I would put it, you know? Work towards recreating history, towards, you know, the revealing of truth. And people should not hesitate to recognize truth even when it puts their own identity into question.

In this way, Imani Tafari-Ama attempts to appropriate what she considers the best of the history of Rastafari in her 'Revisionist Rasta' perspective, grounded in the essential humanity of figures like Jesus and Selassie I.

With her open syncretizing of Rasta with African traditional elements, she parallels the syncretizing of some African 'Rastas' who adapt their own revision of Rastafari, affirming the humanity of Selassie and drawing from traditional religion, Christianity, Islam, Eastern religion, and in some cases the Rosicrucian influence in Dennis Forsythe as well.

Such an African is Majek Fashek of Nigeria, who is one of the most exciting innovators in African reggae. Riding his song 'Send Down the Rain', which has made him an international star, he uses his musical platform to address both his peers in Africa ('Africans Keep Your Culture') as well as diasporan Rastas (in such sensitive moves as his reverential covering of Bob Marley's 'Redemption Song').[18] As one form of African 'Rasta', he writes and performs with a global audience in mind. On his *Spirit of Love* album, for example, he consciously addresses songs like 'So Long' to both those in the old world of Africa and those in the new. Jesus regularly crops up in those songs. In 'I Come from de Ghetto' Jesus is extolled as a ghetto hero (along with Mohammed, Steve Biko, Socrates, Martin Luther, Buddha, Mandela). 'Light' is noted as being in Jesus, Selassie, Buddha, Mohammed, and in their resulting religions in his plea for religious accord, 'Religion is Politics'. In this song he seeks to separate these religious figures from the 'political' religions that war in their name. 'So Long' distinguishes Jesus Christ, 'who died for I and I to gain salvation', from King Selassie I, 'who was betrayed by his people'.[19]

Dreadlocked, represented on such 'best of' collections of Africa's reggae as Shanachie's *Fly African Eagle: The Best of African Reggae* (1997), Fashek also adds elements to his perspective from Ethiopian belief. For him, Jesus and Haile Selassie are 'of the same lineage', as he explained to me:

Some of his people was white. Sheba was wife of Solomon, right? Sheba gave birth to Menyelek. So Selassie I is from the lineage of Menyelek. And so, Solomon is the link. So, Ethiopia was linked with Solomon ... When you check the Bible, it say that Jesus is the son of David, right? And you have Selassie I, the son of Solomon, see?

So, rather than the return of Jesus, to Majek Fashek, 'I see Selassie I as the redemption of King Solomon.' How does he relate Jesus and Selassie? He explains, 'At the same time, you see, I'm a Christian, and, you see, a "prisoner of conscience." That's the message I've been opening. So, you see, Selassie is "Christ conscious." ... Haile Selassie I is Christ conscious. Jesus take Christ conscious.' This is a Christ consciousness that Selassie 'attained', that Majek Fashek sees also attained by Mohammed and Buddha (an inspiration he calls 'the light' in 'Religion Is Politics'). As he explains:

So Mohammed was Christ conscious. Selassie I is Christ conscious. You know, many masters, Buddha, all of them, you know? Because Christ is Holy Spirit. He is the highest priesthood, which he said that. To call Christ, I cannot, to define Christ like that. So all that, which he said that, it's a priesthood, a living priesthood.

For him, Jesus has a unique task, 'I see his death as unique, you know? He saves the whole world. His death saves the whole world, the universe, you know?'

His view is that 'Christianity gave birth to "Rastafarianity." So, you see, when you say Rastafari, you're talking about Jesus Christ. You're talking about Christ, that is Selassie I come in a kingly character.' Is his view, then, the same as that of many traditional Rastas? Not exactly:

Jesus is the master, you know, the master prisoner ... He break the chains. He broke the chains of death ... and that is why all the masters give him their respect. So every master always had to start with him. So, Selassie I had to start with him. That's how they got call him 'Jesus Christ.' They got call him Christ. Selassie I obtained Christ consciousness. That is why Jamaicans see him as Christ. If you obtain Christ consciousness, you become call Christ. He said, 'What I've done you can do. What I've done you can do.' That's what I read in the Bible he said. 'What I've done you can do.' Yes, so, Selassie I I see a multiplication of Christ. You know Christ has multiplied in you. He has multiplied in me. He has multiplied in everyone that believes. So, Selassie I believe in Jesus Christ.

The distinction Majek Fashek observes is a subtle one. Because of Haile Selassie's diligent spiritual pursuit of the mind of Christ, he attained that mind and people began to see Christ manifested in him in a 'kingly character':

That is why he multiplied in him and that is why people are seeing him as Jesus Christ in his kingly character. You know what I'm saying? In his kingly – the same like God – as in his condition. I'm not saying that he's Christ. You must get this straight.

For him the key is all people getting to 'Jah', 'the Father', and 'no one can reach the Father except through the Holy Spirit'. So, he pleads in the song 'Holy Spirit', on Interscope Record's *Spirit of Love*, for the Holy Spirit to take over the world. He realizes:

> It's very hard for people to believe in Christ, because they don't see Jesus Christ, ever see this man before – just that. Yeah, nobody has seen God before. So, now he revealed the Holy Spirit, which is the Comforter, that always comfort us, which is the still voice, inner voice, and this is the still word of God. And so the stillness of your inner self is what will lead you to the Christ consciousness. You can obtain Christ consciousness.

For him, this is the meaning of Jesus' teaching 'I'm the way of life. No one cometh to the Father but through me' (John 14.6): 'It means that no one can reach the Father except through the Holy Spirit. Because the Father has the Spirit ... he is an immanation, is the true image and likeness of the Most High.' Into all this doctrine, he mixes a heavy dose of syncretism, having learned from his mother that people reincarnate fourteen times before they achieve a purified state. How many of these lives one has lived so far, he believes, can be noted by the lines in one's palm. All good people are striving to reach God, he affirms:

> There are people who are Buddhists. There are people that are Moslems. There are people who are Rastafarians. They have a right to be what they are. So, you see, now we choose. I choose Jesus Christ as my master. Is my master. You know what I mean?

What he means is that 'you can obtain Christ consciousness'. Majek Fashek's concern to respect all religions and urge people to progress peacefully in their attempt to reach God is a central concern shared by most leading African 'Rastas' like South Africa's Lucky Dube. In songs like 'Together as One', this best-selling artist challenges his hearers to recognize the image of God in all people: Rastas, Indians – all. In his song called 'Jah Live', which is not the song Bob Marley released to answer those who criticized Rastas' disbelief of reports of the demise of Selassie I, Lucky Dube takes a wider theological perspective, noting that while Rastas refer to the Deity as Jah, Moslems as Allah, and the 'Englishman' as God, all are referring to a single God, thus unifying this song's message with that of 'Together as One'.[20]

Nigeria's great Sonny Okosuns in his reggae song about Jesus, 'King of Kings', extols Jesus as the 'Son of God', 'King of Kings', 'Light of the World', and recounts Jesus' great acts of dying for 'you' and 'me', being raised by God, healing the sick, raising the dead, opening the eyes of the blind, ordering the wind and the waves to obey. Therefore, he thanks Jah for Jesus. On that same album he includes a respectful song entitled 'Mohammed', noting in the album's liner notes, '"King of Kings" and "Mohammed" are dedicated to religious tolerance'.[21]

The Ivory Coast's Kone 'Alpha Blondy' Seydou, whose 'Come Back Jesus (My Lord, Come Back Light)' is a hauntingly beautiful reggae plea to Christ to return and end war, appeals to such religious and political leaders as 'His Holiness Pope Jean-Paul II', 'Shimon Perez', 'King Hassen II', 'Yasser Arafat' and others to pay heed to Martin Luther King's wise words, 'Learn to live together like brothers otherwise we will parish (sic) together like idiots' on his *The Prophets* album. He makes a special plea for uniting 'the sons of Abraham', 'Jewish Israelis and Palestinian Israelis'.[22] His own 'God Is One' song can be found on his World Pacific album *Masada* (1992).

Further, most African 'Rastas' seem to have adapted Rastafari into a previously held Christian perspective: they respect the emperor as a great leader, but they regard Jesus as Christ. Some appear as Rastas but identify as Christians, as does Nigeria's Musical Power and the Roots Vibrators band, who in Angus Power's 'Rasta No Go Dirty' reveal they 'act' like Rastas, but are not since 'Rastas believe in Rastafari' and 'me believe in the Trinity, Jah, Christie and Holy Spirit'.[23]

Several years ago, when I interviewed the members of Jamaica's Black Uhuru, Duckie Simpson complained about the Marxist military persecution in Ethiopia and the denial of belief in Haile Selassie in Africa:

> I don't think I want to be living there right now. There's nothing there. I don't want to be down there with some guy looking to get my head. Man, they're against people who praise Selassie in Africa, man. You see all those sufferation going on down there? Yeah-h-h-h, they blaspheme. They got to pay the penalty. In this modern time people are suffering like that? Something's wrong. We was telling them men. But they say they kill the emperor and they get Mengistu? Well, you have to live with that!

Today, the persecution of both Rastas and the Ethiopian Orthodox Church has quieted in Ethiopia. And across Africa a few exceptions have even begun to extol Selassie as God. One notable one is Ras Kimono of Nigeria, whose 'Rastafari Chant' hails Haile Selassie I with all his crowning titles, identifying him with Jah.[24] How have some moved to such a position after virtually all Africans (including Selassie) have denied Selassie's divinity since the 1930s? Ras Siam and Ras Isha of Negril shed some important light on this current theological shift. Its origin, they reveal, is in Jamaica, not in Africa. When I pointed out to them that doctoral students of mine from many different parts of Africa reported to me that no Rasta they know in Africa regards Haile Selassie as God, but simply as another African king, and furthermore that most Africans with whom I have talked cannot fathom why Jamaicans consider Selassie to be God when his own people did not consider him God, and that his denial of his own divinity is what Abuna Yesehaq conveyed to them directly from the emperor himself, Ras Isha replied, 'That's why I say a king have no honor in his own country.' But Ras Siam disagreed with me:

> I may call you straighten up now. I was in Kingston amongst Peter Tosh, Bunny Wailer, Bob Marley and some very great scholars, bright scholars who are able to open the light focus of brother eyes who lock up the light teachment. And I do remember sitting down at Peter Tosh yard in his house. You know clothes basket?

How large a clothes basket is? Those man will have at least 3 full clothes basket collected with letter from all part of the world. Those man will have all 5 people reading letters and it's so funny – you saw a letter coming from all part of Africa but giving thanks to the bredrin them to open up their eyes to worship the King, and to see the King, and to know His Imperial Majesty Haile Selassie I. We have received basket upon basket and boxes of letter. I remember sometime when some of the letters have been reading, it even made the heart leap that the bredrin will says to another in the bredrin – individual bredrin – 'Till I want you hear this one letter!'

So, worship of Selassie is being exported from Jamaica to Africa.

Still, the vast majority of Africans I have encountered in my research are similar to the outstanding Nigerian reggae star Victor Essiet of the Mandators, whose protest songs like 'Power of the People', 'Injustice', 'Apartheid' are as penetrating as his praise for Jesus is devoutly poignant in 'Thanks and Praises' on Heartbeat's excellent collection of his songs *Power of the People, Nigerian Reggae*. In 'Thanks and Praises', he sings:

Yes children, give thanks and praises to Jah Almighty Father
The ever Living God
Give Jah thanks and praises
Oh Jah Jah children
Jah Jah people uuu-uuu
Jesus Christ . . .

If Jah never love me would I be around today,
If Jah never care for me would I be standing here
If Jah never love me where would I be today
If Jah never care for me would I be standing tall so . . .

He sent his only son to die for we here, so we might live on,
Sent his only son to suffer for we now so we may be strong
and so they crucified Jesus Christ
And they turned his back on we the simple ones.

He has risen up, the king of kings, Lord, oh children,
He will not let you down and will never deceive you

They crucified Jesus Christ and they turned his back on we the simple ones
And he has set the children free, with the blood on the cross so
Give Jah thanks and praises, Oh Jah Jah children, like I and I.[25]

In Victor Essiet's lyrics we see the impact of Diasporan Africa back on the motherland. Rastafarian terms like 'Iwah' for 'hour' and 'I and I' for 'we' are used to depict a thorough-going Christian cosmology. While 'Jah people' and 'Jah Jah children' are also Rasta terms, the use of 'Jah' as a designation for God is common within Africa's 'spiritual' churches, like the one Victor Essiet attends. 'Yeah, I go to church', he informed me. 'Mount Zion, yes, that's a spiritual church.' As he explains the impetus of his lyrics:

I am from a very, very mystical and spiritual family and I am from a Christian family. In life we have been kept alive, in fact, through miracles and I like to share the truth about miracles. I have lived beyond life's physical and seen things that has happened and that has made me also to live not only in physical but in spirit. It's not just a cheap talk, but it is a talk that I have a duty to extend to people in the world as a whole that we have a life deeper and better and more happy than the life we're living right now. And that we have more hope even in death than even the life we're living, you know? So, that is why I've gone through a lot of things. In the song, I'm giving thanks and praises for the things that he has done, because of where he says that those who believe in him will not suffer shame or be disgraced. And so, I give thanks and praises for the sweet life because Christ gives life. And I give thanks and praises for the shelter. And I give thanks and praises for the food he has given, for all things he has done for us. So it is exactly what I have experienced that I'm trying to pass it on to the people.

'What' Victor Essiet 'experienced' was the cruelty of Nigeria's civil war that murdered his sisters and uncle, brutalized his family, and left him a destitute refugee struggling for survival on the streets of Calabar at the age of 13. When stability returned, he infused his experiences into the lyrics of his 'bubbling' Ibibio reggae music. Born with his hair already dreadlocked, he is forever explaining his music to people who assume his music is 'all about ganja and violence':

Sometimes some people see me and say, 'Hey, you have dreadlocks, do you believe in this, or do you believe in that?' But I tell them that everyone – as Christ said – you don't have to judge, you know, unless you be judged too . . . What I'm seeing is that like a lot of people who have been listening to my songs and a lot of people are drawn near. And most people who thought it was like all about ganja and violence who start to look at it like, 'Yes, I think it's not about all this. And we want to sit and we want to listen to it.'

Central to Victor Essiet's message is the conviction that 'Jesus is uniquely the Son of God. He brings us the gift of life. He is Lord of Lords, do you understand?' Like most Africans singing reggae, Victor Essiet observes a distinction between Jesus and Haile Selassie. Asked how Jesus would differ, he explains:

Because he conquered hell and the dead. He gives us love and sets we free for iver. We talk about Haile Selassie. Haile Selassie was just a man who, you understand, was also saved by grace – you understand? – that cannot save. Haile Selassie was a man saved by grace like anyone of us, who has sin and come short of glory of God and he is fully saved by grace and the mercy of God Almighty through the sacrifice of Jesus Christ, the Lord of love and the Savior of all mankind.

Asked, for further clarification, if he would subscribe to the idea that Haile Selassie and Jesus were uniquely God in the same way, he replies firmly, 'No, no, no, no. No, no, no.' Of Selassie, he confirms, 'I respect him.' But of Jesus, he explains:

Jesus Christ is uniquely God among us. When I talk about Jesus Christ, my heart happens to light up every time! You understand? And when you know him, you will live, despite the troubles, despite the struggle, despite the sorrow's grief. He will not let you down. That's why I'm singing that song. I said, he was crucified, and his back was turned against the simple ones. But he has risen up as the King of kings and Lord of lords. And, he won't let you down. He won't deceive you. And so, ever since he is and he will be and he has been. He never change. So, the same thing with God. So, that is my view and this is not a cheap talk. This is not a joke thing. Because this is where I stand and I will not move from there.

But despite all the accommodations to salvage a place for Jesus in Revisionist Rastafari from Jamaica to Africa, some Rastas, particularly some groups in the United Kingdom, have not gone the route of their Jamaican or African 'bredrin' and 'sistren'. Unable to separate Jesus from the horrors done in his name, they do not find Jah through Jesus. For these, Jesus has become an anathema.

Jesus as the White Man's Myth

Monica Lambett, whose Rasta name is Maniah Mani, is a delightful woman who, strangely enough given her position on Jesus, pleasantly plies her trade as a higgler, or business woman with a stall, with an outspoken Christian partner named Victor in the Brixton marketplace near Coldharbour Lane in one of London's more concentrated Rastafarian areas. As Maniah Mani, she is No. 2 in the House of Africa (House of Israel), a Rastafarian organization. When I met her at her stall in Brixton, her group of Rastas was even then engaged in what they termed the 'Denounciation of Jesus Christ'. What does that mean for these British Rastafarians?

> Well, it means that he have been placed in the character of the Beast. Because, you see, it's really the 'Denounciation of the Church' ... I mean, at the moment, what we've actually done, we've caged his spirit onto Haile Selassie and, you know, say, 'Well, this is it.' But there's no way. It can't be possible. Because there's no way Jesus Christ have ever in the New Testament be known as the elect of God. And Haile Selassie is claiming that title. So that's a different thing.

So, if Jesus was not the elect of God, who was he? Maniah Mani replies succinctly, 'Baal!' Baal?

> Yeah, and they've been carrying that image from Egypt. But this time ... we are actually – we in the House of Israel – is actually talking about the restoration of the throne. They don't want to keep it because they abolished it in Ethiopia. America have taken power and they've turned it into a Republic. So, we're at this stage now of concentrating on the reestablishment and the Denounciation of Jesus Christ.

Like Maniah Mani, Rastas in the United Kingdom, whatever their view of Jesus, seem to share an intense orientation toward Ethiopia. As we noted earlier, one of the most visible is the articulate director of Ras Tafari International Consultants, Ras Seymour McLean, who operates out of London's Wandsworth area. As opposed to Maniah Mani's group, he takes the more traditional Rasta position that equates Jesus Christ with Haile Selassie, as he explained by letter to me:

> The questions concerning Jesus Christ can be answered from your Bible. Revelation 5 v 5, and the Book sealed with seven seals. Revelation 19 v 12, a new name that no man knew, but he himself. Revelation 19 v 16, who is the King of Kings, Lord of Lords, Conquering Lion of Judah today? What is His new name?[26]

However, Ras Seymour shares with Maniah Mani the passion for Ethiopia, having been engaged in a multi-year quest, petitioning the government, the Queen, the Archbishop of Canterbury, among many others to have returned to Ethiopia the sacred relics looted during the British Invasion of April 1868, as we saw in an earlier chapter.

Yet Rastas like Maniah Mani prefer to choose between Jesus and Selassie. They believe one cannot serve both. In this they are reminiscent of the exclusive declarations of Leonard Howell in *The Promised Key*:

> Legislators said one man cannot serve two masters. Ministers say they can't work with Adam and Eve, and work for King Alpha and Queen Omega the same time. Abraham the historian said despise the both of them; lawyers said you have got to find fault with them, the judge said leave the Alpha and Omega out, because they are black and skin for skin.[27]

The irony here is that Howell was paraphrasing Jesus (Matthew 6.24, Luke 16.13), but now Jesus' teaching is being used by these contemporary Rastafari to exclude Jesus himself. Still, the sentiment being expressed by Maniah Mani is not necessarily a new one within Rastafari.

When Professor George E. Simpson, the first researcher to publish articles on the Rastafarians, assessed the Rasta preaching he heard in the early 1950s, he saw a similar sentiment to Maniah Mani's at work. At 92 years of age, when I interviewed him, Professor Simpson still had a clear recollection of his dramatic introduction to the Rastafarians. In an unforgettable encounter, they literally burst into the Revival meeting he was researching. He explained to me:

> When I was there in '53, Christians and Rastafarians were bitter rivals. And, as you may know from some things I wrote, I worked in a Revival Zion group, the best one in Kingston at that time, which was just across the street from a very important Rastafarian group [Joseph Hibbert's group]. There were actually scuffles in the street sometimes as people from these two groups got into arguments. And one night I was there when a group of Rastafarians came in and broke up the Revival meeting, saying that 'We worship the true God and you people are not!'

What was at the heart of these Rastafarians' objection? Professor Simpson explained:

They said, 'You're worshipping a dead God; we're worshipping the living God!' And they began to shove, push the chairs around and push the people around and so forth. No one was hurt. But there were arguments and scuffling and so forth in the area between those two meeting places.

On this distinction, Professor Simpson found these early Rastafarians consistent, persistent, and vehement:

Ras Tafari was the living God and they ridiculed people for worshipping a dead God and said that they worshipped a living God: Ras Tafari. That I heard many times.

Therefore, when reports of Haile Selassie's death circulated in 1975, Simpson heard Rastas attributing such 'rumours' to white people, whose God was dead and who consequently wanted Rastas' God to be dead too:

I heard them say and I heard myself from some people I saw in Jamaica after 1953 that Haile Selassie was not dead. He was still living and the rumour that Haile Selassie was dead was just a rumour. And it was a rumour. It was a false report by white people to smear Haile Selassie and to ridicule the movement and so forth and they didn't believe that. They believed that Haile Selassie was still alive. That was a very common thing to hear.

Who would spread such a rumour? For Maniah Mani the explanation seems clear: only those who would worship the arch divine villain in the Old Testament, the worshippers of Baal, would do such a thing. In the vision of Rastas like Maniah Mani, a stiff competition is being waged in the Bible's pages between Jesus (the Hebrew Bible's Baal) and Selassie (the true messiah). She declares:

Well, he is Baal, isn't he? ... Yeah, it couldn't be Selassie. We're not claiming that Selassie is God at this stage. All we're claiming H.I.M. to be is Elect of God, according to the information received. And also carrying the – coming under the – divinity of the Alpha and the Omega. Well, the only thing that I have ever known about Alpha and Omega that it was Alpha the first letter of the Greek alphabet and Omega was the last letter. But, I didn't know that there was a throne somewhere in the world that was carrying a title on it: The Alpha and the Omega. But we actually go and connect up this Ethiopian dynasty.

The competition between the false god and the true God extends for this British Rasta right into the present age. Reading Genesis 38, her group sees references to modern times. The passage in question involves Judah, one of Israel's patriarchs, taking a Canaanite wife and producing a son named Er. Genesis 38.7 tells us, 'And Er, Judah's firstborn, was wicked in the sight of the LORD; and the LORD slew him.' At Er's death, his father attempts to fulfil the custom to have children produced in the widow by a second son, thereby to be reared to inherit the blessing and property rights of the first. But the second son Onan is greedy and does not co-operate. He dies too. Finally, Judah promises a third son to the widow, but does not fulfil this promise. In an act of desperation Er's widow disguises herself as a prostitute, seduces her father-in-law, Judah, and bears a child to him, thus dramatically reminding him of his failure to fulfil what custom demands, that she be provided a husband from her father-in-law's family to secure her first husband's inheritance. In this very ancient account of greed, treachery, justice, and vindication, Maniah Mani believes she has unlocked a contemporary secret. She knows who Er really is:

> Do you know 'E R'? Well, we find that on a throne. It's now known as Elizabeth Regina. Well, it's associated with this Judah, you see? Well, something went wrong along here. Well, it went very seriously wrong because someone went and did something along here. This is Judah. And this is supposed to be his firstborn son 'Er.' But something happened with the wife.

The 'something' that 'happened', for Maniah Mani, was a 'conspiracy', one which also can be found in the book of Ruth, as she notes: 'Yes, there's a conspiracy in Ruth. You see, the conspiracy started at the very early stage. They even went into details. Ruth isn't a very long chapter. And to say that it was something to do with they were going to make here.' The passage in Ruth to which Maniah Mani refers is 4.11b–12, 'The LORD make the woman that is come into thine house like Rachel and like Leah, which two did build the house of Israel: and do thou worthily in Ephratah, and be famous in Bethlehem: and let thy house be like the house of Pharez, whom Tamar bare unto Judah, of the seed which the LORD shall give thee of this young woman [Ruth]'. As she understands these verses, 'It's a famous name in Bethlehem. You see? A famous name in Bethlehem. And there it is in all this shit. And Rachel and Leah and this is going to be a noted name in Bethlehem. And it's the same Tamar.'

As a leader in the 'House of Israel', Maniah Mani feels her group to be enlightened by Jah to discern what is true and what is false in the Bible because 'somebody fickle the book. And put in a new one in there, you see? And start doing some antics.' The 'antics' are that someone in ancient times took Baal and Tamar and made their names Jesus and the Virgin Mary in the New Testament. Then they took the proper government of God that should rightfully fall to the true successor of Haile Selassie, who is in exile in the United Kingdom, and gave it to 'Er', which today stands for the dynasty of Elizabeth Regina, or Queen Elizabeth II:

> I'm talking about a government, because what this is, this is for the formation of a government. You've read it, if you've got it in a book. And we've actually got the successor in our care at the moment, because they're in exile, aren't they? [Haile Selassie's] grandson, because he is the one who is the successor to the throne ... That's why I'm saying we're actually talking about restoration of the throne, because we've got the guy.

Does all of this political talk mean that Rastas like these are a threat to the security of the United Kingdom? Not at all. Their focus is not really Great Britain, but Ethiopia and the restoration of its monarchy. Would they seek to overthrow Ethiopia by means of force? No. they are waiting for God to act in God's time and replace the present government with a successor of 'earth's rightful ruler', from the lineage of Solomon to Selassie. This view illuminates the persistent passion of Rastafarians like Ras Seymour to be a gadfly to petition Parliament to return sacred mementoes to Ethiopia to prepare the land for the return of the throne. It also explains why Rastas like Maniah Mani want to dispense with Jesus. The sooner Jesus is removed, the sooner Selassie's successor will be recognized as the 'elect of God' and the true object of worship, and God will see the time has come to act and restore the throne to 'Israel' (cf. Acts 1.6). For that reason, the 'House of Israel' is engaged in the 'Denounciation of Jesus'. As Maniah Mani explains, 'Something is wrong in there. I'm thinking: Jesus. I think the sooner we get rid of him and call Jahoviah.' The end result of Maniah Mani's theology is to oppose her to traditional Rasta thought; she rejects the idea that the same spirit dwelt in Jesus and then 'reincarnated' in Haile Selassie, as George Simpson heard one early Rasta preacher proclaim.[28] For her that is more a Jehovah's Witness position:

> Because, you know, the Jahoviah Witness actually associate him with Jesus. I told them, there's no way another person can come along here and say it's you and be incarnated in somebody else and when you're not here somebody else come here and stand here and talk to me and I'm talking to you. You [are] you. That would be a mess to jump off. It wouldn't be you.

Though her understanding of the Jehovah's Witness position seems a bit confused (Witnesses accept the Arian position that Jesus is a created being, but not God), her rejection locates her group's position within the findings of two previous British researchers. In 1979, Len Garrison in his influential study *Black Youth, Rastfarianism, and the Identity Crisis in Britain* noted:

> The Emperor, however, denied suggestions that he was Christ Incarnate, but for the Ras Tafari brethren he is the living God. And even though deceased the Emperor is considered to be spiritually omnipresent since like Christ it is believed by the faith that He can never die.[29]

Concerning the emperor, the House of Israel would reject the equation of Selassie = Christ. Such a rejection would also place it somewhere along an ongoing trajectory noted by sociologist Ernest Cashmore when researching his authoritative book *Rastaman: The Rastafarian Movement in England*, also published in 1979. Cashmore noticed that, seeking to strenghten its ties with the Ethiopian Orthodox Church, the Ethiopian World Federation, a prominent British group dominated by Rastafarians, had previously sought to divide Haile Selassie from Jesus:

> Superficially, then, the EWF had brought its members into line with the official Church doctrine, worshipping Haile Selassie as the Supreme Patriarch of the Church without publicly attributing to him any greater status. The prevalent view

in the Church at the time of my research (1977–8) was that Haile Selassie was *the* central figure in the whole Rastafarian movement, but that in many ways his divinity was open to misconception. He was a 'personification' of God but his death bore no lasting effect on the future of the movement for God was implicitly residing in all men. Haile Selassie had personified God for a while: 'How can Ras Tafari be dead when he is in all men? The body of Haile Selassie I may have been terminated but the spirit of God lives in all mankind.'

As Professor Cashmore noted further:

An interesting after-effect of this ideological movement in the Church was that some members eventually felt compelled to concede that they had been hopelessly mistaken in their previous thinking that Haile Selassie was God and that, in view of their new conception, they should renounce their Rastafarian status, admitting, as one ex-Rasta did, that: 'My King is not my God' and 'I am no longer Rasta, my work is for God not for a king.'[30]

For many Rastas, the reactions Professor Cashmore lists became two alternative responses to the devaluation of Selassie I's divine status. Rather than becoming 'ex-Rasta', some who noted 'My King is not my God' became liberalized Rastas who saw Selassie as a significant figure, but not God. Others, choosing the second response, did indeed become ex-Rasta, rejecting Ras Tafari totally.

The House of Israel begins by following the same trajectory in dividing Selassie I from Jesus. However, where it veers off is in what it does after the division. It takes the exact opposite stance to the Ethiopian World Federation's: it rejects Jesus' divinity rather than Selassie's. Yet, these actions are not entirely opposite. Rastas in the House of Israel do not claim Selassie is God. They maintain a lesser position that he is 'elect of God' (not closing the door to elevating H.I.M to divine status). But devaluing Selassie from God to 'God's elect' seems to compel them to devalue Jesus even further, hence the Baal stigma. As Maniah Mani explains:

No, I don't think there's a real Jesus. I think Jesus is Baal. I think Baal is the King Nebba [Nebuchadnezzar, see 2 Kings 24.1]. It's an image that have returned from Egypt. And I tell you another thing, down in Egypt, right? When Jahoviah God went down there, it was a disasterous saddened situation.

For her, such a situation has occurred again to God in the Christian United Kingdom:

The Denounciation mean another disasterous situation, because it look like this Jahoviah God, in the law he said he's a jealous God and we should not no more gods. So when we start pretending this Jesus him – he must be fuming with anger! Nobody want to pray to him. Nobody want to pray to him, you know?

Her focus here is curiously closer to the Jehovah's Witnesses' than it is to traditional Rastafari's in that she does not simply substitute the 'living God' Selassie for the 'dead God' Jesus but emphasizes 'Jahoviah':

> I'm not even interested in Selassie I that, because I don't pray to Selassie I. What
> about Jahoviah? How can Jahoviah be Jesus? No, tell the truth, Mister! It's two
> different people, isn't it?

Yet, she is quick to take offence if one questions whether she has become, in
Cashmore's terms, an 'ex-Rasta':

> Rasta? I'm elect of the House! You see this beast here? Every nation on earth
> dismiss him. And he was wounded by the sword, but him loose. Every nation on
> earth worship him. Nobody never trouble him at all. I think the first person ever
> come and trouble Jesus Christ is the House of Israel.

Other Rastas, however, have also sought to 'trouble Jesus Christ' and one of
these, Jamaican by birth, but also immensely popular in the United Kingdom,
is the legendary Manley Buchanan, known as 'Big Youth'. For him, Jesus is a
'condition'.

JESUS AS THE WHITE MAN'S CONDITION

Manley Augustus 'Big Youth' Buchanan, known in Jamaica as 'The Preacher',
began deejaying in Kingston in 1971, and recording in January 1972. By 1975,
Ernest Cashmore was recognizing the 'magnetic attraction' of his Rasta
message on the 'black working class of London, Birmingham, Leicester,
Liverpool, Manchester and Bristol'.[31]

Particularly, Cashmore notes the impact of Big Youth's song 'Jim Squashey'
in shoring up the flagging belief of British Rastas reeling from the news
reports of Selassie's death.[32] What gave this Jamaican 'Preacher' such power
that he could influence a population of West Indians a world away? He
learned to preach with power, Big Youth explained to me, because he is
descended from another preacher:

> My mother even today is a pastor. Yes, she is. She's a Revivalist. Yes, a spiritual
> woman. I love her, but I'm not of Christianity. I'm of naturality. Seen?

Within Big Youth is re-enacted in microcosm the struggle between the
Rastafari and the Revivalists that George Simpson observed in the early
days in Jamaica. Revivalism is a movement that came from a mixture of the
memory of Christianity from Christian slaves who were captured and
transported to Jamaica, the thin echoes of faith in imposed plantocratic
religion, the subsequent preaching of George Liele and the missionaries who
sought to bring authentic Christianity to the slaves, often in the face of bitter
opposition by the plantocracy, blending with African traditional religion.
Today that traditional religion is expressed as Myal among the Maroon
descendants, Kumina among others, and mixed to a greater or lesser
degree with Christian doctrine in such faiths as Pocomania (often
Pukumina), Revival, Revival Zion and other expressions.[33]

The struggle of Revival and Rastafari breaks out in Big Youth's expressions
with the same force it did when Joseph Hibbert's Rastas broke up the Revival

meeting George Simpson described earlier. And Big Youth knows that battle is a controversial one:

> I'm just as the Lord created me and it's very controversial, you know, to talk about a lot of things. Because, it's long to talk about. It's not just a short story. Because some people would say, 'Boy, he's crazy to say things that way!' But, it's time that people realize and face the truth. Because the Bible tell you that you must not lift up your soul unto vanity. And the Bible tell you poverty is a crime. So, if you follow the way that they tell you things, you wouldn't try to get nice things to be nice to yourself and to be nice even to others, because you just believe in Christianity and think that, because you're so religious, you don't need such things, you understand? So, Christ is just a thing that, when the people want to preach Christ unto this world, they put people in gas chamber.

Big Youth, who sports a mouth full of jewels embedded in his teeth, wears the 'nice things' of his rebellion against an ascetic interpretation of Christianity. But his concerns run deeper than decrying an other-worldly approach to Christianity which he flaunts with creative dentistry. He attacks the way that Jesus himself has been presented by the Church:

> To me, Jesus is a condition. Yeah, a condition that they gave us to believe on. You understand? Because, through a foundation of Jesus, after they take a set of people into slavery, then Victoria was saying, 'Christianize them and teach them of a heaven in the sky.' Seen? So, it's like the opostle Paul now, who preached Jesus. Me no preach. Me haven't talk of Jesus, because Jesus and Moses is of the same condition. Because they don't really tell us the real truth about Jesus. They just tell us parables about him.

And what is the 'real truth' about Jesus, according to Big Youth?

> Me say Jesus is a version that his mother, Jesus' mother, was working with King Herod as what you'd call her a helper or a maidservant, whatever, right? And the king have this maid pregnant which becomes – it's so a disgrace in society – you know what I'm saying? – that they had the boy who work around the house called Joseph, he had to left with her. And you know they give us all these parable and there was a star in the east after this child was born and again [he] live on and perform a certain amount of miracles till the system Babylon kill him. 'Cause there was an exchange for Jesus for one called Barabbas. As we were taught I think 'B.C.,' which is before Christ, because this earth was here before Jesus. You understand? Because the earth is the Lord's and the fullness thereof. So, I deal with naturality. I don't deal with Christianity and religion.

His doubt does not encompass Haile Selassie, however. In his need to choose between them, Big Youth has opted for Selassie over Jesus as Lord:

> Why, H.I.M. are the Kings of kings and the Lords of lords, the Conquering Lion in the Tribe of Judah, which is higher than Jesus. 'Cause, like I said, Jesus is a condition that they give us to believe in, 'cause Jesus and Moses is the same condition.

Like Howell before him, Big Youth sorts through the Scriptures labelling certain figures 'myths':

> Yeah, Moses born under the same condition as Jesus did it. He's just like I said, just a condition that they give people to believe in. Because they used to went in one. In Christianity, when they tell you of Jesus, they tell you of a heaven in the sky to keep you cool and quiet and calm.

In this Big Youth follows a mindset that precedes even Leonard Howell and, one might say, goes back to the doubting temple authorities who, confronted with the empty tomb, Matthew tells us in 28.11–15, bribed the guard to report that the disciples came by night and stole Jesus' body. Seeing the New Testament as creating a legend out of Jesus' life, however, came into contemporary thinking in the thought of the Deist Hermann Samuel Reimarus (1694–1768), David Strauss (1808–74), Ernest Renan (1823–92), and others, prompting scholars like the great humanitarian Albert Schweitzer (1875–1965) to go questing for the 'real' Jesus. Some concluded that Jesus was simply a carpenter who preached love, ran afoul of the constituted authorities, and had a rich myth life eventually grow around him.

Evidence outside of the New Testament records being rare,[34] the quest was naturally a frustrating one, giving place in the 1960s to a 'New Quest for the Historical Jesus', most notably of scholars like Gunther Bornkamm, and resurfacing again in the 1990s in the 'Jesus Seminar' as a kind of third quest. What unites these three quite separate ventures is distrust of the New Testament records and a desire to look beyond them past the presentation of Jesus as the 'Lord of Glory' (1 Corinthians 2.8) to find the human within the accounts. However, though fuelled by post-Enlightenment doubt, none of these quests were essentially hostile to the figure of Jesus to the degree we find in Maniah Mani and Big Youth. Instead, that line belonged more to figures like Hugh Schonfield and Abelard Reuchlin.

The view of many participants in these quests had been that Jesus was a sincere, if deluded, individual, who felt his death would force the hand of God to bring about the parousia and the kingdom of God. To Dr Schonfield, however, Jesus was much more calculating: 'What we chiefly note is that the plans of Jesus were laid with remarkable care for timing.'[35] What were those plans? 'Jesus was convinced from the Scriptures that he was to suffer on the cross, but not to perish on it.'[36] Drugged on the cross,[37] Jesus was able to recover sufficiently in the cool of the tomb to crawl out for a few 'resurrection appearances' before disappearing into the mists of history.

Why exactly a half dead zombie, desperately in need of medical attention, would inspire anyone that he was the risen 'Lord of Glory' is the challenge of common sense. Where he disappeared to, according to those who cherish the resuscitation of the half-dead position, depends on whether one is reading Baigent, Leigh, and Lincoln's *Holy Blood, Holy Grail* (1982) where Jesus stumbles off to Kashmir, Masada or Alexandria, Egypt while his wife, Mary Magdalen, is spirited with his children to Marseilles France to found the

Knights Templar;[38] D. H. Lawrence's *The Man Who Died* (1928), where he creeps away to have an affair with a temple prostitute of the Isis cult; or Michael Moorcock's uniquely imaginative 'Behold the Man' (1967), where a time traveller discovers the true Jesus is actually an idiot child and he himself gets crucified at Golgotha. The last two are self-admittedly fiction, but equally bizarre, but claiming to be fact, is the booklet attributed to 'Hevel V. Reek' titled *The True Authorship of the New Testament*, and offering on each copy a challenge to disprove its claims. What it claims is most parallel to the positions we are exploring. According to author Abelard Reuchlin:

> The New Testament, the Church, and Christianity, were all the creation of the Calpurnius Piso (pronounced Pēso) family, who were Roman aristocrats. The New Testament and all the characters in it – Jesus, all the Josephs, all the Marys, all the disciples, apostles, Paul, and John the Baptist – are all fictional. The Pisos created the story and the characters; they tied the story into a specific time and place in history; and they connected it with some peripheral actual people, such as the Herods, Gamaliel, the Roman procurators, etc. But Jesus and eveyone involved with him were created (that is, fictional!) characters.[39]

According to Reuchlin, Arius Calpurnius Piso's pen name was no less than Flavius Josephus,[40] the great historian, whom everyone naturally supposes to be Jewish, but was actually Roman![41] What possibly could be the motivation for such deception? According to Reuchlin, 'They feared that Judaism would become the chief religion of the empire.' So, 'About the year, 60 C.E., Lucius Calpurnius Piso composed Ur Markus, the first version of the Gospel of Mark, which no longer exists' in order to produce a 'new "Jewish" book' as an 'ideal method to pacify' the insurrectionist Jews.[42]

When that plan did not work, the so-called Flavius Josephus 'this Arius Calpurnius Piso deliberately provoked the Jewish revolt in 66 so he could destroy the Temple in Jerusalem – for the Jews were unwilling to accept his father's story and thereby become pacified by it as was intended'.[43]

What would motivate anybody to come up with such a flight of ahistorical fancy? Though less sophisticated than genuine New Testament scholars who are Jewish like Hugh Schonfield and Claude Montefiore, Abelard Reuchlin's main intention was similar to theirs. He notes:

> Originally, this explanation was designed solely for Jews – for the purpose of preventing their conversion to Christianity. It was not intended for Christians nor other non-Jews. No exclusivism was intended; rather, concern for the faith of others.
>
> The purpose of this booklet was to inform Jewish-Christians and Jewish-Jews of the true account of the creation of Christianity. In the first century A.D., Jews were 10% of the population of the Roman Empire. Today, after 1900 years of suffering persecution, forced conversion, exiling, murder, and finally the Holocaust, the Jews are but $\frac{1}{4}$ of 1% of the world's population.[44]

Now the parallels between the concerns of Reuchlin, of Schonfield, of Big Youth, and of Maniah Mani become clear. Like Reuchlin, who wants to avoid another Holocaust and feels that the elimination of Jesus is the way to succour his people, so does Big Youth, as we have seen, inseparably link Jesus with the 'gas chamber' and the attempt to 'keep you cool and quiet and calm'. The deadly legacy of the pirates who used a ship named the S.S. *Jesus* to thieve a people from their homeland, who perverted the Bible to justify their enslavement in a foreign land, and who used the Christian faith as justification for their continued enslavement, suppression, and destruction comes back as bad news to blight every presentation of the good news about Jesus.

How well Christ himself said, 'The kingdom of heaven has suffered violence, and violent people take it by force' (Matthew 11.12). Any empathetic human being, if he or she inherited the plight of the West Indian descendant of the slave population, including the present writer, might well become culturally Rasta. And that heir would have an understandable suspicion of the motives of many calling themselves 'Christian'. Yet, the miracle of God's grace is that Jesus, shackled and murdered like a slave, proved to be the Lord of Glory, conqueror of death, of oppression, of sin and injustice. And the prior claims of Christ are difficult to suppress. Even in the songs of Big Youth himself, like 'Natty Universal Dread', Jesus is quoted favourably. Like Big Youth, many Rastas have felt a pull between excoriating Jesus and salvaging him. When early researcher William A. Blake wrote up his findings in November 1961, he found just such a tension across Rastafari:

> Many Ras Tafarians believe that Jesus is the Son of God, but in spite of this belief they think of Him as equal with Moses. Moses brought the law of God revealing how man ought to live. Jesus brought the promise and Haile Sellassie is the fulfillment of that promise, in that God has come to live with man. God therefore is a man. On the other hand, there are others who claim that there was no such person as Jesus.
>
> Those who say this, claim that the stories of Jesus are merely another attempt of the white man to prove that God is white. The Gospels are only propaganda towards that end. They therefore have no regard for the Gospels.[45]

Like Big Youth, these Rastas have given up Jesus and Moses to the oppressors and are clinging only to Selassie. But many other Rastas find themselves loath to lose Jesus, God's elect and their 'brother man', simply because he has been subjected to a blond-hair, blue-eyed captivity by the overlords. Instead, in the wake of the death reports of Selassie and a new evaluation of what the emperor actually revealed about himself, they set upon their own quest for the meaning of who Jesus is.

Luke 4.16–19 records that one Saturday morning in Nazareth, Jesus read aloud Isaiah 61.1–2a, explaining that he had come to 'proclaim release to the captives' and 'let the oppressed go free' (NRSV). Now, ironically, these 'oppressed' are engaged in nothing less than attempting to free Jesus himself from the captivity of the chains of imperialistic mythology plantocratic downpressors have placed upon him. He has become the captive Rastas are attempting to let go free.

Freeing Jesus from the Chains of Myth

Casual listeners to Rastafarian reggae might well conclude that all Rastas are hostile to Jesus and believe him to be simply a white myth to keep Blacks pacified. Certainly the members of the Wailers appeared to give that impression, particularly Peter Tosh, when he declared himself against Christianity in songs like 'You Can't Fool Me Again', where he names it the return of slavery, 'Crystal Ball', where he calls for a 'lock down' of churches, and the acerbic 'Stand Firm'. In this diatribe (what the Old Testament calls a *meginnāb*, a mocking, derisive parodying in song), he snarls that the 'Parson' is a 'pirate' who tells him he must die to be 'saved', 'love' and 'take' Jesus Christ to be 'the light', confess his sin to be pure, and get baptized. This advice he calls 'madness', 'fantasy', and 'ignorancy' of those deluded by the disguised devil.

Yet he extols 'Yesus Christos' in the spoken prologue to 'Rightful Ruler', lamenting 'confusion' about 'the lamb that was slain' in 'high places' that causes 'Anti-Christ forces' to war against 'JAH children' in 'Recruiting Soldiers', and paraphrases the Thomas Shepherd/George Allen hymn 'Must Jesus Bear the Cross Alone (and all the world go free)' to depict the plight of the persecuted Rastafarian in 'JAH Seh No'. Then, in an unusually gentle moment in 'Nah Goa Jail', he dreams of a day when priests and ministers will be the Rastas' friend (because they hand out free ganja (!)). 'Nah Goa Jail' is on the same album that features 'Come Together', his song about learning to love one another.[46]

Again, Peter Tosh and Bob Marley together wrote and sang in their anthemic 'Get Up, Stand Up' that the idea that one must die to go to heaven in 'Jesus' name', in order to get one's full share of life's goodness and one's full rights, is an 'easing kissing game'. Directing people to look for 'great good' to come out of the sky is to attempt to 'fool' them, and preachers who proclaim such a message have no idea of the real value of life, having fallen for fool's gold and 'half' the real story: that God is not alive up in the sky, but a living man, so one must look to earth for heaven.[47] One might rightfully wonder from these songs if the Wailers shared Maniah Mani's hostility to Jesus as the mythic Baal, bane of the true gospel. Not at all, Bob's son Ziggy Marley explained to me:

> Yeah, well, let's take Yesus Kristos, man. Yesus Kristos is the man who we look up to and we take after him. Is him we follow in the lifetime. Him is the way a man should be on earth. That is the example that we follow. Him is a perfect example for us to follow.

For Ziggy, Bob's concern in 'Get Up, Stand Up' and 'Time Will Tell' was the same as his own concern in 'Wrong Right Wrong', when he sings, 'The Bible was changed just to suit King James'.[48] The intent was not to attack Jesus, but hypocrites who lie in the name of Jesus. For, as we saw in our opening quotation from 'Time Will Tell', for Bob Marley the Jesus who was crucified on Calvary belonged to the dreadlocked oppressed, not the baldheaded oppressors. These latter are the targets Marley rails against in such songs as 'Crazy Baldhead'. They are those who build penitentiaries as they build schools in order to brainwash with the message of a 'God above'.[49] But he applies Jesus' adaptation of Psalm 118.22–23 in Matthew 21.42, Mark 12.10–11, Luke 20.17 ('The stone that the builder refused shall become the chief cornerstone') to the future destiny of the Rastaman in songs like 'Cornerstone' and 'Ride Natty Ride', using the image of the dreadlocked crucified Christ who conquered death to proclaim the oppressed Rasta dread will rise again.[50]

Another misunderstood reggae great is Frederick 'the Maytal' 'Toots' Hibbert who wrote in his beautiful but blistering 'Careless Ethiopians' that diasporan Blacks have 'lost their way' and are actually calling 'upon Anti-Christ' when they pray for 'a God to come from outer-space'. In this practice they have been led astray.[51] At first glance, this Jamaican musical patriarch seems to have shifted from Christian affirmation to Rasta suspicion in his four decades of recording, since back in the liner notes of his Studio One 'spiritual' ska album, *Never Grow Old*, recorded when he was only 19, he and his group members were identified as all being members of a church choir. True to choir form, on that album he sang two rousing gospel songs, 'Hallelujah', which exults 'in the name of J-e-s-u-s' 'I am saved' and 'to Christ we are bound to win' and 'Matthew Mark', which pleads to God to give him a 'mind to serve Jesus everywhere', Jesus being identified as 'my Lord'.[52]

Was this Jesus he obviously loved so fervently at age 19 now an anathematic Anti-Christ to him 30 years later? In 'Careless Ethiopians' was he referring to Jesus' second coming? No, he explained to me:

> I would just referent to people who would them hurt, who don't know themselves. Rastafari who don't know themselves, among people who don't worship Rastafari, who don't know themselves. They just calling toward God they cannot see and where you see people just their serving up Christ. 'Cause Christ is in us and the wrath of the people is the wrath of God, you know? So, if I say 'Christ,' I'm talking about God. If I say 'Jesus,' I'm talking about God. If I'm talking about 'Jah,' I'm thinking about Christ, you know? They're the same man. But he have a lot of name – plenty, plenty name. His last name is Rastafari! So, you know, that's the way it is. So people calling upon Anti-Christ each night and day, praying for a God to come from outer-space God. They don't respect who they see and there it is, so they live by their each other. And they fight and they curse and they quarrel. And if you know that God is in you and you can see God in the morning call to you and so, which is your brother which you should respect, then you would never make war upon your neighbor.

Here again in Toots Hibbert's thoughtful lyrics is the division of the Anti-Christ, the Anti-Jesus of those who war against their neighbours, an otherworldly Jesus, unconcerned and uninvolved in his creation, juxtaposed against the Jesus who taught in Matthew 25 that he was present as the neighbour you see each morning.

The former is the 'Jesus in the sky' blasted by so many Rastas, like Mutabaruka in his 'I Am De Man', or again in his 'God is a Schizophrenic', where he warns against a 'universal lie' of god coming down from the sky to die, catechizing his listeners on 'Say', to choose as a synonym 'Man' when they hear the word 'God'.[53]

Ras John Moodie in his book *Hath ... the Lion Prevailed ... ?* explains it this way:

> If Christianity was true as we know it today, the world would be in peace. For Jesus was a peaceful man. There are so many professed, religious people in the world today, yet more than half the world's nations are at war. Something is wrong. According to one of England's Queens, the Bible holds the key to England's greatness. Well, not only England, but the rest of the Satanic Kingdom. They have used the teachings of Jesus and the rest of the Bible to suit their own evil dreams, while keeping the people blind to their hypocrisy. To understand the Bible, one has to be guided by spiritual insight by the Comforter. One has to know oneself and must be aware of where one fits in this vast knowledge of the world.[54]

So what 'spiritual insight' does John Moodie share about Bible understanding?

> About two thousand years ago, the Greeks and Romans saw the world as a revolving blob, ready to explode just as it is today. From life to death and nowhere else. Then came this knotty headed black man conquering the minds of the people. (The Pope, John Paul II worshipped a black woman as the Mother of Jesus). He even, at the end, conquered death. His people did not recognize him, but the Greco-Roman Empire did. They realized he had good medicine, and as a result, they killed him and suppressed his teachings. Then they were ready. Christianity was let loose well-polished with Greco-Roman paganism.[55]

Small wonder, then, that Rastas who have been taught this position are reluctant to identify with the Christian Church, though not with Jesus as the liberated 'Yesus'. And their attempt to separate Yeshua from the Church created in his name goes back to the very foundations of Rastafari. In the detonation of emotions set off by Mussolini's invasion of Ethiopia, the pages of *Plain Talk*, Jamaica's black forum for debate, exploded with protest from those choosing the emperor over the Pope.

F. G. Ried Pastor, of Montego Bay, demanded to know, 'Is Mussolini a Papal Henchman?', warning 'only the sword of emperor Haile Selassie will bring the Italian dictator to his senses'. 'Mussolini is in every respect a Papal Henchman', he concludes. 'Give Rome her former power, and she carries on slavery as of yore.' 'Mussolini refers to white-slavery in Ethiopia, and argues about its suppression ... I am quite certain that the Ethiopian monarch is not a slave-master, and if slavery is going on in Ethiopia Haile Selassie will suppress it in time.'[56] L. F. C. Mantle saw the Italo-Ethiopian conflict as an attack of biblical proportions, like Goliath attacking David, and begged for the United Kingdom to remember 'we the Western Ethiopians had been very successfull in time of wars towards the British Empire', so to allow involvement:

I am only praying that Great Britain or properly speaking His Majesty's Government will give us a chance to get over; then we will pay the Italians or Romans the said trick that they played with Jesus.[57]

At the crux of Mantle's complaint is a sense of betrayal by churches that would not protest when '"Father" said that his followers must fast and pray that Mussolini wins the war' against Haile Selassie who 'is solar master. Haile Selassie means the "Power of the Trinity"'.[58] Mantle separates Christ and Selassie from the Roman Catholic Church. And he also separates Christ from the established Christian Church in general which has taught 'we was piloted to heaven to drink milk and honey after death, destructively', and 'taught our Lord's prayer that "thy kingdom come" here on earth and thy will must be done here in Jamaica or in any point of the earth; but instead of it being so we can see the Judases of the Churches still are asking "Is it I Master?"':

> This is my contention, If the Bible is right, I am right. Now these kind of tomfoolery must be cut out for there is no minister or clergy who is trying to follow the footstep of Jesus the Christ Because they are full of hypocrisy, deceit, and superstitiousness. For instance the way you taught us of God and Christ, its a horse of two different colours. I beg to inform you hypocrites that what you have taught us about Jesus, is fulfilling in the land of Ethiopia right now: with the said same Romans or so called Italian or Fascist. These are the said people who crucified Jesus 2,000 years ago, and as we read that after 2,000 years, Satan's kingdom or organizations shall fall; and righteousness shall prevail in all the earth, as the waters cover the sea. But you sky-pilots are still fooling people; we are now in the time that the 2,000 years have expired so you culprits, do not tell any more lies for the Bible is here to condemn all your demogogues Just take a glance at the christian nation that you form apart both in creed and colour.[59]

Back in November 1935, at the time of crisis for Haile Selassie in Ethiopia, major tenets that would form the basis of Rastafarian doctrine were in play. The Pope was reported to have blessed and supported Mussolini against Haile Selassie. Therefore, the Pope was evil. This situation was seen mirrored in Jamaica, where the 'Judases' of the Churches lied constantly to the true believers. As Jesus was crucified by Rome, so was Rome again crucifying him in Ethiopia, just as every day the Church 'crucified' the Jamaican by lying about 'God and Christ' and offering only 'milk and honey after death'.

This apocalyptic linkage of the old and new worlds persists into the Rastafari of today. One of the clearest expositions of such linking in Rastafarian thought can be found in Tekla Mekfet's *Christopher Columbus & Rastafari: Ironies of History . . . and other Reflections on the Symbol of Rastafari* (1993). Ras Tekla writes, 'Who is it that sells the idea of "Competition"? . . . Through manoeuvres of diplomacy, The Papacy, virtually convened "the creation" of the New World. The Pope & Christopher Columbus: legitimizing the idea of a "NEW World", essentially an idea which was born in the imagination of "The Serpent of Eden"'.[60]

Those who compare the accounts of Columbus' and Las Casas' journals wherein the Pope's priests, though seriously flawed, still struggled against the murderous exploitation of the conquistadores, may well be baffled by this statement. But the impetus for this position for Rastas is the definitive action of the papacy and the Church of Rome reportedly supporting Mussolini's Italians' invasion of Haile Selassie's Ethiopia. That event is read both ways in history, backwards and forwards, so the Pope becomes the villain behind Jamaica's slaves' plight and the future Anti-Christ whom the true Christ in Haile Selassie will someday defeat. For, for Mantle, and those like him, 'This is the fulfillment of the two thousand years you told us about':

HAILE SELASSIE EXPLAINED

He shall have a new name, the new name is Haile Selassie which means Power of the Trinity that we had been taught about. The Father, the Son and the Holy Ghost; also in Rev. 5 5 we read, 'And one of the elders said unto me weep not: behold the Lion of the tribe of Judah the root of David, hath prevailed to open the book, and to loose the seven seals thereof.' The book which contained the seven seal were loosed on Nov 2nd 1930 at his coronation ceremony . . . We also read in Rev. 17–14, These shall make war against the Lamb but the Lamb shall overcome them: for he is Lord of Lords and King of Kings and those that are with him are called and chosen, and faithful Rev. 19.16 . . . Be not dismayed wheree'er you tide for God and nature will take care of us . . . On the battlefields of Ethiopia you shall hear our cannon roaring victory, then the handwriting shall be left on, the wall. Then the black men of the world shall rise and stand – for his nationwood.[61]

Essentially, what was happening is that in a time of crisis for Haile Selassie the tools of the Bible, Jamaica's past and present context, and its Ethiopianist spiritual aspirations were all coming into play to evaluate and reaffirm or alter doctrine.

Forty years later, in 1975, a crisis of even greater magnitude struck again. Haile Selassie was deposed and then reported dead. Again, Bibles were opened, history was searched, 'overstandings' were re-evaluated. But this time, Haile Selassie had not simply been exiled. He was reported to have been eliminated. In the absence of the emperor a major reassessment was launched by some of the most thoughtful. New perspectives were considered, but this time they were being done by a more widely global community of adherents.

JESUS AS A PROPHET

The shocking announcements of Haile Selassie's arrest and betrayal were not the only news to come leaking out of Africa. By 1975 an ebb to the flow of reggae had been occurring with such force that it threatened to flood Jamaica with musical response. Ever since bands like Black Blood in the early 1970s had paid tribute to 'Rastiferia', a tidal wave of African reggae groups had come washing over the New World. From Ghana came Kojo Antwi, Okasa Lamptey, the Classic Handels, Felix Bell, K. K. Kabowo, Roots Anabo, the

African Brothers, City Boys, Daniel Amakye Dede and his Apollo High Kings, among many others. From Nigeria came Sonny Okosuns, Majek Fashek, Victor Essiet, E. G. Agbonayinma, Victor Uwaifo, Bongos Ikwue, Ras Kimono, Evi Edna Ogholi-Ogosi, Rasman Maxwell Udoh, Musical Power and the Roots Vibrators, Universal Love. From South Africa rose Lucky Dube, O'yaba, Harley and the Rasta Family, Senzo Mthethwa, the Sons of Selassie and countless others from each of these countries and from across Africa.[62]

When they met Africans, Jamaicans were to discover that few if any worshipped Selassie as God, all of them having watched his rule and its tribulations as next door neighbours. Oluwole Peku Ojitiku, a college-educated insider in the Nigerian Rasta reggae scene, touring with Majek Fashek's Prisoners of Conscience, for example, regards Selassie as a prophet:

> Nobody's perfect all his life. I mean, with the Italian invasion and everything. He's like a guiding light for people to follow. Okay, so you might call him a visionary, a prophet, but you wouldn't call him God. Yes, that's sure.

Previously we noted an escalating view of Haile Selassie is sometimes accompanied by a descending view of Jesus, while a reassessment of Selassie's divine claims can elevate Christ. For a third category of inquirers, however, a re-evaluation of either robs both of divinity. African Rastas like Oluwole Ojitiku fall into this last category. Though reared a Methodist, he saw a disjuncture between his parents, their church, and their culture:

> We [Prisoners of Conscience] all have different backgrounds. My parents were Methodist, for example, and then eventually we ended up – well, they flirt around with spiritualism. But, if you started Methodist background, it's very hard to go too far. But, it's very popular in Nigeria, because the idea of people wearing suits and ties, that might be okay here [in the USA], because it's sort of similar to the culture of the people, but when you start doing that in a totally different culture, you are actually chasing the people away. Because, what they're seeing is not just Christianity and a way of life and love, they're seeing some imposition of how they wouldn't dress in ridiculous heat and different formats of behavior. You're not accomodating their ways of life, the music they want to play. So, I think early on they made a mistake. They sort of chased them away, refusing to allow them to play their music and everything. They actually were imposing their culture. So, that's what scared most people off.

In college he relativized his view of faith:

> When I was going through college, [I] sat down and read a whole bunch of stuff and different philosophies. You know, the thing is that if you grow up in a different background, then you have a different way of looking at things. So, I can objectively sit down and take it and say, 'Okay, this looks like Greek philosophy, or this looks like this, or this looks like this.' I just don't accept it because I'm forced to. There's nothing forcing me to. If I wanted to be, I could be a Shango worshipper and I wouldn't be out of place, you understand? So, though it's a matter of being born in a church, you can sit down and actually look at it properly.

For him, assessing Jesus 'properly' is to divest him of divinity, just as he does not regard Selassie I as divine: 'Jesus is not Jah, though the Methodists, you know, go around telling you how Jesus is the Son of God and everything.' So, who then is Jesus? For Ojitiku, he is an avenue:

> I'm always thinking of God. So, when it comes to Jesus, it's that this is the avenue that's been open to me to get to God, but it's not like the Christian thing of how Jesus is the one who would save me. And Jesus and the cross and the crucifixion, sort of avenues that supposed to lead me to God. So, I only use Jesus when I want to implore God for something, but I've sort of always felt that that's just the link between God ... I mean, there is a Creator and there is a God and, from what I've read in the Bible, God does love me and Jesus Christ came to establish this fact.

Rather than divine, then, for this Nigerian Rasta:

> To me he might be more a prophet, definitely, but definitely more than a prophet. But I mean, I don't know about this 'Son.' These are concepts that are beyond me to understand, about somebody saying, 'He's the Son of God,' 'He's not the Son of God.' I'm not a theologian. I just want to get along and practicalize whatever beliefs I have in this short little time that I have and do something that's going to help other people. I mean, pretty soon you're going to die anyway, as I see it. So, I don't accept things I don't totally understand.

The perplexity this thoughtful Nigerian feels is similar to that felt by those confronting Jesus: his disciples, the crowds, and (most lethally) those who held power in Jerusalem. Herod, Luke was told by his informants, was very confused about Jesus (Luke 9.7–9). From some he heard reports that John the Baptist, whom he had beheaded to please his wife, had risen. Others contended that Elijah had come back to life and still others speculated that Jesus was one of the ancient prophets supernaturally returned. Herod kept trying to see Jesus and his anxiety, along with his pathological need to control, no doubt fuelled his interest in complying with Jesus' arrest and examination.

Jesus asked his own disciples, 'Who do people say that I am?' (Luke 9.18–27, in a key conversation that is recorded as well in Matthew 16.13–20, Mark 8.27–30). While Luke does not specify when the event took place, choosing the vague 'it happened' (*ginomai*), both Mark and Matthew place the conversation on the road to Caesarea Philippi, when Jesus suddenly turned around to his 'posse', so to say, and asked literally, 'Who are people saying I am?' The disciples' answer is substantially the same in all three gospels. In Matthew 16.14 they reply, 'Some, John the Baptist, others, Elijah, and others, Jeremiah or one of the prophets'. Mark 8.28 records, 'John the Baptist, and others, Elijah, and others that you are one of the prophets', and Luke 9.19 states, 'John the Baptist, but others Elijah, but others that one of the ancients has resurrected'.

Then Jesus homes in with his own penetrating examination: 'And all of you, who do you say I am?' In each version, Matthew 16.15, Mark 8.29, Luke 9.20, Jesus' question is identical. Peter speaks up in all three versions, 'You are the Christ' (Mark 8.29), adding 'the Son of the Living God' in Matthew 16.16, and 'of God' in Luke 9.20. Some Rastafarians share these ancient Israelites' and the contemporary African Oluwole Peku Ojitiku's speculation that Jesus is a prophet.

While some Rastas, as we shall see, have widened their 'overstanding' to Peter's confession, others do echo the crowds. Jesus is identified as a prophet in the song 'Let's Give Praise and Thanks' by the great rock steady band the Melodians, known for their beautiful rendition of the classic 'Rivers of Babylon'. Reminiscent of the old gospel shouter, 'Everybody Ought to Know (Who Jesus Is)', 'Let's Give Praise and Thanks' quotes Jesus' famous 'Love your neighbour as you love yourself' summary of the law and the prophetic teaching (Mark 12.29–31), adjuring the listener to 'listen to the words of the prophets'.[63]

Identified as a prophet, Jesus is highly regarded since prophets are honoured in Rastafari. Many feel that the great Marcus Garvey played John the Baptist to Haile Selassie's Jesus. We saw earlier Moses extolled in Jah Lion's 'Black Lion'. Peter Tosh, too, honoured Moses, Elijah, Jeremiah in '"Moses" the Prophets' on his *Bush Doctor* album, claiming they are still walking the earth, judging the wicked today. The early researcher William A. Blake observed in his day:

> Many Ras Tafarians believe that Jesus is the Son of God, but in spite of this belief they think of Him as equal with Moses. Moses brought the law of God revealing how man ought to live. Jesus brought the promise and Haile Sellassie is the fulfillment of that promise, in that God has come to live with man. God therefore is a man.[64]

Over a dozen years later, O'Neal A. Walker recorded a similar view, critiquing the implications of the Rasta position of paralleling Jesus with Moses:

> The Rastafarians' equating Jesus Christ with Moses might appear reasonable on the surface but it is really playing down the divinity of Jesus Christ. Indeed, Jesus Christ was a prophet in that He had a specific message and purpose, but He was also the 'Begotten of God' (Jn. 3.16). In fact, God is revealed in Jesus Christ and Jesus Christ is also God. This is the mystery of the God-head. (Jn. 1.1, 11.30)[65]

Some Rastafarians, however, have come to share O'Neal Walker's discontent with limiting Jesus to being a prophet like Moses. These also harbour Oluwole Ojitiku's sense that Jesus is 'more than a prophet', sensing too that he has opened an avenue to God. And their quest has taken them back toward Christian orthodoxy.

7 Roots Christianity

THE TRINITIES IN RASTAFARI

Since Rastafarians universally agree that Ras Tafari Makonnen was the black king crowned in Africa according to Ethiopianist prophecy, and since in Amharic he was crowned with the title Haile Selassie, 'Might of the Holy Trinity', all Rastas must believe in the concept of a divine Trinity. At least they must deal with it. Even those traditional in Rasta doctrine or pulled to syncretize with other more unitarian religions or hostile to the Christian Church who might like to dismiss the flagrantly Christian concept of the Trinity are forced to formulate some sort of response. Some of these dealings may get fairly creative, as in the case of Leonard Howell and, perhaps, Claudius Henry and Prince Emmanuel Edwards, when the Rasta enters himself into the Godhead. Or, as Cuthbert Gustav explained the belief of his Rasta sect on St Lucia to me, 'Haile Selassie is a prophet. This is what all Rastas believe.' 'I am Jesus. That's right. I am Jah. Jah is inside.'

Many Rastas, as we saw in the case of Junior Taylor, recoil against such presumption. Michael Rose, too, replied to my query 'Would you consider yourself Jah?' with a clear and simple, 'No'. In these responses, such Rastas are following a guide laid down for them by Marcus Garvey himself who taught, 'There is no human limit. The only limit is transgression on Divinity.'[1]

But even when a Rastafarian observes this distinction to the extent of being basically unitarian in viewpoint, a perspective on the Trinity must still be negotiated. Lindon 'Half Pint' Roberts, for example, who, for over a decade, has performed succcessful and thoughtful deejay style hits from his signature song 'Level the Vibes' to his 1998 reflection on Jesus and others, 'Let We Be', on his Artists Only! album *Legal We Legal*, separates 'the Almighty', who is 'Supreme', from 'the workers' who represent God and, therefore, are 'God', in the sense that 'you, me, and the whole entire universal all is of God'. One such worker who was appointed to do a 'special task', is distinct and in some way 'more supreme' than others, is the pre-existent 'Yesus or Yoshua', who was 'Son of God'. With other 'workers' 'before him' like Michael and Gabriel, the archangels, and those after him like Selassie I, he represented the Almighty. In addition is the Holy Ghost or Holy Spirit, who is the 'Sense' the Almighty 'would use' 'to do his work'. Such a position is reminiscent of functionally unitarian Christian theologians who refer to Jesus as a unique individual in whom God meets humanity and the Spirit as the power of God that acts. Such a Trinity he sees paralleled in humans: 'The trinity really consists of your biological part, your emotional, and your spirit. That would be the Trinity in humans – the three in one and one in three.' Through this tripartite composition of humans he sees the 'Holy Trinity' operant, the Almighty 'manifest himself through you. You may not even imagine that they're doing or see them do anthing. But, he can because he create all things.'

Apparently, only Rastas who find themselves most pulled to syncretize with other religions, like the Nigerian Rastafarian Oluwole Peku Ojitiku, will demur on the question of the Trinity with a hesitant, 'Well, I don't know . . . I don't know this Trinity and not Trinity and there's so many confusing things. And people keep putting their own ideas on top of it.' Most other Rastas will affirm it. And, though they see themselves as 'god-men' (because the spirit of Jah dwells within them), they will posit a trinitarian Godhead that is distinct from themselves.

But to say that Rastas are by and large trinitarian in doctrine because their orientating locus of faith, Haile Selassie, has the concept built into his identity, does not necessarily mean that Christian history would recognize their trinitarian formulas anymore than it would the Masons'.

Of Rastafarians, who, as we saw, drew on such rich sources as Masonic ritual to formulate their beliefs, one might also ask what the exact divine content of any given Rasta's trinitarian belief might be. The answers are fascinating.

Earlier we considered the perspective on Selassie's suffering in the work of Joseph Hill of Culture, one of the great composers of reggae, whose consistently tuned gift for lilting melody and memorable lyrics places him at the top of reggae's contribution. We noted Jesus is present in his version of 'Marriage in Canaan' on *Wings of a Dove* and also in 'Sufferer' on *Three Sides to My Story*, but also a hostility against Christianity as it is practised in such songs as 'Christian' or 'Rub-a-Dub Style'.[2] In these he attempts to separate Jesus from the fallen church, since 'Jah Alone a Christian' (as he alternately titled his song 'Christian'). We noted, for him, Jesus and Haile Selassie are 'one family', 'which are the same', 'same flesh, same blood', 'between one and one and three: Father, Son, and Holy One. Three in one and one in three.' Since Haile Selassie is Jesus returned, for him, 'and being persecuted once more', therefore, 'the Trinity is right. Yes. Yes.' But within that Trinity is God (which for him is a 'title' for 'His creation, yeah, it's supreme, because it's your creation', 'God is a surrounding spirit'), the Holy One, and Jesus who is returned in Haile Selassie.

The elders of Negril, Ras Siam and Ras Isha, gave a unique response when I mentioned the Sophia movement that is currently positing a female deity behind such passages as Proverbs 8.22ff. Citing Marcus Garvey's observation that, while God has no colour, since the white race prefers to see God as white, Blacks should view God through their own spectacles, I observed, 'What women are saying is since males are seeing God as male, they're positing God as female. Would you think that would be okay?' Although Rasta is always presented as nearly hopelessly patriarchal and often in practice that appears to be the case, Ras Siam, who, like Joseph Hill, holds fast to the traditional idea that Jesus reincarnated in Haile Selassie, replied:

> God as female? I gonna tell you now, the breasts that I saw God with – he's the Lord of begin without end. That Lord of begin, of beginning, without heself begotten. So, he was suckled from the breasts of the sky. He was suckled from his own breast of the sky. The mama art the whole creation, you see, represented a woman, seen? The woman with God. Because the Trinity means God, the Mother, and Son. God which is the Father, and I and I , the Son of God. And Mother Earth. All atoms. Because it's three in one, three in one.

Matriarchal Sophia advocates might find themselves in unexpected proximity to the re-imaging of such dreadlocked patriarchal Rastas. But who is Jesus in such a formula? Is Jesus still a component? 'Israel King is Israel God and Israel Father', Ras Siam replied. 'Christ and the Father is the same', Ras Isha added. 'He say, "I am the Father." He say, "I and the Father are one." Yeah, he went to the Father when he die." 'So', I said, groping for clarity, 'in a sense, Selassie I and Jesus were the same spirit? or the same person?' 'They were the same person', said Ras Siam. 'The same person', confirmed Ras Isha.

Ras Siam and Ras Isha and the Rastafarians who follow their teaching in Negril are self-confessingly trinitarian, then. But their trinity is comprised of God the Father, who is Jesus and Haile Selassie, God the Son, who is comprised of a composite of all true Rastafarians, and Mother Earth, who includes the rest of creation.

Tony Rebel, whose contributions to dancehall, we noted, are among the finest in the genre with music that is compelling, lyrics that are rich in allusion and brimming with ideas, and ethics that are dedicated to upbuilding the hearer,[3] also believes in a trinity. 'We see God as a plural. God is very plural. We don't think it's one person.' 'You mean like the Trinity?' I asked. 'Well, or more', he replied:

> You see what I'm saying? We know it's a government. It's not one person, because in the beginning He said, 'Let us make man' and in the beginning there was a Word. The Word was with God. The Word was God. That's a speaking of more than one person.

For Tony Rebel, Jesus is God, 'Because what I'm saying is that it's a plural. So, it's not him alone. There is the Father also. And there is where we think that he has returned again: His Imperial Majesty Emperor Haile Selassie.' Are Jesus and the emperor the same person for Tony Rebel? Not exactly. They are 'of the same personality. All was created by the Word, or all have that divine power.' Were there others who had that power besides Jesus and His Imperial Majesty? 'Yes, definitely', Tony Rebel observed. 'So', I reasoned, 'it's more like – now, if I got you clear, there's Father, Son, and Spirit. Okay. You said that. And that's the plurality?' 'Or maybe more', Tony Rebel replied again. Maybe more? 'Yeah,' he explained, 'I think they are like the Creators. They are like that Government, because no matter how you have like groups, you have like leaders. And they are like the leaders. Jesus is God.'

Then, would Martin Luther King or Marcus Garvey fit in the Godhead? No, for Tony Rebel, 'I see Martin Luther King as a king. A great black leader. Yeah, Marcus Garvey's also a great leader. Yeah, maybe he's like a forerunner. Yes, he's more like John the Baptist.' Might the additional members of the Trinity be comprised of Buddha or Mohammed? 'I knows nothing about Buddha. I knows nothing about them. I just hear about them.' Would he be content at this point with just identifying Jĕsus and Haile Selassie as a part of the Godhead? 'Uh huh', he consented. But, like Benny Hinn in his unrepentant moments, Tony Rebel leaves the door open for the Government of the Trinity to contain a few more officials besides Jesus and the emperor. Still, for him such divine positions are not held by other humans. Are Jesus and Haile Selassie unique in the fact that they are more God than we are? 'If they are more God than we are?' he reasoned. 'Well, we're the children of God. And if we are the children, we supposed to be different from the Father. So, the Fathers remain different from us.' Tony Rebel truly retains a great degree of mystery in his concept of the Godhead.

Ziggy Marley, too, believes Jesus and Selassie are unique. Quoting Jesus' words of Matthew 18.2, Mark 10.15, Luke 18.17 in 'Pains of Life' as 'Jah said if you ain't like a child you can't enter Mount Zion', he readily agrees to the question, 'Are you suggesting there that Jesus is Jah, since they're Jesus' words, but you say Jah said this?', with a swift reply: 'Jah and Jesus, yeah'. And Haile Selassie? 'Same spirit, but not physical in the same dress.' But to the question 'Would God have come any other time besides Yesus and Selassie I?' he is more hesitant: 'Well, I don't know. You know, he's mysterious. Sometimes he comes like he's a begger, a poor man, sometimes.' But Ziggy Marley affirms a Trinity of Father, Son, and Spirit, but as 'linkages': 'There're linkages between the three: that Father, and the Son, and the Spirit. Because the Spirit is a part of inside of every man, every man has a spirit . . . I can understand that in a sense of there's the Father, and the Father send the Son, and the Spirit is in the Son.' So, in this formula the spirit within humans is also in the Son. But, Ziggy Marley does not see this as making him a 'Christian'. At the question, 'Would you consider yourself in the best sense, not in the hypocritical sense, now, but in the best sense, a Christian as a Rasta?' he replied, 'Christian Rasta? No, man. Me consider meself a Rasta.' Would he use the term 'Christian' at all? 'No. No'.

Another self-consciously Rastafarian dread who affirms a Trinitarian Godhead is Alvin 'Keith' Porter, perceptive songwriter for the respected roots harmony group the Itals. In the reggae classic 'In a Dis A Time' he sings, 'Although they say them sell Jah fe 30 pieces of silver, Jah Jah live forever', quotes John 3.16 in 'Rastafari Chariot', and Matthew 22.21, Mark 12.17, Luke 20.25 in 'Temptation'.[4] He sees these references as pedagogically motivated:

It's just to point out to people because some people read and don't understand. So what I in these lyrics try to point out to people, you know, that he's one. He's called 'Jesus.' People call him 'Allah.' You know? They call him 'Jah.' He's known in all different names. You know they call him 'Jesus Christ.' It's the same. It's the same Universal Power. The same Almighty.

To him Jesus and Jah are the same because, 'It's the power that manifested in all: the Father, the Son, and the Holy One. Because Jah loveth the world that he gave up His only Son.' Why is he so open to a plurality of names for God? He sees these as necessary steps in arriving at worship of the Almighty Universal Power:

> People used to praise wood and stone. People praised like silver or gold. People praised like house, animal – you know? So, I would say, if someone were gaining knowledge and they're looking at things in the world and they see Selassie and say, 'Well, this man, you know, he's the creator. This one is the one Jesus Christ that lived in the flesh,' they should also let him be.

For him, Selassie worship seems a stage toward gaining knowledge of God or Jah. Still, Jesus, for him, 'was unique': 'It's like the power manifested. He had that power.' But, even further, he states, 'Remember, he's the Almighty.' Would Selassie also be considered a part of the Trinity?

> Well, whoever that Power is on, they down. So, Selassie – you'd have to say that. Because, he was the only one that was found worthy to open the book and broke the seven seals for us. So, now, like I said, thus so it was written, so it must be done and said. It's just a reincarnation of things, then, everything that is read to me. It is a reincarnated world that we're living in.

But Keith Porter stops short of adopting the traditional Rastafarian formula: Jesus came in the old dispensation; Haile Selassie came in the new:

> Well, see, if you're going to say it in that way, then you're going to try to differentiate the Powers, you know? Yeah, you can't differentiate the Power, because He's forming in one. In one is all the time.

Keith Porter extends his inclusive view to sincere Moslems praising Allah or sincere Hindus praising Vishnu.

> It's just a changing of names, you know? And in this dispensation in the Western world they have divided understanding, so people said like, you know – 'Oh, Christianity.' And, you know, people say, 'Rastafari.' It's just a way of saying of 'Holy unto the Almighty.' The same. But, is one Almighty, that only One that created the stars. If you go ahead and praise whoever you want to praise, you know, or whatever you want to praise, as long as you praise sincerely – you know what I mean – He heard that prayer.

So, for him, is a sincere prayer to Allah or Vishnu the same as praising Jesus or Selassie I? He assents: 'Definitely. Definitely. Exactly. Because there's no one Father for this people and one Father for that people – it's one.' One thinks here of C. S. Lewis' similar view in *The Last Battle*, wherein kind actions and sincere prayer done in the name of the false god Tash are assigned to the true God Aslan, while vile cruelty and false prayer done in the name of Aslan are assigned to the Satanic Tash.[5]

The Itals' complaint in their scathing song 'Too Much Religion (in Babylon',[6]) which rails against too many denominations, is aimed against people being 'divided' ever since the time 'when Moses went up into the mountain to receive the commandments, people were divided' What appears at first blush to be simple syncretism, a melding of all beliefs if the believer is sincere, is actually a bit more complex. The goal, Keith Porter explains, is to arrive at worship of 'The Father, the Son, the Holy Spirit: that's the Powers. Now the Powers remain between both of them, now the Father and the Son, the Holy One of Israel, that is the Power.' And while Jesus is 'one of the Powers', and 'the Almighty', for him, if 'someone sees Selassie and seen as one that the power is handed down onto', does Selassie become like a window to the Almighty? 'Exactly'. He explains his conception by analogy:

> If you find like five airplanes in science – like in computer – and all those other big technical things in the world like all those satellites there whatever they have like that. All those science and those high powers coming from this Power. So, this Power can move in all directions, which is the same Jesus.

Therefore, questions such as whether Jesus Christ was black he answers in adapted Garveyian fashion from his hermeneutic of pluralism:

> Which ways that he was aren't significant to me, because he can appear in all different forms. You've just got to see him as how you see him. You know? If you see him as a white person, you know you hold onto him. If you see him as a black person, you hold onto him. Because, like I said, it's just a name. Just a name. Because He's God and chooses the name.

Since the Universal Power is what counts, Alvin 'Keith' Porter feels freedom to speak in both Rasta and Christian language:

> I can get up and say, 'Hail! Hail this Selassie I!,' because Selassie I is a Power of the Trinity. So I can hail Selassie I anytime. I can go down, say, 'Jesus Christ Almighty!,' you know, because I'm praising him the same way. You see? I just got to be sincere.

Some Rastas, however, have moved even further along the path toward reclaiming Christianity within a Rastafarian schema. As we shall see, these move on a continuum between modalist monarchianism and a fully historically Christian orthodoxy which has been recast in a Rastafarian formulation.

The Ancient Bridge

In the early 320s the rhythm of the workday of the docks of Alexandria was swinging along to a nautical beat. The sea shanties of the longshoreman were, to them, as rhythmic and compelling as reggae is to many today. And the content one of the city's popular pastors had cleverly wedded to their tunes had turned their musical chestnuts back into hits. 'Before the Son was – he was not!' boomed the sailors and the townies as they loaded and unloaded the vessels. The merchants found themselves tapping and snapping along to the beat and before long these new hits from Alexandria were sailing out to sea and being traded along with merchandise all around the Mediterranean.

The genius behind this theological songbook was a grey-haired elder named Arius, who served a church in the Baucalis section of town. He had been a student of a meticulous scholar named Lucian, renowned for his close reading of the biblical texts, whose expositions were in conscious opposition to the free-wheeling allegorical readings of some of the earlier teachers. Lucian ran Antioch's catechetical school. Such schools were the earliest type of formal seminary, where new Christians as well as Christian youth were taught the faith. Each teacher infused his own training and expertise throughout his pedagogical approach. For Lucian, trained as a neo-Platonist, his emphasis was the absolute transcendence of God. Plato had viewed matter as little more than a prison for the soul, which was always striving to break free and pass upwards to the spiritual realm inhabited by the great, impassible God, in order to spend eternity with God contemplating the forms of which material life is but a dim and imperfect reflection. A sincere Christian who was martyred in 312, Lucian nevertheless filled his teaching full of this pagan distillation and his students imbibed deeply. One student, drunk on the teaching, was Arius, for Platonism had recently come back into vogue as a neo-Platonism reshaped by the philosopher Plotinus (d. CE 270) through his writings being edited for popular consumption by his anti-Christian student Porphyry. Neo-Platonism flowed like a waterway between pagan culture and the Christian faith that sought to reach out to it. Many travelled down it, seeking a passage between these incompatible belief systems. That it was not a reliable intercourse became evident when the theology of Alexandria revealed a treacherous shoal where orthodoxy marooned and rotted.

Arius, as Lucian before him, affirmed the neo-Platonic view of the transcendence of God. Only God is eternal; only God is unique, only God is indivisible. Therefore, he reasoned, God's essence of being can never be shared with any other being. Whatever Jesus was as the Son of God, Arius concluded, he could clearly not have shared the ultimate divine essence.

Arius' concern with separating Jesus from the Father is echoed to a degree in the Rastafarian theology that seeks to separate Jesus from the Almighty. One of the best worked out of these positions is that held by Somala, the dreadlocked Rastafarian poet from Dominica, and puts his views, considered earlier, in another light:

> According to what the Bible says, Jesus is not really Jah, but is thus come through Jah to bring Jah. He bring Jah, so, technically, he is Jah. Because, in order for Jah to set example for man, he have to come with a man as man to set principles. Haile

Selassie and Jesus is the same man that just come in different forms. So, back to the
original question now – no one is as fixed, you know? He talk about 'our Father,'
so different is like which is the dress of all of we – so, he just like one of we still.
Just like a man, because he's a man, because all of we is one, so he talk about 'our
Father.' He's part of we; he's one of we. But where he comes Jah now is because he
knew Jah before we, you know, because he comes direct from Jah to we. So, then,
there in this form we consider Jesus Christ is Jah. You know, it's like he know
where the Maker and he come down. So, you know, it's Father, Son, and Spirit,
you know? In Trinity's strength and courage. It's the I-Threes all the time. Yes,
they're a Trinity all the time. So, it's like each of them both know one.

In the schema of Somala, and Rastas like him, Jesus (who is also the 'same
man' as Selassie) is less than God but dwelling with God in a relationship that
is called the Trinity. The third component of the Trinity for him is 'the Holy
Spirit [which] is a life that move with the wisdom, a source of energy, a mystic
force that lifts you'. This force, he says, is like 'electricity', but 'we're not only
talking about electricity, but about energy itself' that is available through the
example of Jesus:

> Because people don't always took of the cup and then rewash right in the cup and
> we have another set of cup and then have maybe more power and the same power.
> You know, it all depend on what you want to do. It's why the current always
> linked to Jesus the cup.

So, Jesus, though less than Jah, was linked always to the perfect power
source through the constant energy of the Holy Spirit, since he willed this
relationship even on earth. Not only does this view preserve Jah from
expiring with Haile Selassie, but it protects Jah's uniqueness from all
incarnations by making Jesus (and his reappearance in Selassie) a lesser
being than God. And it casts God's Holy Spirit as God's energy current that
fills Jesus up with divine power.

Such a position parallels at certain points Arius' concerns. This particular
Rasta position protects God from death. However, following a path like
Arius', dismissing the full incarnation of Jesus as unthinkable, since it posited
that the great, immutable God could take on decaying flesh and suffer and
die subject to the penalty of the fall and suggesting God must have appointed
a creature, the first of creation, made by God to redeem humanity, is to
jettison the central message of the New Testament. Lose God's incarnation,
death, resurrection, and redemption and the heart of Christianity is stopped.
Without the Gospels' unique, primal message one has a different faith, as the
Church responded to Arius. What he was teaching was not the historic
proclamation handed down from the disciples of Christ's disciples.

Alexandria's Bishop Alexander was appalled and so was his secretary
Athanasius, a youth from the country raised because of the power of his
intellect to deacon and then appointed to succeed Alexander as bishop. Then
in presbytery meetings, Arius began to attack the bishop's sermons which
spoke about God's incarnation in Christ, following up such verbal diatribes
by publishing his writings, beginning in 318, expanding the war in which his

waterfront jingles became his most popular public shots. With Athanasius as Arius' most vocal opponent, orthodoxy and Arianism waged a moveable and vicious battle across ancient Christendom. Finally, annoyed at this inter-necine war where marauding bands of either side sacked chapels and murdered clerics, all in the name of the pacifist Jesus, the Emperor Constantine the Great ordered the heads of all churches to convene at a council in Nicaea, the present site of today's Turkish town of Isnik, and after vigorous examination against the Bible and the teaching of early church theologians, Arius' teaching was condemned.[7] The creed Nicaea's council agreed upon comprised a brief set of statements about the Trinity:

We believe in one God the Father All-sovereign, maker of all things visible and invisible;

And in one Lord Jesus Christ, the Son of God, begotten of the Father, only-begotten, that is, of the substance of the Father, God of God, Light of Light, true God of true God, begotten not made, of one substance with the Father, through whom all things were made, things in heaven and things on the earth; who for us [people] and for our salvation came down and was made flesh, and became [human], suffered, and rose on the third day, ascended into the heavens, is coming to judge living and dead.
And in the Holy Spirit.
And those that say 'There was when he was not,' and 'Before he was begotten he was not,' and that, 'He came into being from what-is-not,' or those that allege, that the son of God is 'Of another substance or essence' or 'created,' or 'changeable,' or 'alterable,' these the [universal] and Apostolic Church anath-ematizes.[8]

Immediately the creed delivered a resounding blow against Arianism by establishing that the Father is the Creator. It did so by lifting out the exact phrasing of the Apostle Paul's letter to the Colossians 1.16, which identifies Jesus as the one by whom were made all things heavenly and earthly, 'visible and invisible'. While Arius would agree that a 'first-created' Jesus would fashion the rest of creation, he recoiled at a face value reading of Genesis 1.1 that the Almighty Father was the shaper of all material things. To Arius, a picture like the one James Weldon Johnson paints in his poem 'The Creation' of God sitting down like a mother in the mud shaping Adam was not only blasphemous, it was incomprehensible.

Next, the creed hammered on several key points about Jesus: that he was the 'only begotten' (*monogenas*) out of the substance of the Father, being God out of God, not created. This was the creed's terse answer to the song the longshoreman were bellowing on the docks.

So potent was the result that it not only set its contemporaries straight on Arianism, but it also set a standard for testing future doctrines that is still recognized today. This creed – or statement of belief (from the Latin *credo*, 'I believe') – which was forged at Nicaea has become the unifying statement linking all Christendom. And its tenets about Jesus not only form the primary walkway on which the tenets of Rastafari have progressed, but it is also the single most important doctrinal bridge that links the two faiths together. It is the ancient and sturdy footbridge between them. It provides the common ground.

On 2 September 1928, Marcus Garvey addressed a gathering at the Century Theatre, Westbourne Grove, London in a lecture collected by his second wife Amy Jacques Garvey and E. U. Essien-Udom in their third collection of his writings and speeches. Chiding his British audience because business and military interests regularly followed the London Missionary Society, he announced:

> You have come into our homes, deceived us in every way under the guise of Christianity – but do not you ever believe I am not a Christian. I believe in God the Father, God the Son, and God the Holy Ghost; I endorse the Nicene Creed; I believe that Jesus died for me; I believe that God lives for me as for all men; and no condition you can impose on me by deceiving me about Christianity will cause me to doubt Jesus Christ and to doubt God. I shall never hold Christ or God responsible for the commercialization of Christianity by the heartless men who adopt it as the easiest means of fooling and robbing other people out of their land and country.[9]

Garvey's words rang with power and he was able to transcend the barriers of culture, race, and context that set him apart as a sojourner from one of the United Kingdom's former colonies and draw both his old world audience and any anomic former Jamaicans among it before the judgement seat of his position because he appealed to a common authority that predated and presided over himself, his audience, the London Missionary Society, and the scoundrels who camp-followed the society and perverted its evangelical intentions. Garvey appealed to the universally accepted definition of the gospel that had a prior claim on them all: the creed established at Nicaea.

Thirty-seven years later, on 15 January 1965 a world away in Addis Ababa, Emperor Haile Selassie I hosted the 'Venerable Heads of the Oriental Orthodox Churches' in conference. Five days later at that historic gathering, the title 'Defender of the Faith' was officially bestowed upon the emperor. Addressing the august assemblage at the commencement of the sessions, the emperor confessed his faith in Jesus Christ and concluded his remarks with this charge:

> Holy Fathers, as the spiritual descendants of the Apostles of Christ you have an eminent responsibility, which responsibility would include the improvement of the relations of laity with clergy and of church with society.
>
> We hope and trust that God will guide the discussions here according to His will and that His power will assist Your Holinesses in finding common solutions to common problems in the spirit of amity and concord. May God who helped the 318 Fathers of the council of Nicaea enlighten and help us all.[10]

Whether reproving a group of errant followers or encouraging a gathering of faithful leaders, both Marcus Garvey and Emperor Haile Selassie I adhered to the definitive, primary orthodox Christian creed of Nicaea.

If the insights of astute Rastas like Barbara Blake Hannah and Alvin 'Keith' Porter are correct, that Rastas who begin with Haile Selassie will eventually follow his example to get to Christ, then the creed of Nicaea is the bridge over which the emperor will take them. Rastas who ground themselves in the teaching of Marcus Garvey will also end up in the same orthodox location.

The great Frederick 'the Maytal' Toots Hibbert, whom we quoted earlier, provides an apt example. Toots Hibbert is the quintessential Rastafarian. A namesake of Joseph Hibbert, a founder of Rastafari who is argued by some to be the first, rather than Howell, to preach Haile Selassie, Toots aligns with Hibbert's Ethiopian Coptic church. Rather than dreadlocked, he wears the beard of the earliest adherents of Rastafari:

> I have my beard. Your beard make you to be more Rasta than anything else, because all the wise men, they have to have their beard. You have some wise men don't have no beard either. But all those great men that work in the hospital — what do they name those guys again — those guys that work in the hospital? — they call themselves 'professor,' right? So, once you have your beard. And do you know why you have your beard? Your beard is called the 'quickening spirit.' If someone asks you a question, which you can't really do, in other words, maybe you don't know, Bill, standing up to questions somebody ask you, you just touch your beard and you find argument right away to satisfy that question, yeah, man!

A thoughtful man, whose conversation is interspersed with common sense and a gentle island humour, he is not given to pretension. Asked if he is a descendant of Joseph Hibbert, he is careful to establish that he cannot verify such a claim: 'No, I'm not sure ... not really the founder, but I know the doctrine'. Though he prefers to call himself the Maytal on stage, he retains the designation 'Toots' for family reasons: '"Toots" is a nickname, you know, it doesn't have anything to do with my career, but people make it up something to do with my career, because really my name is "Maytal".' 'I was called by my brother, bigger brother when I was a little baby, he told me he was the one who called me "Toots".' Yet, this modest man has much to boast about, for, although many claims are presented for coining the word 'reggae', in 1967 he was the first to put it on a song. His disarming account gives a measure of the humility of this outstanding artist:

> When I was — me and my two bredren [Nathaniel 'Jerry' McCarthy and Henry 'Raleigh' Gordon] was just in Trenchtown, we was living in Trenchtown and we were going to do some recording on one Tuesday. And we was just making joke about each of them and other, grin at people, you know? So, well, you see this word by 'streggay' ['Yeah, raggedy people who look raggedy. People who don't look tidy; those call them "streggae" in those days'] by laughing at other people, you know? Streggay. So, I just turned right around and said, 'Let's do the "reggay."' And I wrote the song about that too. It's just a simple two words, I

mean, which two line song – not really! (laughter) But it's a very good rhythm now.

As one who consciously draws from the roots of Rastafari, Frederick Hibbert orients himself from the starting point of the teaching of Marcus Garvey:

I love people who wear long locks and I love people who comb their locks, but I'm coming from Marcus Garvey, the tradition of Marcus Garvey ... He's of Christ, you know. And he's greater than all those other man that you call great, you know. He put black and white together. You know, people should unite and be as one. Here comes justice ... So, all of these mans that are coming over, I don't put none before Marcus Garvey. Marcus Garvey is one of the greatest. So, I'm coming from Marcus Garvey.

Where has Marcus Garvey taken Toots Hibbert? To knowledge about Jesus:

When I was much [younger I] get out some knowledge and then I get more knowledge and I keep on getting, seeking out God and so, you know? Yeah, but Jesus I right around, because you're all around when people look at it and they different. I look at him as a black man and a special man. He's the Son of the Father. Yeah, he's the Son of the Father.

What does that phrase 'Son of the Father' mean for someone as central to Rastafarian reggae as Frederick Hibbert? The answer may appear surprising, but not given his Garveyite leanings. 'Would you see Jesus as Jah or Haile Selassie returned?' I asked. He immediately replied:

No, he's Jah. He's Jah. Jah is the Almighty. Jah is the Son. Jah Is Christ. Jah is the Father. Jah is the Son, you know? And Jah is the Son, you know, and Jah is the King – the only King.

Would Haile Selassie also be Jah, or the Father? Not to the Maytal, Toots Hibbert. Jah is distinct from Haile Selassie:

No, that would be the one who created it – the whole heavens and the earth, created all mankind, created Selassie, created Marcus Garvey, created everyone of us. No, it can't be above Jesus. Jesus is Christ.

Where the Maytal's concern focuses is in establishing Marcus Garvey's agenda: 'I only say that he's [Jesus is] black.' His emphasis, as is Garvey's, is on the Black Christ. And, he is also concerned about the unity of God:

I just want you to know that Jah is the same person as Jesus. Yeah, he's just one person. But people try to make him in different, different, different, different, different churches, in different Rastafari, everybody think different, you know?

And what of Haile Selassie? If for the Garveyite Rastafarian Toots Hibbert Haile Selassie is a created human like Marcus Garvey and is not the return of Jesus, since Jesus is Jah in the Godhead with the Father and the Holy Spirit, who for him is Haile Selassie? A great human, he explains:

Selassie I is a body to himself. Yeah, he's a body to himself. All the great mans them, into their own body to themselves. What they do is written. If they do good, it's written. If they do bad, it's written. So, you know, we cannot change those things. As I told you before, Jah created everyone of us. And created Selassie I, created all the great mans them.

But, despite what looks like thorough-going Christian orthodoxy, even with an Eastern flavour of determinism, Toots Hibbert is not about to go running back to the Seventh Day Adventist or Roman Catholic churches of his youth: 'No, because I can't see the message of the church.'

Though he will sometimes visit ('Yet I will go and listen what they saying. I will listen what they're singing, everything, you know?'), he prefers to follow Marcus Garvey, 'the greatest of them all'. Because of his afrocentric approach to Jesus Christ, to Toots Hibbert, 'Marcus Garvey is more a preacher of Rastafari, you know?' When I observed, 'I have the most profound respect for Marcus Garvey. He was a Nicaean Christian', he agreed, 'Yeah, man. Martin Luther [King], you know, all these great man, that is where I'm coming from.' So, Toots Hibbert is a Christian, but a particular kind of one, he explains:

> I am a Christian, but different kind of Christian: Rastafari Christian. What 'Christian' mean: people who try to do good at all times. Don't deal with politics; don't deal anything that you cover up the Spirit of Jah, you know? Don't deal with violence; don't deal with a lot of things. So, you don't have to go to church to be a Christian, but you learn that you have to go to church to be a Christian. But I learn that the Church is the people. People is. You're a church.

What does it mean to him for people to be a church? 'We should live good among each other, for the church is one foundation. Every church is one foundation, which is Jesus Christ made it.' In that sense, 'We're part of him, we're part of each other, you know, too.' So the Church is each individual. This idea is widespread in Rastafari. The more Selassie-oriented T. 'Ijahman Levi' Sutherland (author of paeans like 'Jesus Selassie I Keepeth My Soul' on Ras Record's *Africa*) affirms his 'born again' 'body' is 'a church' in his song 'The Church' on his Island album *Are We a Warrior*.[11] In a rare Wailers single, reportedly written for them by the great Rasta sage Mortimer Planno,[12] the old standard 'Crying in the Chapel' is even reworked into 'Selassie is the Chapel'.

Like these (and most Rastas), Toots Hibbert is a critic of the Christian Church's failures and sings scathing songs of criticism about them, like 'Revolution' on Dynamic Sounds' 1974 *Roots Reggae* album. But, like Sister Margarett E. Groves, a poet of the 'Nyiah Bingi Order',[13] who warns about 'wolves among our Rastafari brothers ... have sold out their brothers, because of the power of "Silver and Gold"', he is also careful to separate himself from what she terms 'traitors, entering the brotherhood'.[14] 'I am not "Rastafarian",' explains Toots Hibbert, 'I am Rastafari. One of them is commercial. True Rastafari is faith. Good faith and good will. And so you have many, many different Rastafaris.' In his brand of Rastafari, grounded in the Garveyite adherence to the Nicene creed, he affirms an afrocentric approach to Christian orthodoxy: 'The Trinity is the Christ, is the Father, you know, is the Father and the Son. And the Holy Spirit. That's what we call the full name: "the Holy Trinity of love and power who sees us in danger hour" '.

Not all Rastas whose Trinity consists of Father, Son, and Holy Spirit have moved as far toward historic orthodoxy as has Toots Hibbert. Some concretize statements like Toots' that Jah and Jesus are 'one person' into a theology that ends up truncating the persons of the Godhead. In this is illustrated one constant truth that one notices about church history, that rejected views continually reassert themselves. Creeds that correctly expound and apply Bible passages preserve the reasoning of earlier minds who dealt with heterodox teachings and after examination found them wanting. They provide a helpful guide to future Christians when these views adapt themselves and reappear in changing dress. Such is the case of Nicaea's Creed. In addition to Arianism it also corrected an ancient attempt to understand the Trinity and still preserve the monotheistic unity of God. Termed dynamic monarchianism or modalism, this way-station along the road toward orthodoxy taught that God appears in different modes or manifestations. One theologically engaged Rastafarian I encountered who had worked out a modalistic view of the Trinity is the Montego Bay Rasta Byron Antonio Beckford. To him, Jesus is 'the creator', 'He created all this you see: the sea, the sand, all.' Further, Jesus and Jah are the same: 'the Creator'. Is Haile Selassie God? No, to him, he is 'the greatest man':

> He is the king of all kings, the king of Rastafari. No, you see, he is a man. The greatest king. The king of Rastafari, He said that when he came to Jamaica. He spoke through an interpreter, you know? He said, 'I am not God.' I saw him when I was a little boy.

Tony Beckford became a dreadlocked Rasta because of 'the love. They are very loving. They are very accepting. Rasta got two coins, he gonna give you one. They love everybody. They love and accept me.' To him, Rastafari and Christianity are 'the same thing, to love everybody. It's the same.' But he is not universalist in accepting Islam or Buddhism: 'Some people worship the sand or the sea or that rock over there (points). They think differently than we do, you know? But the Bible says not to worship that.' 'So, would you accept that [as acceptable] worship?' I asked. 'No', he replied. Yet he differs from Nicaean orthodox Christianity in his understanding of the Trinity. He is concerned with preserving the concept of God's monotheism, not falling into the worship of three gods. 'There's just one God', he affirms, but then adds, 'Just one God, one person'. The orthodox formula is one God in three faces (*prosōpon*) or persons. 'I don't know about that Trinity', he demurred. But the one formula I described that resonated in him was reached when I offered: 'Well, would you say God was the Creator of the Old Testament, then he was Jesus in the New, and then the Holy Spirit?' 'Yes, that's it. Just one God, one person!' he agreed. Rather than existing in three co-existent persons, for him, God passes through three modes. In a later refinement of modalism, called Sabellianism, God was presented as choosing to manifest at different times in any one of these temporary modes, irrespective of when in history the time might be. In this schema, sometimes God might appear as the Father, sometimes as the Son, sometimes as the Spirit. But the key difference is that in modalism, or Sabellianism, these manifestations are temporary. In orthodoxy, the three persons co-exist eternally.

In Christendom, the modalistic view can be found today in what are called the 'Jesus Only' churches, for example, in many of the Apostolic churches among predominantly black denominations and United Pentecostal churches among white denominations.

In Rastafari, Silburn 'Mosiah' Morrison seems to express the view in his book *Rastafari: The Conscious Embrace*, when he exhorts his reader, 'Because this is the age of the Last Days, the world must address itself to creating the reign of unification and democracy. It must uphold the ideal that Christ is our Father, our Son and our Holy Ghost.'[15] Praising 'Jah Rastafari', his ideal is that 'Real Rastas are Christianity personified. They uphold the ideas and beliefs of Jesus Christ and believe in the Trinity of His Reign.'[16]

Sometimes reggae musicians, who are exploring doctrine even as they are entertaining, can be moving through a stage of Christological formulation, as appeared to be the case of the great musical stateswoman Judy Mowatt, author of such classics as 'Black Woman' and 'Slave Queen' and former member of the distinguished, 1997 Musgrave Award winning I-Three, in songs like 'Get Up Chant' and 'Who is He?' on her beautiful 1987 *Love is Overdue* album. While P. Dave Richards' 'Get Up Chant' appears syncretistic, suggesting that whatever the hearer conceives God to be, one should praise God for setting humanity free, her own gospel-reggae crossover 'Who is He?' touches on modalism.[17] The lyrics for 'Who is He?' ask who was crucified at Calvary and answer the 'Father God'. This theological stopover is a oneness view termed 'patripassianism' that was rejected by the early church. As lawyer and apologist Tertullian (c. 225) explained, this view suggests 'the Father himself descended into the virgin, was himself born of her, himself suffered; in fact that he himself was Jesus Christ'. 'It was Praxeas who first brought this kind of perversity from Asia to Rome', points out Tertullian in his colourful courtroom style. 'He put the Paraclete to flight and crucified the Father.'[18] Rastafarians have explored this view because of their theology that Jesus and Selassie I are the 'same person'. Therefore, practices like Ras Michael's to interchange 'King Negus' or 'King Rasta' or 'Selassie' with 'Jesus' or 'King Jesus' in songs like his beautiful rendition of 'Marriage in Canaan' on his excellent *Know Now* album would inevitably end with 'the same person' on the cross. If Haile Selassie is God's 'Fatherly' manifestation and Jesus is God's 'Sonly' manifestation, but they are the *same person*, then the recorded lyrics of 'Who is He?' would take this theology to its natural conclusion, placing Selassie on the cross in a type of patripassianism. Oneness doctrine, with all of its strange, theological permutations, is one of the choices facing Rastas still attempting to choose between regarding Haile Selassie as Jesus the Son returned, or Selassie as the appearance of the Father, Jesus being separately the Son. For Rastas who have moved beyond worshipping

Selassie as God to worshipping Selassie's God, Jesus, such oneness theology in either its simple modalistic form or Sabellian refinement sometimes becomes a way-station.

However, despite appearances caused by the espousing of patripassianism in 'Who is He?', such was not Judy Mowatt's view. Underscored again is the lesson that assessing someone's views by appearances is always speculative and often misleading. Only by direct revelation can one know spiritual truth. In Judy Mowatt's case the modalistic view was another Rasta's emendation to her original lyrics for 'Who is He?':

> Yes, 'Who is He who gives us so we can give? Who is He that gives us life so we can live? Who is He that shed His blood of Calvary? He's our Father God.' And I remember I was sharing those lyrics with a brother who is a fellow member then from the Rastafarian faith and he didn't mind the song at all. But I had Jesus Christ in it and he said, 'No, because the Christians going to believe that you and them are one. Yes, Christians, they're gonna think, you know, your belief and their belief is the same thing. So, don't put in Jesus Christ, just put in God. Because God is general.'

In deference to the brother, Judy Mowatt accepted the alteration; however, in reality she was still singing about Jesus Christ:

> So, I saw the truth and I was revealing the truth, but it never get out the way it should have been, you know? But, that song is really a lovely song. I'm gonna do it over though, you know. I'm going to rerecord. I'm gonna sing it the right way.

Despite her respectful deference in allowing the lyric change, Judy Mowatt had already moved along the road of Trinitarian 'overstanding' to recapture the heart of Christianity. Following the emperor's leading into Nicaean orthodoxy, she converged with the parallel path that Marcus Garvey blazed for others like Toots Hibbert. Such resultant Nicaea-defined Rastafarian Christianity, as we shall see in the next section, has become a most helpful afrocentric corrective for the mother faith. It can serve to break Christianity from the Euro-American stranglehold that, while doing much good, has also produced such bizarre corruptions as plantocratic Christendom. In this, Nicaea-guided Rastafari contributes to the good work being done to revive and reform Christianity by the burgeoning two thirds world orthodox perspectives on the faith, as detailed in books like our *The Global God*. Those entering Christian orthodoxy from Rastafari can bring a sensitivity to pruning away the sixteenth to twentieth centuries' overemphasis on often destructive Western Euro-American-centred, imperialistic utilitarian, or non-biblical, non-orthodox, interpretations that have enervated Christianity. They can help revitalize the faith by calling it back to its primary focus of loving God through serving Jesus Christ and treating one's neighbour as one treats oneself.

'ROOTS CHRISTIANITY'

Of all the sincere and devout minds I encountered in my twenty years of interviewing Rastas, among the most astute and probing is Judy Mowatt's. As most Rastas, she was reared a Christian:

> Yes, I came out of the church. You know, because my grandmother was a Christian. My mother, before she was deceased, she was a evangelist in the Church of God. She was in New York. I came out of the Roman Catholic. The reason why I'm sure we came out of the Roman Catholic is that we were very poor and the St. Vincent de Paul Society really took care of us, you know? And I think it came out of that experience of not having and these people are so kind to us why we became a part of.

By the age of 18 or 19 she had already begun to explore 'Rastafari doctrine':

> I was living in Bull Bay out in Nine Miles and you have a large community of Rastafarians out there called the Bobo ... up in the mountains, in the hills. And their philosophy was that their leader was God ... Prince Emmanuel is God and Haile Selassie and Marcus Garvey is a part of the Trinity.

In this schema, Jesus would be the same as Prince Emmanuel 'because he said, "The Father and I are one"':

> But, Emmanuel be God the Father, and so they see Emmanuel as God the Father. Yes, [Jesus] would be the same ... and then Marcus Garvey would be like the Holy Spirit. Because they said Marcus Garvey lived out before Christ was born. And he was the foreteller – the person who foretold about Christ.

The Bobo Dreads became Judy Mowatt's first stopover in Rastafari:

> They said that His Imperial Majesty is the Almighty. All right? So, I was searching and I was listening to the different Rastafarian views. I was listening to the different views and then I find that none of them – none of those that I mention appeal to me. Until I search and search until I became a member of the Twelve Tribes of Israel. All right. In the Twelve Tribes of Israel, when I became a member, my understanding – the Prophet, Gad is the Prophet – he is the founder of the Twelve Tribes of Israel. And what I learned from him is to follow the teachings of the Bible. He said that we are to read the Bible a chapter a day. And we got the teaching from His Imperial Majesty that His Majesty says, 'Men sees their hopes and aspiration crumbling and they know not whither to turn. But they should know that the Bible is a rallying point for humanity and guidance for their future actions.' So, we started reading our Bibles. But to my understanding from the brethren was that His Imperial Majesty was the reincarnated Christ; that's what I was told. But, in reading my Bible, and listening to what I'm hearing on the outside, it was a little conflicting. Because, the Bible was telling me about Jesus Christ, especially the Acts of the Apostles was telling me about Jesus Christ and here I am learning about His Imperial Majesty. So, what I did, I converted in myself; I converted everything I read about Jesus in respect of His Majesty. I say,

well, it is Selassie I it's talking. And when I should say Jesus Christ, I say Selassie I. The point is made and it is very powerful and my heart sanctioned to it. Instead of saying Jesus Christ, I would say Selassie I. You know? But, I did not know, as you said, Lutheran, they follow Lutheran. So, some Rastas follow Selassie's teaching, but they worship Christ. Right? Right! But I, at that time, my Christ was Selassie I. Right? Now, I am not going to tell you that that was the teaching of the Prophet himself because he didn't come out and tell me that. I don't know if he had said it to anybody, but in greeting, when he would greet the house, he would say, 'Selassie I.' And I would think the person who you worship is the person that you would speak of the most.

Immersing herself in avid and regular Bible study, she was focused on Psalm 87 by the Twelve Tribes' teaching. This brief psalm reads:

(1) His foundation is in the holy mountains.
(2) The LORD loveth the gates of Zion more than all the dwellings of Jacob.
(3) Glorious things are spoken of thee, O city of God. Selah.
(4) I will make mention of Rahab and Babylon to them that know me: behold Philistia, and Tyre, with Ethiopia; this man was born there.
(5) And of Zion it shall be said, This and that man was born in her: and the highest himself shall establish her.
(6) The LORD shall count, when he writeth up the people, that this man was born there. Selah.
(7) As well the singers as the players on instruments shall be there: all my springs are in thee (KJV).

Yet, while her teachers were seeing this text as proof of the Bible prophesying about Haile Selassie as 'the man' born in Ethiopia, Judy Mowatt was progressively realizing something quite different:

We again were told that there were 2 scriptures – many scriptures – but 2 in particular. Psalm 87: 'His foundation is in the holy Mountain. The Lord loveth the gates of Zion more than the dwellings of Jacob.' If you look at that. And what it is really saying in a sense, because it says, 'Glorious things are spoken of thee, O city of God. I will make mention of Rahab and Tyre. And to them that know me.' Now, and Ethiopia, it shall be said that that man was born there. But, it is saying, along with these cities, along with Ethiopia, it shall be said that that man was born there. *There* in Zion. Now I'm learning. Because I was one of them who used to tell everybody, 'Read Psalm 87 if you don't believe me. Read Psalm 87 because it speaks of the man who was born there.' But, we don't really follow. When they just look at Ethiopia, that's what they hold on to. But, when we look at the whole chapter, we see that it is Zion and of Zion it shall be said that this and that man was born in her. You can read it for yourself . . .

So, we as Rastas, then, we really thought, because it said this and that man was born in her, His Imperial Majesty was born in Ethiopia. So we are convinced, but not understanding that because of our own misleadings led us into a deception. All right, the next chapter in the Bible that really convinced me was Revelation chapter 5. Yes, there it said John never saw no hope for mankind and he wept much and there was a voice that said to him, 'Behold, weep not, for behold the Lion of the Tribe of Judah hath prevailed to loose the seven seals.'

Now, the lion of the tribe of Judah is what we held on to, because His Imperial Majesty had the title, 'The Lion of the Tribe of Judah.' And nobody couldn't tell me then that the Lion of the Tribe of Judah is not His Imperial Majesty, because he bears the title. Now is recently I learnt that all the kings of Ethiopia, they all have the title. All right? Right.

One by one, she discovered that passages used to establish the divinity of Haile Selassie, like Acts 2, were really 'speaking about Christ'. Trying to be loyal to what she understood to be Rastafari, she would faithfully centre on these three scriptures: Psalm 87, Revelation 5, Acts 2:

Those were three of the biblical chapters that really ministered to me in my time of Rastafaria. Because, when I'm witnessing to people, those were the scriptures I introduced to them. And as it convinced me, I trying to go where I could to convince others. But, I found out after a while I became empty. Yes. After such a long, long time of knowledge, having a lot of biblical knowledge and thinking that I am a child of God because reveal to me in so many different ways. And even when I was with Bob, I remember it was during that election period and Bob Marley was shot at at 56 Hope Road and before it happened I saw it in a dream.

After 22 years, I still wasn't quite sure about my belief. But, because of my association with the organization that I was in, and I meet with the others and everybody's saying the same thing. And I'm sure people will tell you, when you speak with people from the Twelve Tribe of Israel, if they're honest enough, they'll tell you that they believe that Selassie I was Christ. But, for me, they said that the Gad man, firstly he never told us that Selassie was not God.

But, he never clarified and said, 'Brothers, I just want to let you know. You, probably, some of you have a belief that His Imperial Majesty is God and some of you might not have a belief, but I want to clear it up once and for all that he is not God.' He never said that. So, there were people in the House of Israel who some had a mindset that His Imperial. Majesty is Christ returned. And some people knew that it was not so. But the people who knew did not communicate with those who did not know. All right? And it was my belief, and many others'.

Recent public clarification has cleared up the matter. On 13 July 1997 on Jamaican radio station IRIE FM's programme *Running African*, the Prophet Gad did just what Judy Mowatt had hoped he would do. He declared: 'We see Christ, and that die and rose again, and that die for our sin, we see that person. So that is, you know, a different teaching, because is not many see this teaching, that Christ is the person.'[19] When the interviewer pointed out, 'Recently we've had much debate on this program *Running African* and other programs about the Divinity of His Majesty the Emperor Haile Selassie as it relates the return of Jesus Christ. What are your thoughts on the matter?', Prophet Gad replied, 'Well, Christ is to return and sit on the Throne of David, so I strongly believe that, you know, Christ is going to come and sit on the

Throne of David.' The interviewer was quick to highlight, 'You said something very important here and something that may disturb the Rastafarian Movement in Jamaica. Christ, You're talking about the return of Christ.' At that the Prophet Gad stated firmly: 'Yes I am talking about the return of Christ who is going to sit on the throne of David.' 'Are you making a differentiation between Jesus Christ and Haile Selassie?' the interviewer then asked. The Prophet Gad clarified the point, 'Yes I am making a differentiation. Because Christ the same yesterday, today and forever. And even after His Majesty say, Him saved not by the man character but by the blood of Jesus Christ.' The interviewer concluded this excellent interview by toasting 'The Prophet Gad. The man who boldly declares Jesus Christ.'

Along a similar trajectory to the one the Twelve Tribes' leader was travelling, Judy Mowatt herself was moving. She too had become disenchanted with the practice of confusing with Haile Selassie Scripture texts about Jesus Christ:

After 22 years of being Rasta, I was losing out now on my belief. It was running away from me and I couldn't catch it. I didn't believe anymore. All I had was my religion. All I had was Rasta. And if Rasta is leaving me, my self esteem is going, my life is going away from me. And I don't know how to put my hand on it to hold it back now. And I was really – I thought I was going out of my head. And I didn't want nobody to know what was happening to me. I would sometimes catch somebody by the side and said, 'Do you really think His Majesty is God?' And they would say, 'Yes, man, I believe that!' So, I said, 'Okay, let me leave it like that. That person is not like me, not feeling like me.' So, I started going to Church on the Rock. I went to various churches and I remember one night in particular a brother took me to Bible Teachers' Ministry on Half Way Tree Road. And the preacher, she was a preacher from Fort Lauderdale, Dr. Mary Banks. And she was preaching and the message was really strong and it moved my heart. But, when it came to the altar call, I decided I would not go. Yes, it's a big step. But, I am not going to go because I am not a member of the church, number one. And I do not believe that I need a publicity that I would engender. But, when I saw the last person, I thought – I just felt something call inside of me said, 'It's time.' And I said to the person next to me, 'Excuse me!' And I went up. Yes, when I went up, the lady said to me, 'If you did not come, I was coming to get you!' She met me halfway. Halfway going up! She said, 'If you did not come, I was coming to get you. And, she held my hand and I went up. And when I went up, this elder she prayed only for me. She said, 'Lord,' what I remember hearing her said. She said, 'Lord, she has searched for you in many different places – various places – and the image that she has of you is a false representation of you.' And, I'm saying, but how is somebody exposing me life like this? I don't want everybody to know my business. But – how she know? You know? How she know all of this? Because I was really searching now. And I left. I didn't know what to do because I didn't want anybody to see me changing, but, as you say, I'm searching. So, I would go on stage and I would say, 'Greetings in the name of our Imperial Majesty, Emperor Haile Selassie I, the First.' I greet them in the Lord and Savior Jesus Christ, who is this day revealed in the personality of His Imperial Majesty. But, I keep saying it. But, more and more I'm saying it, I'm only like a sounding brass. And a tinkling cymbal. Because it is only lip service I'm paying now. Nothing is coming from my heart as it used to be before. That intensity is not there. So, anyway, I went out and I was doing the same thing.

But such a tension cannot remain without demanding to be resolved, especially given the Twelve Tribes' fervent emphasis on study of the biblical records:

As I said again, my intention was Christ, to add Christ in, because that's what I saw in the Bible. Now, Gad man teaching in the Twelve Tribe of Israel force you to read the Bible. And His Majesty insist that we read our Bible also. Then, when we read the Bible, His Majesty say, we'll find the truth in ourselves.

The truth she found was that 'Jesus is the Son of God':

Jesus was with God from the beginning of creation as the John 1 says, 'In the beginning was the Word and the Word was God.' And the Word, it is Christ. The Word is Jesus Christ. In flesh, came in flesh to die for our sins. So, I believe that Jesus was God because he said when you look at me you see the Father ... the Father gave him a human body where Mary was overshadowed by the Holy Spirit and she became pregnant without a man touching her. And so he came in a human form to relate to human beings and to reveal to human beings the kingdom of his Father, to reveal to us the kingdom of God. And also to die for our sins. Because in order for us to become a part of that kingdom we could not be a part unless he gave his life and, giving his life, his blood shed so we could be a part of that kingdom, and most of all for us to be born again by the Holy Spirit for us to be a part of that kingdom.

And what of Haile Selassie?

Selassie? First of all, I would say every nation has a king. And, you know, the black race should also have a king. Because, I mean, you have a king in Japan. I don't know if he's dead now. I think the last king that they had was in Japan – or emperor. But, every nation should have a king. And also as our people, our king is His Imperial Majesty ...

When I found Christ, I dreamt I saw His Majesty smiling with me. Smiling like he was saying, 'My darling' or 'My daughter, I'm so glad you've found the truth.' Yes, I saw him just smiling. Yes, sleeping, that's a dream. He never said anything. He was just smiling. So, I said that smile was giving me the assurance that 'I am glad that you have found who you were looking for.'

I've learned, when you start seeking, then you will find. But, if you have a dead mindset that says, 'I don't want to learn anymore, because this is what I know,' you'll never know anymore. And you might be in the darkness for the rest of your life. And the light is around you, but you'll never reach it because of what you are holding on to. So, when I was able to release what I was holding on to and started seeking for the truth, truths and little bits and pieces came. Evidence started to pose and say, 'See, His Majesty himself said this, you know?' So, if it is coming from the mouth of His Majesty, what more do I want?

Yes, you see, I've always been trying to get near to God. I've always been seeking God from I was a child. But, as I said, in the Rastafarian faith, His Imperial Majesty was my Christ. But, when I decided now, it was as if God say, 'This is enough.'

Today, she is outspoken in pointing Rastafarians to the fuller revelation she has found in Jesus Christ:

My message to my Rastafarian brothers and sisters is that I have found the truth. And His Imperial Majesty that I used to worship, he said that in the Bible you will find truth for ourselves and, when I read the Bible, Jesus Christ himself said, 'I am the way, the truth, and the life. No man cometh unto the Father, but by me'. And I've discovered that truth is not information – truth is information, but it's not totally information and it is not totally fact – but it is a Person, and that Person is Jesus Christ. And, if they want to know truth, they should follow His Imperial Majesty. And Bob Marley also said, 'Give us the teachings of His Majesty, we no want a devil philosophy.' And if we read the teachings of His Imperial Majesty, then we will find out that it is Jesus Christ. He said that he's saved by the blood of Jesus Christ. And that is what I want them to find. Because in it they'll find the truth for themselves.

At the end of his life on earth, Bob Marley himself followed the teachings of His Majesty into the church the emperor gave to Jamaica. On 4 November 1980, the dying Bob Marley was baptized into the Ethiopian Orthodox Church. When Marley died six months later, Abuna Yesehaq, the archbishop presiding over the Ethiopian Orthodox Church in Jamaica and the Western Hemisphere Diocese, presided over his funeral. We noted earlier that the abuna consistently taught:

The emperor was not God to the Ethiopian people and other nations. He was a religious man who was elected king of Ethiopia. While one can appreciate the respect, love, and devotion given to him as a clergyman; it is my duty to speak the truth and to strongly advise my brethren and sisters, young and old, to be aware of the commandment of God: 'Thou shall have no other gods before me – for I am a jealous God.' And they must turn their hearts and walk in the right direction, which is the Lord Christ, without whom salvation is impossible.[20]

Today, Judy Mowatt notes a movement among younger Rastas into the Ethiopian Orthodox Church:

I see some young Rastas being members of the Ethiopian Orthodox Church. They're moving towards that church because over the years – and I just ask you to – it's no disrespect – but, over the years, the church has always projected a white Christ. And it was not that Christ was white or Christ was blue or Christ was black, it is the essence of Christ that we need to worship, not color. But what I think has kept Rastas outside of the church is the teachings, you know? And there was a teaching that they worship Christ. There was always this white picture of

Christ in the church. They could not explain the history of the black man. Because, as black people, they want to know about their view, especially the men. They want to know where they are coming from and where they are going. And this is why you find that inside of the Muslim religion and inside of the Rastafarian religion it's male. It attracts a lot of males, because it gives the history. It tells you of the history. Now, in Christianity in the churches, you just hear about God and you hear about doomsday. That was not right now, but first time when I was looking at the church, and it does all these 'don'ts, don'ts, don'ts.' You cannot do this. You cannot wear your hair this way. You cannot wear jewelry. You cannot – you know what I mean? And that kept people outside of the church. Now, when a lot of Rastafarian get to find out that Jesus Christ was not blond hair, blue eyed, and he was born in a geographical location where it wasn't white people lived in that area, but it was people of color, then they look at the church as a big lie. You know what I mean? They said the church is a big den of – they are liars, because they have been deceived by the church. So, they have their church like this. Now, for me, for God to lead me inside of the church, because sometimes I ask myself, I close my eyes and I try to see where for 22 years I've been one place. And well, yes, they did some things to me, but what they did I could have stayed. And maybe they did it because I was to go. 'Cause I didn't have any feelings for there anymore. And when I close my eyes and I see myself, I see myself same place at that little church where I am right now [Holiness Christian Church in Kingston, Dr Samuel Vassell, pastor]. The Spirit has led me there and that's where I am. And if the Lord lead me to go back to the Twelve Tribe of Israel, so be it. But I don't have the feeling. I don't have the desire, you know? I really don't. But, the Twelve Tribe of Israel, yes, what I learned you can believe. You can believe something. You can believe that – yes, Jesus Christ is the Son of God and it is not His Imperial Majesty, and you can be a Twelve Tribe member.

In that sense, as we have seen from the Prophet Gad's declaration, the Twelve Tribes have moved to a position similar to that of the Ethiopian Orthodox Church, with perhaps the exception of that Church's monophysitism, its beliefs in 'one' (*mono*) 'nature' or 'natural condition' (*phusis*) for Jesus Christ, emphasizing Jesus' divinity as being primary, his humanity subsumed within or filtered through it.

Since Ethiopian (and Coptic) Orthodoxy adheres to Nicaea's Creed, it is in full accord with all orthodoxy in East and West in recognizing Jesus as fully God and fully human. But it is distinct in viewing Jesus' humanity as being contained in his divinity. Ironically, with Rastafari's emphasis on God as 'a living man' in its various incarnational teachings, the Twelve Tribes of Rastafari appears closer to western Protestant orthodoxy than either to Eastern orthodoxy or, particularly, to its extreme, non-Chalcedonian monophysitism. In fact, the Twelve Tribes is so close to Western Christian doctrine that some outside the Twelve Tribes label Twelve Tribes members as Christians rather than Rastas, as does Imani Tafari-Ama:

Because, when you look at the way people in Twelve Tribes, for example, with Judy Mowatt's conversion, Twelve Tribes are more Christian than Rasta livers, if you understand what I mean. Because of the emphasis on Jesus Christ and the 'who has been this day revealed in the personality of His Majesty.'

The articulate Twelve Tribes Rasta, Brother Marcel Goffe, is well aware of these charges:

When you hear of the Twelve Tribes, for example, we have been accused of being – this is Jamaican terminology now – we have been accused of being 'Jesus boys' – and we're not Rastas, you know?

Judy Mowatt herself has confronted such disapprobation:

On the Rasta side they are saying that I have sold out; I'm a traitor; I have betrayed them. I should not have done that. And I mean it has caused a lot of serious animosity – hostility. Yes, it has generated a lot of hostility from the Rastas. And what Pastor Vassell has taught me that I must just ask the Lord to just fill my heart with love. Because, it is in loving them you're gonna win them. Because, even when they come up against me, you know, and they will say, 'So you're so? Let me ask you something now. So, you're this and you're that?' For example, when I say in myself, 'Lord, fill my heart with love. Let me answer this question now with love, give them a loving answer.' And so, I will answer them. I remember a brother said to me, 'So, tell me something now. I hear something now. I hear that you're with the church.' I say, 'Yes, man. Yes.' And he said to me, 'So, you move off some of your locks too?' I said, 'But, who it belong to?' I said, 'It's mine. Right?' So, I knew he was coming with a ferocious behavior, but to it I responded with a soft answer, just turned away the wrath. And he left me and I said, 'Any more questions?' And he said, 'No.' I said, 'All right. God bless you' . . . I'm a Christian now. But, the Twelve Tribe of Israel, they say they are Christians. When I was in there, there was a song that a brother wrote and sung. He said, Rasta are Christian people; Rasta are righteous people, because they believe in Christ.

So vociferous has the reaction of some Rastas been that they have been given a name, 'the Bun (or Burn) Jesus' movement, and popularized by such young deejays as Capleton (nicknamed 'The Prophet', for such searing apocalyptic songs as 'Mark of the Beast' and 'Escape the Judgment'), Sizzla, Bounty Killa, and the dynamic Anthony 'Anthony B' Keith Blair. But, despite its name, Anthony B assured me, the movement is not an attack on Yĕsus Christ:

No, not Christ. We cannot burn Christ. Christ is a Son of the Almighty. And no said – we never said, 'Bun Christ.' Even when we said 'Bun Gezus,' we never say 'Christ.'

So, what, then, is being denounced? 'The misconcept, you know, but not the man himself':

He's the man from Nazareth, you know? The Son of God, you know? Yeah, God him say, 'The cycle of earth,' you know, 'is one in three and three in one, you know? And he said, 'No one come into the Father but through the Son,' you know? Yêsus Christ is the living testimony of the Almighty that he manifested in flesh, you know? Yeah, it's the same way. It's just the concept which I show the people that this concept is wrong. I say the concept of how they put Gezus to you is wrong. Well, the people who got to say Yĕsus Christ, you know, because, when we see Yĕsus, we see Yĕsus as a saviour. We see Gezus as a Greek word. So we see Gezus as a word that starts with a G ... It is a misconception, when you say Gezus to praise. You should praise Yĕsus Christ. You have to write Yĕsus because there was no J. There was no J in Hebrew, you know? There was Y.

Who cares? The 'Bun Jesus' Rastas care deeply, as the renowned and very vocal dub poet Mutabaruka explained to Jamaica's distinguished talk show host Ian Boyne: 'This Jesus they teaching is causing all the problems we have today.'[21]

For Mutabaruka, 'Jesus is a concept from Europe. We lick [burn] Jesus. I never say anything against Christ.' Echoing Dennis Forsythe and H. Spencer Lewis and the Rosicrucians before him, Muta snorts at the idea that 'Christ returned in Haile Selassie': 'Christ never went anywhere. The black Christ manifest in man. But, Christ is not an individual man, but a "way" which is manifested in man.' For him, 'Burn Jesus' is as old as the Nyabingi movement in Rastafari: 'Nyabingi is the core of Rasta. They have said "burn Jesus" from the beginning, but it is now being heard more publicly.'

Some 'Burn Jesus' reactors are making themselves heard so publicly that they are duplicating the actions George Simpson saw back in the 1950s when Rastas from Joseph Hibbert's group broke up the revivalist meeting he was attending.

Judy Mowatt comments on just such a disturbance at a church service recently and on similar actions aimed at intimidating both Christians and Rastas who espouse Jesus:

They disturbed the church so badly when church was in session, yes, that the church members had to go to the leaders of the movement to complain. They had to call the police, so it's that bad. I remember I went to a Tony Rebel concert in January of this month, January 15th [1998], and, I mean, when you saw the flags, and you hear the 'Bun Jesus,' everybody 'Bun Jesus! Bun Jesus! Bun Jesus!' And I was to perform. And my daughter and my niece was with me. And my daughter said to me, 'Mommy, I told you that you should not have come, you know.' I said, 'Are you afraid?' She said, 'No, Mommy.' And I said to Marsha, 'Marsha, are you afraid?' And she said, 'No.' Then I said to myself when I saw what was happening, I said, 'Lord, I'm not going to say a word to these people. I'm just going up there and sing my two songs and come off.' And I heard a voice. This is not a verse in the Bible that I have ever rehearsed, but it said, 'If you deny me before men, I will deny you before my Father and his angels.' And I was shocked. I had to straighten up myself and say, 'Yes, Lord.' And I went up there and I did the first song and nothing came out of my mouth. I did the second song. Nothing came out of my mouth. And when I did the third song, I said, 'Listen to me, people. I don't care what you want to say about me. But, recently something spectacular, significant, has happened in my life and I have always talk about, used this theatre as a platform to talk about my life to inspire people. And it has happened that I have found Jesus Christ and I'm not ashamed to talk about it. Well, some people 'buned,' but I heard some people applauding. Yes! And then the next song now, I started to tell them what His Imperial Majesty said, remind them what His Imperial Majesty said about the Bible and what His Imperial Majesty said about Christ. And I just finished that and I came off. But, people were shocked to see how I did, but it wasn't me. God just needed a voice and so we have to be vessels. Yes, we have to be vessels. But like Jonah, who didn't want to go to Nineveh, I had felt like him, because I was afraid when I saw everybody around, they're 'burning Jesus' and the people are so violent that you think that they would want to hurt you physically. And so I did like this. And then the Spirit was still, 'All right, if that is what you're going to do – well, don't even count on me!' You understand? 'I will deny you!' And I so straighten up myself and I say, 'Yes, Lord.' And I went up there and I found rasses came to me and said, 'Sister, that was good, because we don't believe in Selassie I as God either.' Some of them came back and they said it. One woman, I don't know how she got backstage, she said, 'I am a Christian. I don't go to these places. I've never been to these places. But, I came only because the Spirit of the Lord asked me to come to pray for you while you were there.'

'Bun Jesus' leaders appear to be ambivalent about such violent reactions. Anthony B deplored the disruption of this church service, when I told him about it.

No, that's not the way to do it. You know, that not appropriate, because, as I say, His Majesty teaches us tolerance, you know. His Majesty teaches us militancy, you know? Mussolini just bomb Ethiopia and the fascists and His Majesty go to Geneva Conference. He didn't go there to war, a go some talk. He go there to address the League of Nations, said, 'Today for me, tomorrow for you.' So, we got to use humbleness and do it, you know?

But, Anthony B also added:

This is the way people do it in Jamaica. The way they do. What I'm saying is that you go into church and maybe to me saying 'Selassie I' and maybe 'Fire Bun Jesus.' You take offended because you feel I should be saying 'Gezus' too. Seen? But I don't feel offended when you don't say 'Selassie I.' So why should they feel offended when I say? Bob Marley say he feel like bombing a church, now that he know the preacher is lying ['Talking Blues'].[22]

The 'Bun Jesus' attack is also coming from another quarter, as I saw at a lecture by Mortimer 'Kumi' Planno that I attended on 11 May 1998 at the University of the West Indies, Mona campus. Both the 'Bun Jesus' backlash and the response of Rasta elders erupted during the question and answer period, when a young man, wearing a fez, and quoting Black Muslim leader Louis Farrakhan, who had spoken recently in Kingston, 'bunned Jesus', denouncing Bob Marley as obsolete, demanding the Bible be abandoned to Whites, attacking oriental business people in Jamaica, and charging Blacks to withdraw from the rest of Jamaica and work alone on their unity.

After stopping the young man for commencing with the 'wrong attitude' and disrespecting the memory of Bob Marley, and making him start again, but this time respectfully, Mortimer Planno strenuously disagreed. Planno declared that God and Christ are to be respected and pointed out that Emperor Haile Selassie himself had commissioned the Amharic translation of the Bible. When the young man continued to attack Chinese ownership of businesses in Jamaica, Rastas across the audience spoke up in dissent, protesting that the Chinese, East Indians, and others had all come to Jamaica to better themselves and were part of the nation. Mortimer Planno added that only the Blacks had not come voluntarily, but now all had to share the nation.

The previous evening I had attended Artistic Expressions, the monthly gathering of musicians, poets, story-tellers and other artists, at Kingston's Crown Plaza Hotel and heard Euston Lee, one of Jamaica's outstanding poets, who is of mixed Chinese/Jamaican parentage. In a poignant poem he deplored the prejudice against Jamaicans of Chinese extraction that had recently been stirred up again by Farrakhan's programme to polarize people and isolate Blacks from others.[23]

Commensurately, the Rasta elders in the Planno lecture audience corrected the young man. Alan Martin of the UNIA declared that he had studied Rasta deeply and had earlier pointed out that Rasta had been among the first to be environmentally sensitive. He informed the gathering, 'These youngsters are saying "Burn Jesus," but I don't see retaliation.' He noted some who are calling themselves 'Rasta' might be saying 'Jesus Burn', but no Christian was responding by saying 'Selassie Burn'. Christians were continuing to respect Rasta and the emperor, and he called on Rastas to be doing the same with Christ and Christians. Afterwards, Ras Alan made a point of coming over to me to make certain I was not offended and he thoughtfully disassociated Rastafari from the young man's diatribe, watching carefully as I wrote down his words: 'The traditional elders are not condoning this action or belief. Our fundamental beliefs are that the Deity should be respected. The burning of the Bible, the burning of the name of Jesus Christ is not condoned by the elders.' When I pointed out Selassie was a defender of Ethiopian Christianity, he said, 'Yes, as a defender of Ethiopian Christianity, he, the emperor, should be seen as a *defender*.' 'These are tares among wheat. We're not happy with the things these people are saying.'

What, then, makes Jesus Christ-following Rastas different from Christians? As Mutabaruka told Ian Boyne, 'You cannot be a Rasta and not say "Haile Selassie"'.[24] What a Rasta says about Selassie I, however, is what distinguishes Rastas from one another. Some still proclaim the 'new name' for Christ that Mortimer Planno reaffirmed when he answered his rhetorical question: 'Can Rastafarian be a Christian?': 'The Rastaman carry Christ into the African country. I have been to fifteen African countries ... Every said Jesus. Every said Christ. But we call him this new name and watch the mountains tremble!' Such are the Rastas who struggle with Selassie's disappearance, as Planno did, declaring, 'His throne last forever and ever. I don't say Selassie dead and dry up.'[25]

Others like the Prophet Gad and Brother Marcel Goffe fit Selassie into the loyalty they are declaring to Jĕsus Christ and the identification they are maintaining as Rastafarians. Marcel Goffe explains:

> As a dread I shall stick to Jĕsus Christ. Jĕsus Christ is Marcel Goffe's personal Lord and Savior. Yeah, well based on Scripture, which I hold dearly to and accept all of it, he's the Son of God.

Would a Rasta like Twelve Tribes' intellectual Marcel Goffe conclude that Haile Selassie would be Jêsus as well?

> No. Haile Selassie is the 225th descendant of King David. He sits upon – he sat upon the throne of David. I see him as a divine king. Based on the lineage and based on his acts he's done for Jêsus Christ . . .
>
> His Majesty is not the returned messiah. I prefer to leave it like that, you know? He's not the returned messiah. And we are looking for the return of the messiah to come back and sit on the throne of David. Scripture, Acts 2, says he will rise up Christ to sit on the throne of David. In his first advent he sat on no throne. And where's the throne? And Revelation says he shall sit on the throne of his Father. Because at that time him sit with him Father riding on his throne. Him must come back and take charge of the throne that was promised, because, as I said, it is unfair for all the kings sat on the throne of David *all* that lineage of kings the promise was. But, the King of all kings never sat on that throne. And the promise is, he going sit on it. I don't *think*. I am confident that when the right time comes, personally from the clouds he come, landing in Jerusalem, and sit on the throne of David.

Such 'overstanding' he sees not so much as the development of a doctrine, but as progressive enlightenment about Jĕsus in Twelve Tribes' Rastafari. In fact, he believes the distinction between Jĕsus and Selassie has been implicit in the Twelve Tribes for a long while, but not made explicit on account of a desire to foster discovery learning in the adherents:

> I would say that the teaching that Christ is Jêsus Christ and Haile Selassie is Haile Selassie was being taught long time in the organization, but like a schoolroom, you teach and is not all 'a.' And there are students going to get 'b.' Some others 'c.' Some going to get 'c,' you know? And probably like by the ending of the third term – and you have three and a half terms – by your reason start make a man say what proceed from myself, because it is good when the organization leader say 'a, b, and c.' But, it is better when the student understands for themselves why there is 'a, b, and c.' You understand what I say? So, it is one thing to say the president taught right, but it is all which I accept. I accept it, not because he taught it, but because I see it for myself, personally, you know? So I am saying, I can recap and say that I believe that that teaching was there long ago. But, like, for me, I couldn't tell you. If you had called me ten years ago, I couldn't have this conversation with you, being a member at that time. You understand me? And I would be dishonest to say otherwise.

Such a maieutic approach was also necessary, he believes, because so many Rastas enter the Twelve Tribes with firmly held divergent views:

> The Bible and his teachings were just slapping me in the face. You know what I mean? Because, you have to understand that a lot of brethren, before the Bible, you have a concept, a preconceived idea of what is what, you know? So, yeah, when you're reading, or you might start putting the pieces or the piece of the puzzle in the wrong places just to make it fit the way you want it, you know? Eventually, you realize it don't work like that.

Despite his sincere confessing of Jĕsus Christ as his personal Lord and Saviour, what makes Marcel Goffe distinguish himself from church attending Christians?

> I don't think you personally acknowledge me. When I say you, I don't mean *you*, but, you know, I don't think a lot of the churches. I think that's a question a lot of people asking, why is Twelve Tribes members different from a church? I would say, we accept the Monarchy as part and parcel of. It's very important to me – the Monarchy. Because, based on Scripture, based on my reading in the *Kebra Nagast*, there is definitely a link between Ethiopia's monarchy and David, right? I think that people have discovered that, and that His Majesty himself is based on this. And he is of that lineage, the seed of David. So, for us, the teachings of His Majesty are part and parcel with the Scriptures. I find it very important. As a matter of fact, for my part, the teachings of His Majesty led me to accept Jesus Christ, to adopt the Christ as my personal Lord and Saviour.

Extensive reading of the emperor's speeches has convinced Ras Marcel that Haile Selassie was himself a follower of Jĕsus Christ: 'He's a Christian. He's a thorough, he's a devoted Christian.' Therefore, he concludes:

> I'm a follower of Ras Tafari's teaching, he being on the seat of David, still a Christian, definitely. Rasta are Christian people. There's a song that one of our members have done 'I'm a Christian.' What he meant, he was an orthodox Christian, because, again, the churches out there don't like lot of them – let me not say that – some people out there don't like Selassie, don't know Selassie.

But, for Marcel Goffe and his house:

> I'm a Christian and I can't make any bones about that, you know? And His Majesty is really important. My wife actually told me that it was His Majesty who led her to Jĕsus Christ. And she cannot point to a more appropriate example. She read a lot about him, had him probably not so straight one time, you know, a clear understanding of what we read in the Scriptures. And reading the history of Ethiopia and His Majesty's words, she became crystal clear and joined what was what, you know? Crystal clear.

Such a message of unity between Rastas and Christians Marcel Goffe is delighted to share:

> This, what you're hearing now, probably for the first time, or a few recent for the

first time, about Rastafari Christians, it can go out. It only can do a world of good. But, people need to know in it. People need to know. And I think Brother Gad taking the airways last year and talking was a start. A matter of fact, he's going be on the radio again. Which ought to be out very soon. Those things, some of the communication, you'll be able to get it.

But unity does not mean uniformity. Being a Rasta Christian still distinguishes him from other Christians, since he staunchly maintains a place in biblical prophecy for Haile Selassie, the Ethiopian monarchy, and the throne of David in Zion. Brother Marcel explains: 'There is an important link between the Ethiopian Royal House of David. The Ethiopian Royal Family and David. It's a family line.' How such a link will affect the future he may not be certain, but that it will, he is:

So, for me personally, I can't say to where Israel is going to carry; I don't know that. But, what I know for sure, the message we want to tell people, is that the Davidic throne is very important, and, if the king on the throne obeys, he will be filled with the Holy Spirit, which is basically accepting Christ as Lord and Savior. Filled with the Holy Spirit, Christ is in that person. The person is not the Christ. But, what I'm saying, but for me, for Marcel, the throne of David is very, very important. In more ways than one. I'll give you an example. I think the throne of David for those people who are unsure about God and the Bible it show without a doubt that God is real.

So, for me, my message is, I don't know what they'll do to [you]. Some will curse you. Some brethren don't like the answer that His Majesty is not the messiah. Okay? But, for me, I believe that the king is/was – because, I don't know if him pass away, I couldn't say that. I don't know. Okay? His throne was divine king. Because sitting in Christ, I mean he was now seated upon that special throne. And, you know a man by his works.

In the case of Haile Selassie, the emperor's faithfulness to Christ helped him to fulfil prophecies about continuing David's earthly kingdom. This Marcel Goffe and Rastas like him want the Christian Church to realize:

As you're a Christian, then, be an informed one . . . This is from Psalm 89, verse 3 and 4. It says, 'I have made a covenant with my chosen,' and 'I have sworn unto David my servant, Thy seed will I establish for ever, and build up thy throne to all generations.' All generations means all generations. It doesn't mean to me as some church people would have it, would think, that when Christ came in his first advent, there was no more need for our earthly king. But the Scripture says, 'Build up thy throne to all generations.' Okay? And I'll go further and say, His Majesty being a Christian king, not a Jesus. He is a descendant of King David. Actually the 225th Christian king of the lineage of the Solomonic kings. So, I'm saying now, based on this Scripture here, and others, right? I am saying, why is it? I was asking the question, why is it that the importance of the monarchy is something that the churches, to me, bypass?

For Rastas, this issue is of key importance, built into the significance of the name through which they identify:

> I was saying that a lot of people who to me are searchers of the Bible, of Scripture, of truth, find His Majesty to be not just an ordinary man, but a regent, a divine person, a one to exalt. Because Israel exalts their kings. So when we shout out, 'Selassie I!,' it's with understanding, you know? And those are things, again, that people don't understand. Because it's a name. The name means something great. The name means part of what the Trinity would stand at. I mean, who is the Trinity? The Father, Son — so if a man takes on a name like that, it shows the reverence a man has. I mean, if you give a child a name that you like — you know what I mean? I mean, you look up and you say, 'Well, "Mango" means a sweet something.' You may not want that name, because that name affects something that you want in you child, you know? So, I'm saying now, exalt a king! Among church people, they laugh, 'Oh, Selassie I!' Always big laughing and jeering, you know? Again, it's lack of understanding. I don't put it down to anything more than that, you know? But, I would say that I've always been very careful who I talks to. You might think of that that I'm talking to you still.

But Ras Marcel is not recommending the kind of veneration toward which a few Roman Catholics are moving in appearing to elevate Mary to a co-redemptress. Instead, he is positing a place for a line in prophecy that does not simply end with Selassie:

> You see, for me as a Rastafarian, a follower of the teachings of His Majesty, as an Ixample, a Christ-like person, a divine person, divine don't mean God. When you look in the dictionary, doesn't really mean that. What it means is Christ-like, God-sent. All right? A light of God. Okay. For me, His Majesty said, he told he is a Christian from which we are told, hear it? That interview. Same as he was interviewed in Italian. And 'My lineage is coming from the time of' — I'm not quoting, right? — 'from the time of the union of Solomon and the Queen of Sheba. And mine will continue,' and he mentioned in that same speech that there's a crown prince and that there is also a heir. Because there's a heir, because there's a grandson who is next in line. He's in England right now.

Though he realizes some Rastas stop with Selassie, he does not:

> I go further, I wouldn't say it stop there. Because, he has a son who died recently. He has a grandson. Again, I don't want to say the Twelve Tribes of Israel, because I'd rather it be Marcel, right? Just Marcel. The lineage continues for some Rastafarians. I don't want to start going into what a lot of people think, but for some Rastafarians, they don't see anybody after His Majesty who is worthy to sit on the throne.

Fundamentalist Christians who have posited the Pope, Saddam Hussein, the United Kingdom, the United States, and a myriad of other people, places, and events as prophesied in the Bible may have less problem with seeing one more human fitted into the apocalyptic scheme than either they or Rastas imagine. The incarnational uniqueness of Jesus as the only way to God is what keeps Christians in fellowship with one another, not unified scripts and storyboards of God's forthcoming parousial extravaganza.

One bridge-building Rastafarian who identifies himself as Rasta and Christian to the extent of being baptized into a Christian church is the celebrated Tommy Cowan, Jamaica's famous promoter and producer and husband of the renowned 'reggae songbird', Carlene Davis. A Rastafarian for many decades, Tommy Cowan's 3 May 1998 baptism at Kingston's Family Church on the Rock, where his son Che pastors on the staff of head pastor and gospel reggae star David Keane, sent shock waves through the Jamaican entertainment industry and its Rasta connection.

A full page article on the front page of the following *Sunday Gleaner's* arts section annnounced, 'No Change for Born-Again Tommy: Yes Indeed!' On tour with Carlene Davis in Singapore, Cowan told *Gleaner* reporter Reginald Allen, 'I don't see a difference because Rastafari as far as I am concerned, and for the time I have always known, has always been a Christian faith, borne upon Christianity.'[26]

A week after the article appeared, Tommy Cowan explained to me that, like the Prophet Gad and Marcel Goffe, he also maintains a place for Selassie in his world view, and, like these others, following Selassie led him to Jesus Christ. Although he had been reared a Christian, Brother Tommy was repulsed by 'the name "Jesus" ' being 'used to enslave' Blacks and the refusal of 'many of the churches in the early churches' in the Caribbean to 'condemn slavery'. As a result, 'in my search as a Christian, I went into Rasta':

Yeah, and doing my search up in Rasta. Because I saw 'When ye shall come again as the King of Kings, Lords of Lords, Conquering Lion of the Tribe of Judah,' and 'He shall be of the line of David.' And did Selassie fill that role? Because I search for Selassie. Selassie pointed to Christ. And if you look into his works you will see even in his first 25 years of ruling in Ethiopia that he built over 3,000 churches.

And he not also built the churches, but he demanded that each church have a school that teach theology and, even in the educational system of Ethiopia, he thought that theology had to be accepted on a higher level than all other subjects. And he taught saying that we in Ethiopia have one of the oldest version of the Bible and for whatsoever language it is written it will mean one and the same. It's a guide to your past, your present, and your future. Within the Bible you'll find the truth for yourself. And when you search a Bible, Jesus says, 'I am the way, the truth, and the life. No one cometh unto the Father but by me.' And so you see His Majesty was quite into Jesus and I believe that he had that purpose of God as a man of God. Because, he was a very, very deeply rooted man of God and found that his thing was to point his people back into righteousness. Because, even myself, why I went into one of the searches, was that people would say to me, 'Look here, why look at the Bible? It was written by King James. He's changed it around.' But, His Majesty said, 'No, don't watch that. It remains one and the same. It's a guide to your past, your present, and your future, wherein you'll find the truth. I once heard the truth. You find it for yourself. And for myself,' he says, 'Jesus says, "I am the way, the truth, and the life." '

Affirming Jesus Christ as his personal Lord and Saviour and Haile Selassie as his 'Ixample' of how to follow Christ, he explains:

> I am still a Rasta. Yeah, because it's his teachings. It's just like Bob Marley; Bob Marley said, 'Give me the teachings of His Majesty. I don't want the Devil's philosophy.' What is the teachings of His Majesty? His Majesty is a final way to Christ . . . Even when I tried to say, 'Let me see what somebody else is saying,' I couldn't find. Because, the man himself – if you pointed me to you, I start listen to what you're saying – because somebody pointed me to Selassie. And I was hearing what Selassie's saying. Selassie's saying, 'Jesus!' He's saying, 'God!' He never made a move. He never woke up one day. He never had a meal. He never went to a war or anything or made any instruction – even when he was in his kingly position, or as a governor of territories in Ethiopia – he never made any decision without God revealing that decision to him. He was such a high man of God, very deeply rooted into God. And if you should read the books about him, you will see his life is documented day to day. It all begins with prayer. There was a time in his life when he went into prayer as much as eighteen hours a day. And even when he was locked away – why they have never found his body, or could never present him as a dead man – because that's never proven – all he was doing was praying. And I believe that he got so high into God – well, he got so high! You see, he got so very much, so deep into God. Because, I mean, I've read other people's stories. I've read Billy Graham. I've read everybody. I've seen of what Benny Hinn – and I've watched this. And I've seen how deeply rooted they are in God. And I've never seen a man so rooted in God like Haile Selassie. So, I believe that God gave him the power to be, like he said, the son of God.

But Tommy Cowan draws a distinction between the sonship available to Selassie and that incarnated in Jesus:

> Well, I never had my mind in him totally as Jesus Returned. I tried to see where he was Jesus Returned, but he kept saying, 'Jesus!' So, it has never been there. But, what I do believe is that his teachings were so rich. And, you see, but what I said to you before is the identity problem why people still as Rastafarians come. Because, you're taught of slavery. You're taught of how the church rejected slavery and pointed to a blue-eyed Jesus. And they say, 'No, that's a false Jesus.' So you move away. They would rather to look and say, 'Oh, here's a king of mine who's a righteous man and who's of the line of David. So, I will follow him. But anytime I hear that name – other name – I'm arms up' Because, the understanding is not broken down. But, I believe that that understanding is going to regroup now. Because it's not all Rasta, sects of Rasta, that believes that His Majesty is Jesus Returned. Yeah? Some believe that he carries the Spirit, like the Twelve Tribes of Israel. Anytime they start talking, they say, 'We greet you in the name of our Lord and Saviour Jesus Christ, whose personality is revealed in Haile Selassie.' And, if you go to the Ethiopian Orthodox Church, they look at him as a great king. So, they worship Christ. Bob Marley was baptized in the name of Jesus Christ. So, what can I tell you?

As a dreadlocked Rasta who believes 'that the dreadlocks represented a look of Christ. Christ has a Nazarene look', Tommy Cowan feels comfortable maintaining Rasta ties and identity while also joining his wife, son Che, and daughter at Family Church on the Rock. The Jesus Christ 'revealed' to him in the personality of Haile Selassie was Selassie's own personal Lord and Saviour. He has followed and continues to follow Selassie to Jesus Christ.

One appealing term I have heard for such a position was suggested to me by Djate Richards, a multi-talented, world-travelled dreadlocked Rasta from Dominica who supplements his own career of songwriting and performing with stints touring as lead guitarist for the distinguished roots harmony group Culture. As a Rasta who has lived in Jamaica, the United States, and in other parts of the world, he has moved toward a futurist Rasta perspective that presages what Rastafarian theology may well become as it mainstreams as a reform movement in two thirds world Christianity. As he speaks of his religious journey, he reveals a theology that has progressed from the Rasta reaction to slavemaster co-opted 'Christianity', through reactive black theology, into full reclamation of a 'sufferer's Christ', on through the shortfallings of various Christological formulations to a final Nicaean christology that both the true Haile Selassie himself and global Christian orthodoxy would recognize. His journey began by looking toward Africa, so much so that the Jamaicans with whom he lived responded by naming him accordingly: 'Djate is an African name. It means "to be true, strong, or like a lion"'.[27] From his insatiable interest and research into Africa he came to distinguish Haile Selassie from Jesus:

> From my personal observation and my experience and my reading, it tells me that he's a defender of the faith, and the emperor of Ethiopia. Because, when he was coronated as 'King of Kings,' 'Lord of Lords,' 'Conquering Lion of the Tribe of Judah,' as he got his new name, 'Emperor Haile Selassie the First,' he became the 'Defender of the Faith.' Because I believe he went to church every Sunday and prayed just like I and you, or you and I, on a regular basis, you know, to the Father. Because, we all know the Supreme Being is the Spirit within each and every heart. So, that's his relation.

As a self-identifying Rasta, Djate Richards has great respect for the emperor, but does not see him as the return of Christ:

> He's the king of Ethiopia, you know? And he was a great king – as far as, you know, an African king. Now knowing the philosophy and the true vibes to deal with the way mankind is, I mean, it's difficult for me to go on and say, well, you know, he is the real messiah, the original Christ, because we know when Christ come again what it's going to be like. People might debate that. That's debatable. But I'm a person I look at things on a broad basis and I don't go by what people say. I go by what I feel and what I read and what I know is right.

What he has read has been the writings of the emperor himself. Therefore, he feels he is more 'Selassian' than Rastas who have not studied the emperor's own revelations about himself:

A lot of times, you know, a Rasta's a person who is of Rasta faith or supposedly Rasta faith; they probably don't know the wholeness of what it's all about. Because they grow their hair in dreadlocks doesn't mean they're Rasta. A Rasta goes a long way. You need to read. I tell you, if you read, even Emperor Haile Selassie write books. I mean, he had a biography. I read some stuff in there. And I absorb all that stuff from him as a person writing, and so it would be difficult for me to say something different from that what he himself has said. See, Christ said something, you go with that. You can't go against it, because that's what he said. And if you go against it, it's like – well – he didn't. That's already written once. So I go with what Emperor writes. And he doesn't write telling you that he's God. You see what I'm saying? Because he have to respect that quality, but he goes to church. He's the Defender of the Faith. He's a human being like us ... For whatever happened in Ethiopia with him and his people – I haven't experienced that. I don't live in Ethiopia, I'm not Ethiopian. So, I don't really feel like talk about stuff like that. However, but I thought he was a smart person. He meant well.

On the other hand, 'As far as Ioses Kristos – which is Ethiopian for "Jesus Christ," which is really the correct pronunciation, Jesus, of course, that's the same you have the word ...' he explains, 'which is God, you know?'

But, as a Rasta, he prefers to use 'Rastafari' rather than 'Christianity' to term his belief:

You know, I'm seeing it from my point of view. Yeah, Rastafari, yeah, because Ethiopian Orthodox Christianity, that's what it is. And the Emperor Haile Selassie was 'Defender of the Faith.' So, if we, as followers of Rasta, which 'Ras' in Ethiopian means 'head' – it's a title – or 'priest,' it translates to 'head' or 'prince' or 'chief.' ... 'Ras' was the title given to him because he was the son of the king. And his name was Tafari. Jamaicans, the Rastafarians, they put both together and call it 'Rastafari,' which is really two words. Sometimes people think it's just one word, but it's really two. You have to try to understand. It's one way to look at it from the Rastaman's point of view, because he's down to earth and don't really deal too much of the Babylonian system. You know it's more earthy. When you said 'Christian,' we all know it's like quote unquote what Rome wanted to do with Christianity. You know, it's more than just a religion; it's about economics.

So, does Djate Richards see Rastafari as a way of rescuing Christ from Christianity?

Yes, in a sense, what is just language is just all a name change. Yeah, but if you really break it down, it's the Ethiopian Orthodox Christianity. And 'Rastafari' is just the way we just call everything, because we form the church as one ... It started so because everyone wanted to know their roots. Because you and I is no different, really we come from the same place. We might have a different impigmentation, but that's just because of the different region that we live in over time. Yes, I mean, you meet a person and you can only judge them correctly by their characteristics, not by their color. You have good and bad in everyone. There is a positive and a negative side to human beings, whether he be black or white, you know, Chinese or Japanese. It doesn't make no difference.

So, Djate Richards has summoned up an 'overstanding' to recommend to inclusive, historically sensitive contemporary Rastafari: 'It's important for us to know the fundamentals of what Rasta is all about. So, Rastafari is really saying, you know, the Rootsman Christianity. Yeah, Rastafari, that's what it's all about.'

This phrase, 'Rootsman Christianity', captures the heart of what he is conveying and what he believes Haile Selassie himself was conveying, which is to worship not the emperor himself but Ioses, or Yeshua, or Jãsus Kristos, 'his God, which is my God', because 'the same God you have is the same God I have':

> Because, I mean, from his books is what I know of him to be the Defender of the Faith, I mean, going to church and doing everything. Of course, you have to have that spirituality. And, then, for a physical man to be going to church, and others worship him as God? I can't understand that, you see? Because to me, if he's going to church and he's telling you that he's not God, he himself is saying that.

But, as with many loyal Rastas, he still sees a didactic dimension for those who begin by worship of Haile Selassie:

> Most Rastamen look on him, call him as a Godhead figure, which, if you want to look at it, it can be interpreted that way, because we are all gods in a sense. Made in the image of God. So, your son is you. So, we can look at it that way – *that way* – but to call the Ultimate, you have to go to the Highest Spirit, which is really Jah, as Psalm 68 write it out and copy it out: 'J-A-H.' . . . Because, I mean, no one dare call himself 'God' but Jah . . . I read my Bible a lot, you know? I try to read. Sometime I'm tired, but I still find time to read and I find much joy in reading things that are spiritual than any other things . . . I analyze and see how people try to interpret what Christ has done for us.

As Djate Richards, Marcel Goffe, Tommy Cowan, the Prophet Gad, Rastafarians across the movement are engaged in trying to interpret what Christ has done for humanity. Which way will this vibrant and vital theo-logical-psychological-sociological (and in some instances political) con-sciousness-raising identity movement called Rastafari go religiously? Will it forge a new faith or actualize the liberating possibilities for the future of global Christianity?

We have noted two major streams that have come down from the founding of Rastafari: one more biblically oriented, its source in initiators like Joseph Hibbert; the second fed more by Eastern religion from founders like Leonard Howell. Using Ethiopian Emperor Haile Selassie I's image as a head-water point, Howell's pantheistic view, emphasizing God being in each human, progressed through the pivotal work of Dennis Forsythe and inculcated in its journey such wide influences as Masonic ritual, Hindu cosmology and Rosicrucian theology. Today it has flowed into the Revisionist Rastafari that posits a Christ spirit in each human as a part of Jah. The other stream progressed through the channel of Ras Tafari Makonnen, the man, following the actual emperor's direction back to His Imperial Majesty's own God: Jesus

Christ. This stream has widened into the Twelve Tribes' affirmation of Makonnen's image as Emperor Selassie as providing black humanity's quintessential earthly ruler, but his Lord Jesus as the unique salvific Christ of God among us, directing Rastas both into Jesus Christ-worshipping Rasta communities as well as into Christian churches.

Is Rastafari a separate religion from Christianity? The answer is yes and no. While Rastafari resists simple categorization, yet for the sake of summary, what is represented today as Revisionist Rastafari could be viewed as Howell and his colleagues' legacy of a new Eastern influenced Afro-Caribbean religion. What is represented today by Rastas who have sworn allegiance to Jesus Christ as their unique personal Lord and Saviour and have entered the Ethiopian Orthodox Church, remained in Twelve Tribes' Rastafari, or joined other Christian churches could be seen as developing from Hibbert's stream, slowly dispensing with the Eastern-oriented avatarism of his view and adhering more to Nicaean Christian orthodoxy to become a two thirds world Selassian roots reform movement for Christianity, a new development in the Afro-Caribbean Christian family: a 'Roots Christianity'. Dreadlocks and prophecies about Selassie's lineage notwithstanding, Rastas who espouse salvation through the unique lordship of Jesus Christ as God among us are both Rastas and Christians just as Messianic Jews are recognized by Christians as being both observant Jews and fervent Christians. Both would be part of the Christian communion. Like Lutheran Christians who follow Luther to Christ, these are Selassian Christians following the emperor to Christ.

Christologically, the key question Christians should be asking Rastas and the key question Rastas should be asking Christians is the question Jesus asked Peter and his other followers in Matthew 16.15, 'But who do all of you say I am?' As a person confesses through words and actions, so is she or he.

Conclusion

Our examination of the range of Rastafari's message about Christ first centred on the figure of a black Jĕsus, as it developed in the 'Ethiopianist' philosophy of the heirs of the Africans who were kidnapped and enslaved in the New World. We saw how the Ethiopianist movement sought to fix itself on a single messianic figure, trying out one after another until it was focused on Prophet Alexander Bedward.

It endured Bedward's failure until, considering itself fuelled by a reluctant Marcus Garvey, it seized upon the crowning of Emperor Haile Selassie of Ethiopia as providing it a possible contemporary black messiah. Having drawn both its theological concepts as well as its adherents out of Christianity, it sought to incorporate this 'living God' with Jĕsus, either positing him as the return of Christ or a manifestation of God the Father. Some, however, rejected the idea that Selassie was God, a position that gained strength when the emperor was deposed and reported deceased. Others maintained a belief in the emperor, choosing him over Jĕsus, whom they considered a myth. As Rastafarians sought to find a place for the emperor to accommodate his changing fortunes, they also sought to establish one for Jĕsus. Among the theories expressed were that one or/and the other were merely human, prophets, enlightened teachers, avatars (manifestations of God). Some suggested that God is in fact human and therefore they themselves were God. Finally, most moved with a trinitarian view, predicated on the fact that the name 'Haile Selassie' in Amharic, the contemporary language of Ethiopia, means 'Might of the Holy Trinity'. But these trinitarian formulas were often very strange to Christian ears, containing, among other suggestions, Haile Selassie, Mother Earth, the Rastafarian. Some even posited a Godhead comprised of more than three persons.

As Rastafarians have continued to study the Bible, the writings of Marcus Garvey, and the speeches of Haile Selassie, increasing numbers have been following these three routes into a 'Roots Christianity' that is Nicaean in its basis, but freed of a blond-haired, blue-eyed, Western definition of Jĕsus and of Christianity. Those who are ignorant of, or who have ignored, what the emperor has written and the example he has set in his own person as a devout follower of Jĕsus Christ, on behalf of other sociological or political concerns, however, have continued to develop Rastafari as a separate religion from the emperor's own.

The religious choice here before Rastas is to worship the emperor as God or to worship the emperor's God: Jĕsus Christ.

For Rastas stopping at the first juncture, the faith they have created is not one shared by the object of their faith, according to any shred of historical or literary evidence he has left them.

For those progressing toward the second *telos*, following the emperor himself into Nicaean orthodox Christianity, the potential to act as a reform movement within burgeoning global Christianity is vast.

That this is already happening among the trailblazing Rastafarians who journeyed to Ethiopia was indicated to me by Abba Paulos, Patriarch of Ethiopia and the head of the Ethiopian Orthodox Church worldwide. Perhaps the abuna's observation can summarize the Christian response toward and hope for the Rastafarians. He wrote to me:

> Regarding the Ras Taffarians, as you have indicated it is reported that they have been worshipping our late Emperor Haile Sellassie I as God. But to my knowledge, I have never come across any Rasta who claims to believe in the Emperor as God. More often than not, it seems to be an exaggeration. If this is true, it is a completely mistaken notion and a grave heresy. If there are still members of the Rasta Community who hold on to such a belief, I do hope that they will rectify their mistakes as others are said to have done so. Emperor Haile Sellassie as a devout and wise king had a deep love for God and our church. He was a pious Emperor who strongly defended the faith and protected the church. During his life time, he has explained to the Rastas his correct stand by emphasizing that he is a human being and should therefore, not be worshipped as a God.[1]

The key for Rastafarians who truly wish to follow Selassie is to trade worship of the emperor for following the worship example of the emperor, that is, not to worship the emperor as God, but to worship the emperor's God: Jĕsus.

Over the centuries, the centre of Christianity has changed. At first it was nurtured within the Jerusalem church of the disciples of Yeshua. As apostles, the ones sent out by Yeshua, these early believers realized they were being called to share the good news of Yeshua's death and reconciliation of humanity with God with the non-Jewish nations. Shortly thereafter, persecution expelled the Jews all over the known world and the heart of Christianity centred on the most stable centres of the Church: Rome, and the intellectual hub Alexandria, Egypt, and through the latter to North Africa. It travelled on to the seat of the eventual first imperial protector of the Church, the Christian Emperor Constantine's Constantinople. As the centuries have added on, new centres have sprung up as the good news of Jĕsus has attracted nation after nation.

Today the centres of Christianity have expanded to the Orient, where Korea has some of the largest churches on earth and leads the world in teaching techniques of church growth and of the practice of effective communal prayer. South America has become another centre of vast church growth. And all across the world in China, Africa, the Caribbean, Christianity flourishes. Its impact rebounds on European, British, and North American expressions of the faith that centres on God's revelation in Jĕsus Christ.

Into this vast ecclesial mix comes church after church, united by a single confession that Jĕsus is fully God and fully human, the second person of the Trinity commissioned to earth in the Godhead's saving plan to expunge the terminal cancer of sin and restore the spiritual health of humanity.

Does Rastafari have the potential to become yet another two thirds world church: a Selassian Christian Church that follows the emperor's example of worship rather than makes him its object of worship? And if, indeed, it does have this potential, as the 'Roots Christian' position seems to indicate it does, will it be accepted by the rest of Christian orthodoxy?

We have noted that the Lutheran Church is named after Martin Luther (1483–1546). It does not worship Luther. It simply traces its beginnings to his reformation of the Roman Catholic Church. The Mennonites take their name from Menno Simons (c. 1492/96–1559/61), another breakaway Roman Catholic reformer. They do not worship Menno Simons; they merely follow the suggestions for reforming the Church in his *Foundation of Christian Doctrine* (1540). Wesleyan Methodists reform the Church according to the example of John Wesley, but they do not worship him. Named after zealous and influential Christians who became rallying points for reform movements, each of these churches followed a different human example to the single Jĕsus Christ, who is Lord of all Christian churches.

A danger always exists of course that the addition (or occasional substitution) of adoration of a human in place of Jĕsus will cause a church to mutate into a cult, as in the case of Christians following a Father Divine, Jim Jones or David Koresh. Protestants fear that some Roman Catholics in their adoration of the Virgin Mary, especially in her new 'co-redemptress' version, are injecting a new member into the Godhead, making the Trinity a Divine Quartet. This is also what Christians suspect about Rastafarian regard for Haile Selassie. If, however, the emperor is posited as a Martin Luther, leading many to faith in Jĕsus Christ, such reluctance should fall away. Then only the terms of working out such problems as monophysitic doctrine (a dialogue is already in progress among Christianity's orthodox churches) respecting Rastas' own non-salvific interpretations of prophecy, and the not-to-be minimized social difficulties of accepting those with different customs within a united confession, would separate Christ's family.

Barbara Blake Hannah in an opinion piece published in the Jamaican newspaper *The Sunday Herald* suggests that such a Selassian church is being created even now out of the Ethiopian Orthodox Church in Jamaica, as she voiced her objection to a previous article by religious writer Alex Walker. He had observed, 'Rastafarianism is not a black religion as they would have the world believe, but more a blacked up off-shoot of white Christianity!' Walker had challenged:

During the 60 years of their turbulent existence, the Rastafarians have endea-voured to secure recognition from Jamaican society, as well as in the United Kingdom, as a separate religion without success, mainly because the source of their inspiration, their chief philosophical reference, indeed their *raison d'être*, derives from the Christian Bible. The most they can hope for, given the forgoing, is to be able to function within the communion of denominational Christianity.[2]

Rather than accepting as a criticism that Rastafari tried to create its own religion and failed because the prior claim of its Judeo-Christian antecedent was too strong, Hannah argued that joining Christianity is the natural *telos* of Rastafari:

> Members of the Ethiopian Orthodox Church are Christians, and among them are many persons who have come to see Christ through Rastafari. Indeed, the words Ras (Tafari) mean Head = Christ, and, therefore, any man who claims that he is a Ras, must identify himself with Christ. Haile Selassie means: Power of the Trinity, which Trinity is the Father, the Son and the Holy Spirit.

According to Hannah, many Rastas like herself find the Ethiopian Orthodox Church 'the best place in which to worship Christ, God made man'. Though with Revisionist Rastas she sees Rastafari's intention to be developing a 'Christ-consciousness', she recognizes that 'liturgy Rastafarian Christians use in their Ethiopian Orthodox Church, is peculiarly their own yet, wholly Christian'. For her even dreadlocks are a means to increase the Christian identity of Rastafarians:

> Dreadlocks is no new phenomenon among holy Ethiopians. The dreadlocks of the Rastafarian who feels him/herself drawing close to God through the Christ within them, is a direct link through the unknown of time, to this Ethiopian Orthodox Church priestly habit.[3]

Dreadlocks, as we noted, are, of course, yet another Rasta expression of the affinity for 'Christian Jewish' rituals favoured by both Rastas and the Ethiopian Orthodox Church, Rastafarians having adopted them from the Nazarite code of Numbers 6.1–21 (see also Judges 13.2–14), long hair being a symbol of one's dedication to service to God. The Rev Clinton Chisholm, speaker, author, faculty member at the Caribbean Graduate School of Theology in Kingston, and former pastor of the Philippo Baptist Church in Spanish Town, is among the leading Christian figures interacting with Rastafarians. Does he see customs like dreadlocks as presenting a barrier obstructing unity between Christians and Rastas? He counsels, 'No, because I know of a few cases of people who have converted and are in Pentecostal churches and they still have their locks.' For him dreadlocks might actually prove an asset to raising the consciousness of Jamaican Christians:

> From the cultural standpoint, I think they've added quite a strong corrective to the almost anti-black sentiments of some of the churches in Jamaica and in the region. So, they've made us generally more culturally aware, more accepting of ourselves, more at ease with our need to be involved in the cultural expressions of the country. To their credit, they have been leaders in the field.

For the Rev Prof Chisholm, the major barrier would be doctrinal, but even that he perceives as disappearing as Rastafari mutates along Garveyian and

Selassian lines. As a Christian leader, would he accept Rasta as an expression of two thirds world Christianity?

> I would tend to go with the branch of Rastafarianism that would accept the fact that our Lord Jesus Christ is Lord and God and they would emphasize, if they wanted to, black things, ethnic things that are a part and parcel of all African experience. So, it would seem to me that the basic 'scandal' of Christianity would have to be accepted, minus the accretions that are usually associated with it, which could be seen either as European or as non-African. I think for it to be regarded as Christian there would have to be certain fundamental things which would make it Christian as opposed to non-Christian. And one central plank would be a recognition of Jesus Christ of Nazareth as the pivotal person for faith and for practice, which seemingly the group within Twelve Tribes would be moving to now.
>
> This group fully believes that Jesus Christ is Lord and God, not Haile Selassie. So, this is the move that they are prepared to go public on that. So that, it's not a rejection of their obsession, their fascination with Africa. They are still afrocentric in terms of their cultural orientation. But, they would see Jesus Christ of Nazareth as central as God, not Haile Selassie. Selassie would therefore be reduced to a very important African Christian, you know, but not God. For me, that would be a more palatable expression of Rastafarianism. Therefore, Rastafarianism would be reduced to what it probably was in some of the early expressions: a very strong cultural force, even a very strong ethnic force. But the religious overtones would be not radically different from orthodox Christianity.

From both sides, then, through many thoughtful voices, we have heard the potential for the reconciliation of Christianity and Rastafari. Such reconciliation would fulfil the desire expressed in Psalm 133.1, as Rastas render it: 'Behold, how good and how pleasant it is for bredren and sistren to dwell together in inity.'

In Nazareth long ago, Jesus the Christ proclaimed with Isaiah, God's Spirit 'has sent me to preach release to the captives'. The image of a dreadlocked, two thirds world Jesus, released himself from Western cultural captivity, can indeed be a reforming image of wholesome change. His message to the Church can be a wake up call that Christianity is more global and its origins more two thirds world than is testified by its present Euro-American cultural definition. But the 'Dread Jesus' can only do this if it is not cut off as well from God's revealed truth that Almighty God came once and only once to earth to die for all people as a complete and living human being: Jesus Christ, Emmanuel, God With Us, the true Healer of the Nations.

On the Rasta side, indications are everywhere that the concern of Abba Paulos is already becoming a reality. In 1983, Ian Boyne, at the time religion reporter for the *Jamaican Sunday Sun*, reported:

> The Twelve Tribes now accept the entirety of Scripture. They emphasize Jesus of Nazareth and hold that it is through him that all people must be saved.[4]

What is standing in these Rastafarians' way, however, Boyne reports, is the behaviour of Christians:

> But members are still alienated from the established church. They usually refer to what they see as the hypocrisy of those Christians who claim to practice love while justifying many forms of oppression or of those who uncritically accept many aspects of Westernization in the name of their faith yet condemn indigenous black forms of expression as un-Christian.[5]

Stafford Ashani, producer of Jamaican television series *Reggae Strong*, in his well circulated article 'Rasta Now', agrees from a Rasta point of view and adds another dimension to the division:

> Since Independence Rastafari religious belief has not really been the problem; another neo-christian denomination in Jamaica never is. It's the lifestyle of the dreadlocked Rastaman with his uncompromising militant ital culture and Afro-centric world view that threatens the values and the pockets of the status quo.[6]

To him, the function of belief in the divinity of Selassie was to 'challenge' the 'sloth' of Caribbean Christianity and 'liberate Jamaicans from the doldrums of centuries of decaying Christianity'.[7] His inclusive view opens Rastafari to 'anyone of positive conscience; richman, whiteman or baldhead' but warns, 'as long as Rasta remembers Christ's call to "be in the world but not of the it"'![8] As a result, Ian Boyne counsels:

> Now that the largest, most influential body of Rastafarians has moved closer to the orthodox Christian position, the way is paved for serious dialogue and collaboration. The Jamaican Council of Churches' research into the Rastafarian movements has therefore come at an opportune time. The churches have the possibility of reconciling themselves to a large and significant section of the Jamaican population. The challenge they face is to present themselves as genuinely committed, progressive, and aware — willing to share in the hurts, struggles and hopes of the oppressed and alienated.[9]

That opportunity exists not just for Jamaica's Christians and Rastafarians, but for the members of these movements worldwide. In the shared figure of Jesus, on the mutually accepted basis of the Nicaean Creed, Christians and Rastas can unite and complement one another. But in both cases, orthodoxy and orthopraxy must be sincere and pure. Bob Marley's son David 'Ziggy' Marley put this thought well at the end of our interview when I asked him, 'Is there any message about Jesus or anything that you'd like to make sure that I put in the book?' He replied thoughtfully:

> Just follow the example of Jesus Christ. Live, don't talk. Live the life, don't talk it. Live it.

Finally, the only certitude one has about the temporal future in this transitory world is that change is inevitable and it will be totally unexpected. Television viewers have recently been unnerved to see long-dead matinée idols like Humphrey Bogart and Fred Astaire 'morphed' into product advertisements.

On 11 May 1997, London's *The Sunday Times* featured an announcement by Ken Lomax, a 29-year-old Oxford University based inventor, that he had developed a computer technology he named 'Cecilia' that could do something similar with the voices of deceased singers. Needing only a 'range of scales' previously recorded, 'electronic imprints' of any voice could be so arranged through computer programming that an eerily lifelike and accurate rendition of any voice could be 'morphed' into singing any song the programmer desired. At the 1997 London Music Show, Lomax demonstrated the technique by playing artificially programmed selections of new 'songs' by the 'voices' of Maria Callas and Ella Fitzgerald. Music experts were reportedly 'rapturous' and 'amazed'. The next voice to be cloned, he announced, was Bob Marley's. According to *The Times* Arts Correspondent John Harlow, who covered the show, Alastair Norbury of Blue Mountain Music, the company which manages Marley's estate, was 'most impressed', noting that Marley had written many more songs than he had recorded and that a commercial dilemma facing the estate had been the non-existence of any more authentic recordings. Delighted, Norbury responded, 'In a few years' time, with this British technology, that may not be a problem any more.' Lomax envisions this 'musical playstation' on sale to the public in the not so distant future.[10] In that event it might take its place beside the proposed holographic theatre, where viewers can project themselves into films of moving, lifesized holographic images projected in one's living room. A programming component would allow viewers to alter the plot and themselves become villains and heroes. Similarly, with 'Cecilia' in one's home, one can programme the voice of Bob Marley to sing 'God Save the Queen', 'White Christmas', or 'Happy Birthday to You'. The power to alter a singer's choice of material, and with it the lyrical content, has vast implications for the message an artist intends to share.

Rastafarian reggae singers function in Rastafari somewhat like an informal version of the *dâbtâra* of Ethiopia. Historically, these religious and liturgical singers (like churchical chanting Rasta reggae musicians) have moved among the people as emissaries of Saint Yared, the nearly legendary sixth-century musician credited with arranging Ethiopia's Christian hymnody, reportedly while he was under God's inspiration. In an oral culture like Ethiopia's (and like Jamaica's), the religious singer wields great influence and some of the *dâbtâra* became known (as did Leonard Howell) as healers and magicians. Even the Beta Israel, often called the Falasha, or 'Black Jews of Ethiopia', had such singers at one time. Often nearly destitute, as are many Rastafari, Ethiopia's sacred singers also scramble entrepreneurially to survive. With the nationalizing of church property and the loss of ecclesiastical tax money after the abolition of the monarchy, many of the *dâbtâra* were induced to pursue secular markets with their skills, mixing the need for economic security in with their primarily religious message.

Sometimes the pursuit of the former polluted the latter, as the religious message mixed with folk medicine and the *dâbtâra* sometimes degenerated into employing their theological training to produce charms against evil spirits. The key to the *dâbtâra*, notes researcher Kay Kaufman Shelemay, is 'his manipulation of powerful words in sung, spoken, and written forms' and his 'ability to manipulate the sacred and magical', which 'links him simultaneously to the most revered and feared elements in the world of Ethiopian belief.'[11]

In a similar way the Rastafarian through the 'word, sound, power' of reggae music shares a potent religious message that is heard, appropriated, imitated all around the world. The religious message that flows through reggae, as the Ethiopian sacred singer's message, when it is commercialized, can become polluted. But the basic root of each is the Christian message of God's advent in Jesus. In that foundational message lies each's root power.

Perhaps if 'Cecilia' technology alters the nature of music, the religious dimensions of reggae will move out of the control of its practitioners. But, for now, the reggae '*dâbtâra*', has filled Jamaica and the world with a fascinating kaleidoscopic presentation of the figure of a Jesus in dreadlocks, identified with the poor and those downpressed who have been carried away from their homelands in a diasporan exile. For as long as it lasts, may that song reflect the full biblical picture of the true Yeshua/Iesu Kristos/Yĕsus/Jesus Christ as Emmanuel, God Among Us, God's salvific gift for humanity's temporal and eternal liberation from every lethal manifestation of the slavery of sin.

Notes

Preface

1. Junior Murvin, 'Judas and Jesus', *Muggers in the Streets* (London: Greensleeves: 70, 1984), record.
2. Judy Mowatt, 'Who Is He', *Love is Overdue* (Newton, NJ: Shanachie: 43044, 1986), record.
3. Simon Rochester, 'Sweet Jesus', is recorded on Lincoln 'Sugar' Minott, *Ghetto Child* (Cambridge, MA: Heartbeat: 63, 1989), record.
4. Ras Michael Henry, 'He Is Risen', *Know Now* (Newton, NJ: Shanachie: 64019, 1989), record.

Chapter One: The Black Jesus

RAS JESUS

1. Robert Nesta 'Bob' Marley, 'Time Will Tell', *Kaya* (New York: Island: 9517, 1978), record. Quoted by permission.
2. Leonard Howell (under the pseudonym 'G. G. Maragh'), *The Promised Key* (Accra, Gold Coast: Dr Nnamdi Azikiwe, Editor of *The African Morning Post*, Head Office, n.d.), p. 10. Although credited to one 'G. G. Maragh' and purported to originate in Accra, *The Promised Key* is universally accepted to be by Leonard Howell and to have been printed in Jamaica, circa 1935. For a complete text of *The Promised Key* and my commentary on it, please see my chapter, 'The First Chant: Leonard Howell's The Promised Key', in Nathaniel Samuel Murrell, William David Spencer, and Adrian Anthony McFarlane, eds., *Chanting Down Babylon: The Rastafari Reader* (Philadelphia: Temple University Press, 1998), pp. 361–89. Robert Ardrey's *African Genesis* (New York: Delta, 1961) was first published by Atheneum and in Canada by McClelland & Stewart Ltd.
3. Leonard Howell, *The Promised Key*, p. 13.
4. Ibid., p. 8.
5. Ibid., p. 4.
6. John Moodie, *Hath ... The Lion Prevailed ...?* (Boynton Beach, Florida: Hath the Lion Enterprise, 1992), p. 7.
7. Michael Rose, 'World Is Africa', *Sinsemilla* (New York: Mango: 9593, 1980), record. See also such current Christian sources as 'Africa, the

Garden of Eden', Cain Hope Felder, ed., *The Original African Heritage Study Bible*, as well as Cain Hope Felder's *Troubling Biblical Waters* and *Stony The Road We Trod* for Christian arguments for the origin of humanity in Africa and for a 'Black Jesus'. A popular book, currently widely circulated, is John L. Johnson, *The Black Biblical Heritage: Four Thousand Years of Black Biblical History* (Nashville: Winston-Derek, 1975).

ETHIOPIANISTIC CHRISTOLOGY

8. I learned about the black Madonna and Child on a visit to Catalunya in May, 1997. Of related interest is a chapel of the Hermitage of Our Lady of Montserrat in nearby Tortosa. In a beautiful carving on the face of the chapel, the black Madonna and Child are depicted with a number of worshippers at their feet. A five-panel display depicts Montserrat, Sant Salvador D'orta (de Horta), the counsellors of Tortosa at Montserrat, Blessed Frances Gil de Federich and Dertosa (Tortosa). What is striking is that one side of each worshipper's face is black, the other white. Graciously responding to my letter of inquiry, one of the monks, Domingo Escuder of the Seminario Diocesano in Tarragona, interpreted the depiction to mean that, in the presence of the Madonna and Child, the worshippers are partly 'illuminated' (la mitad iluminada), while partly in 'the dark' (la mitad oscura) (Domingo Escuder, letter to author, 7 Jan. 1997). Both holy men, one may note, have the dark side of their faces toward the Madonna and Child, while the government officials have the light side toward them. I learned about the explanations for the statue's colour from an excellent and detailed pamphlet by Josep M. Gasol, *Parque Natural Muntanya de Montserrat* (Catalunya: Generalitat de Catalunya, 1992), p. 5. The Black Madonna has been enjoying a resurgence in current Roman Catholicism (see Ean Begg's *The Cult of the Black Virgin*) and has also been adopted by neo-pagan writers as a goddess image (e.g. see Deborah Rose's 'The Black Madonna: Primordial Ancestress' in the magazine *Spirit of Change* (July/August, 1998), pp. 44–6.

9. See D. J. Bosch, 'Currents and Cross Currents in South African Black Theology', *Journal of Religion in Africa* 6 (1974), p. 1. I am indebted to Dr Edwin Yamauchi for this reference. Readers may consult his own excellent article, 'Afrocentric Biblical Interpretation' in *Journal of the Evangelical Theological Society* 39 no. 3 (Sept. 1996), p. 397, and Mark Shaw, *The Kingdom of God in Africa* (Grand Rapids: Baker, 1996), pp. 114–5. Nairobi Evangelical School of Theology Professor Shaw points out that the young Beatrix Kimpa Vita rose in response to a civil war that had devastated São Salvador, the Congo capital. Claiming the spirit of St Anthony of Egypt had resurrected her at the point of death and was now speaking and doing miracles and healings through her, she declared

Jesus Christ was in reality a Mukongo ancestor, therefore, São Salvador was Bethlehem and Congo the kingdom of God. In her youth, charisma, guiding spirit voice, she recalls the image of a peaceful Joan of Arc. Her fate was similar. Some members of the Italian missionary order the Capuchins instigated her arrest and execution for witchcraft in 1706.

10. Robert Alexander Young, *The Ethiopian Manifesto, Issued in Defence of the Black Man's Rights in the Scale of Universal Freedom* (New York: Robert Alexander Young, 1829), collected in Stirling Stucky, comp., *The Ideological Origins of Black Nationalism* (Boston: Beacon, 1972), pp. 32, 38.

11. Ibid., p. 37.

12. Winston Walker, 'Tin Sardine', in the Meditations, *For the Good of Man* (Cambridge, MA: Heartbeat: 42, 1988), record.

13. Patrick Barrett, Mikey Bennett, 'The Voice and the Pen', on Tony Rebel, *Vibes of The Time* (New York: CHAOS/Columbia: OK 53455, 1993), compact disc. Lyrics used by permission of Patrick 'Tony Rebel' Barrett, granted 8 November 1993.

14. David Walker, *Walker's Appeal, in Four Articles: Together With A Preamble, To The Coloured Citizens of the World, But In Particular, And Very Expressly, To Those Of The United States Of America, Written In Boston, State Of Massachusetts, September 28, 1829* (Boston: David Walker, 1830), collected in Stirling Stucky, comp., *The Ideological Origins of Black Nationalism*, pp. 50–1.

15. Ibid., pp. 49–51.

16. Robert Alexander Young, *Ethiopian Manifesto*, 36–7.

17. A facsimile of 'The Lion of Judah Treaty' and an account of 'the Abyssinian Affair' can be found in The Chicago Commission on Race Relations, *The Negro in Chicago: A Study of Race Relations and a Race Riot* (Chicago: University of Chicago, 1922), pp. 59–64. Of note is that Redding's group, The 'Star Order of Ethiopia and Ethiopian Missionaries to Abyssinia' (which included such members as Joseph Fernon, called the 'Great Abyssinian', and his son 'The Prince') was identified as an 'illegitimate offspring of the Universal Improvement Association and the Black Star Steamship Line', Marcus Garvey's organizations. Observers guessed this group took its lead from an actual visit from the 'Abyssinian Mission' to renew the treaty between Ethiopia and the United States the previous year.

18. Robert Hill, 'Leonard P. Howell and Millenarian Visions in Early Rastafari', *Jamaica Journal* 16, no. 1 (Feb. 1983), p. 25.

19. See Edward Ullendorff, *Ethiopia and the Bible* (London: British Academy/Oxford University Press, 1968), pp. 136–7. Those interested in more detail concerning the pretenders to the title of the coming black universal king can find a detailed discussion in Barry Chevannes, *Rastafari: Roots and Ideology* (Syracuse: Syracuse University Press, 1994), pp. 37–42.

20. Henry McNeal Turner, *Respect Black: The Writings and Speeches of*

Henry McNeal Turner (New York: Arno/New York Times, 1971), p. 176.

21. Ibid., p. 177.
22. Ibid., p. 176.
23. Ibid.
24. See Robert Hill, 'Leonard P. Howell and Millenarian Visions in Early Rastafari', p. 27.
25. All quotations from Robert Athyli Rogers, *The Holy Piby* (Woodbridge, NJ: Athlican Strong Arm Company, 1924), identified by books, chapters, verses.
26. Marcus Garvey, *Philosophy and Opinions of Marcus Garvey*, Vol. 1 (New York: Arno/New York Times, 1968), p. 44.
27. M. G. Smith, Roy Augier, and Rex Nettleford, *The Rastafari Movement in Kingston, Jamaica* (Kingston: Institute of Social and Economic Research, University College of the West Indies, 1960), p. 7.
28. Leonard Howell, *The Promised Key*, pp. 3–4. My commentary on this and all sections of *The Key* can be found in Murrell, Spencer, McFarlane, eds., *Chanting Down Babylon: The Rastafari Reader*.
29. L. F. C. Mantle, 'The Fatherhood of God; & the Brotherhood of Man', *Plain Talk* (24 August 1935), p. 9. Two weeks earlier, 'Dr' Mantle had identified himself:

> I, L. F. C. Mantle, who came here two and a half years ago, and brought the Divine Science of Jesus the Christ and cured thousands of sick people in this Island, some of whom were given over by Doctors, are now enjoying the best of health Deaf, Blind, Cripple, Chronic Indigestion, Gastritis Appendicitis, Consumption, Catar h, Venerial complaint and all the diseases that attack humanity, by touching with my hands. The Science of Jesus the Christ is known by every priest and there is no other denomination that knows the Science of Jesus beside the Catholic. Read Malachi 2, 1 to 7th verse & you will find the deceitfulness of the priests. The Spiritual gifts of men are to be found in 1st Cor. 12, there you will find diversities of gifts. For your perfect health see L. F. C. Mantle and you shall be free from your ailments. Remember the Messiah told us he shall bring healing in his wings. (L. F. C. Mantle, 'In Defence of Abyssinia and Its History', *Plain Talk*, 10 August 1935, p. 3)

By the 15 February 1936 issue, page 7, Mantle's claims were publicly debunked and his titles identified as derived from Ñañigo, the Afro-Cuban power religion of which he was alleged to have been a member. For an interesting discussion of the significance of Mantle's exposure see Ken Post, *Arise Ye Starvelings: The Jamaican Labour Rebellion of 1938 and its Aftermath* (The Hague: Marinus Nijhoff, 1978), pp. 168–9.

30. George E. Simpson, 'Political Cultism in West Kingston, Jamaica', *Social and Economic Studies* 4, no. 2 (1955), pp. 141–3. Caribbean Graduate School of Theology Dean Jean Lee observed this intentional theologizing in interviewing 'Jimmy', a world-renowned, college-educated Rasta

musician, who wished to remain anonymous. 'Jimmy's' criticism of Christianity was that it did not teach 'Race-consciousness', while Rastafari taught 'race-consciousness, identity and cultural perspective'. From these contributions, he told Dean Lee, flowed his black Christology:

> Jimmy, answering my question about the concept of a Black Christ, says that this concept came about because of a White Christ. For me this was a very important insight because here was a Rasta admitting deliberate subjectivity in the idea of a Black God implicitly confirming that this represented a reaction to Europeanized Christianity. He believes that the Bible is, for the most part, the story of the Black man and says that, in reality, Israel is in Africa, separated from the mainland only by the Suez Canal. (Jean Lee, 'The Appeal of Rastafari and Implications for the Christian Church in Jamaica', June 1990, West Indies Collection, Caribbean Graduate School of Theology, Kingston, Jamaica, pp. 4–5)

Christians and Rastas are not the only ones currently engaged in exploring an African aspect for their central figure. Recently, the town of Fremainville, France unveiled a sculpture of the usually blond-haired, blue-eyed symbol of the French revolution Marianne now depicted black as 'Zumba, the Somalilan', whom Mayor Maurice Maillet explains is 'the village Marianne now'. Citing recent racial tensions as having created a 'propitious climate to introduce a black Marianne', the Mayor explained a black Marianne as an attempt to express the inclusive quality of the ideals of the French republic was appropriate, since 'the French people are a mixture' and 'we accept differences' (Charles Trueheart, 'Town Adopts Black Symbol for France', *The Boston Globe*, 17 January 1999, p. A21).

JAH INCARNATE

31. Barry Chevannes observes that Bedward 'led his followers directly into Garveyism by finding the appropriate charismatic metaphor: Bedward and Garvey were as Aaron and Moses, one the high priest, the other prophet, both leading the children of Israel out of exile', *Rastafari: Roots and Ideology*, p. 39.
32. See Timothy White, *Catch a Fire: The Life of Bob Marley* (New York: Henry Holt, 1991), p. 12. Orlando Patterson, in his early article 'Ras Tafari: The Cult of Outcasts', *New Society* (12 Nov. 1964), p. 15, claims, 'Hibbert had been a Master Mason of the Ancient Mystic Order of Ethiopia while in Panama.'
33. Malcolm C. Duncan, *Duncan's Masonic Ritual and Monitor or Guide to the Three Symbolic Degrees of the Ancient York Rite and to the Degrees of Mark Master, Past Master, Most Excellent Master, and the Royal Arch* (Chicago: Charles T. Powner, 1974), pp. 224, 226 n. 1.

34. See former president of Wheaton College (IL) and astute critic of the Masonic ritual, J. Blanchard, ed., *The Scotch Rite Masonry Illustrated: The Complete Ritual of the Ancient and Accepted Scottish Rite Profusely Illustrated* (Chicago: Charles Powner, 1944), pp. 452–3. For my views on the Masonic use of 'Juh-buh-lon' for God, please see my notes on pp. 242–3 in Aida Besançon Spencer, Donna F. G. Hailson, Catherine Clark Kroeger, William David Spencer, *The Goddess Revival* (Grand Rapids, MI: Baker, 1994). For more on abolitionist Jonathan Blanchard's campaign against post-civil war secret societies, see Paul M. Bechtel, *Wheaton College – A Heritage Remembered*, 1860–1984 (Wheaton, IL: Harold Shaw, 1984), pp. 34–7.

35. See Karl Feyerabend's accessible *Langenscheidt Pocket Hebrew Dictionary of the Old Testament* (New York: McGraw-Hill, 1969), p. 295, or Francis Brown, S. R. Driver, Charles Briggs, eds., more exhaustive *A Hebrew English Lexicon of the Old Testament* (Oxford: Oxford University Press, 1968), p. 871.

36. David Hinds, 'Not King James Version', from the album *Babylon the Bandit* (New York: Elektra: 60437-1, 1985), record.

37. Junior Delgado's 'King James' is on *One Step More* (New York: Mango: 9819, 1988), compact disc.

38. Neville 'Bunny Wailer' O'Riley Livingston, 'Rasta Man', *Blackheart Man* (New York: Mango: 9415, 1976), record.

39. Bunny Wailer, 'Bald Head Jesus', *Liberation* (Kingston: Solomonic, 1987–88), record.

Chapter Two: Significance of the Black Christ

THE BLACK JESUS AS INCLUSIVE

1. Kelly Brown Douglas, *The Black Christ* (Maryknoll, NY: Orbis, 1994), p. 55.

2. Marcus Garvey, Lesson 1: 'Intelligence', lesson guides for the School of African Philosophy, quoted in Randell K. Burkett, *Garveyism as a Religious Movement: The Institutionalism of a Black Civil Religion* (Metuchen, NJ: Scarecrow/American Theological Library Association, 1978), pp. 53–4.

3. Kelly Brown Douglas, *The Black Christ*, p. 56.

4. Ibid., p. 5.

5. Marcus Garvey, *More Philosophy and Opinions of Marcus Garvey*, vol. 3, eds. E. U. Essien-Udom and Amy Jacques Garvey (London: Frank Cass, 1977), p. 235. Concurrent with Garvey's response, a battle had been ensuing over whether Haile Selassie was indeed black or Semitic. L. F. C. Mantle referred to 'so much controversy in the *Gleaner*' over 'the difference between the Abyssian and negro types'. Mantle fumed, 'I

beg to say that I am sick and tired to hear so much tom-foolery that the Ethiopians are not Negroes.' He points out that Ethiopians would not use the term 'Negro' because it is 'inferior' to the designation 'black'. He concluded, 'Now, we do not give two d . . . whether he is brown, black or green we admit that he is the King of Kings and Lord of Lords, Rev 17 : 14. And that he is the Conquering Lion from the tribe of Judah, Rev. 5 : 5, and he is the saving monarch of the righteous age who will rule the world with righteousness and power of right but not with might' ('The Restoration of All Things', *Plain Talk*, 31 August 1935, p. 5). Perhaps this is why Leonard Howell continually affirmed Selassie I's blackness in *The Promised Key* with such declarations as, 'King Alpha and Queen Omega are the paymasters of the world, Bible owner and money mint. Do not forget they are Black People if you please' (p. 4). That this ardent hope of Black Jamaica was not a view of consensus is evident in a *Plain Talk* editorial, 'Ethiopians, Negroes? Convincing Argument Aired on Subject', published 21 Sept. 1935, beginning on p. 10. The article commented, 'We have been told by writers that the King-Emperor Haile Selassie is not a Negro, many have gone away believing it to be true, but we shall prove in this writing the contrary. Haile Selassie a Negro Stock' (p. 10). After a column of ethnographical proof, it concluded, 'Haile Selassie is ever proud and ready to acknowledge his racial tradition in whatever place or position he may be [f]ound.' For these Jamaicans, whether that claim was true or not was a serious issue. As Mrs E. Groves of Kingston wrote to *Plain Talk*, '400,000,000,000 Negroes hold Haile Selassie and his domain in the highest esteem, and in our sympathy with him cry out "Africa for the Africans"' (21 Aug. 1935), p. 9.

6. Chancellor Williams, *The Destruction of Black Civilization: Great Issues of a Race from 4500 BC to 2000 AD* (Chicago: Third World Press, 1976), pp. 357–8.

7. Frank B. Livingstone, 'On the Non-Existence of Human Races', *Current Anthropology* 3, no. 3 (June 1962), p. 279.

8. Donald M. Chinula, 'Jamaican Exocentrism: Its Implications for a Pan-African Theology of National Redemption', *Caribbean Journal of Religious Studies* 6, no. 1 (April 1985), p. 47.

9. Ibid., p. 59.

10. Ibid., pp. 47–8.

GOD IN OUR IMAGE

11. 'Vexing Christa', *Time*, 7 May 1984, p. 94. Delores S. Williams, defending her participation in 'ReImagining 1993', drew a clear parallel between Black and Womanist concerns:

> Our re-imaging of Christianity is necessary in order to redeem it from the desecrated imagery of White Christians who snatched Black Africans from Africa in slave ships named Jesus, Mary, Liberty, John the Baptist, and Justice.

Almost two million Blacks died in the middle passages of those ships due to the cruel, inhumane treatment they received from White, male Christians. As a result, we Blacks (who became Christians with historical memory) re-imaged Jesus, Mary, John the Baptist, justice, and liberty. From this centuries-long re-imaging of Jesus emerged a beautiful, redemptive, Black liberation theology ... I cannot help but wonder why the people complaining about feminist-womanist re-imaging ignore the White Christian churches' own long history of re-imaging, evident especially in Sunday-school materials. The Protestant denominations often gave us Black children little cards whenever we went to Sunday school. Many times the cards, containing a Bible verse, also displayed a picture of Jesus. He was tall, white-skinned, and blue-eyed. He had light shoulder-length, straight hair. He wore an immaculate, white, floor-length toga and polished sandals, and his feet were clean. He looked like a White, middle-class, Euro-American male dressed for a fraternity toga party. He certainly did not look dark, suntanned, poor, and ruggedly clothed. He did not look like the Nazarene Jew who walked from village to village, town to town, city to city, healing the sick, raising the dead, praying, and speaking of justice and love.

Through these distorted Sunday-school handouts, White Christians gave us Black people a Jesus in their own image. This image was to be the center of our worship, our 'visual' knowledge of God. If this Jesus is not a product of re-imaging, nothing is. And although certain conservative Methodist and Presbyterian forces have no problem re-imaging Jesus as a White, middle-class, EuroAmerican male, they proclaim feminine images of the divine 'un-Christian' and heretical. (Delores S. Williams, 'ReImagining Truth: Traversing the feminist Christian blacklash', *The Other Side*, May–June 1994, pp. 53–4)

12. 'Loser of the Month', *The Wittenburg Door* (April–May 1984), p. 9.
13. Numerous wonderful books have appeared displaying depictions of Jesus from all around the world. Two examples in which works of most of the painters I cite are reproduced are Masao Takenaka, *Christian Art in Asia* (Tokyo: Kyo Bun Kwan/Christian Conference of Asia, 1975) and Arno Lehmann, *Christian Art in Africa and Asia* (London: Concordia, 1966). See also Frederick Buechner and Lee Boltin, *The Faces of Jesus* (New York: Simon and Schuster, 1974), and for European depictions Marion Wheeler, *His Face: Images of Christ in Art* (New York: Smithmark, 1996). Shusaku Endo, *Silence* (New York: Taplinger, 1976), trans. William Johnston; Robert Siegel, *Whalesong* (Westchester, IL: Crossway, 1981).
14. Eusebius, *The History of the Church from Christ to Constantine*, trans. G. A. Williamson (London: Penguin, 1989), p. 234 (7.18.1).
15. Giovanni E. Meille, *Christ's Likeness in History and Art* (London: Burns, Oates & Washbourne Ltd., 1924), p. 3. Interesting discussions can also be found in Carlo Cecchelli, 'Christianity and Iconography', in Massimo Pallotino, ed., *Encyclopedia of World Art*, vol. 3 (London: McGraw Hill,

1960), pp. 596ff. and Gwenfair M. Walters, 'Postcards from the Past: Depicting God through the Visual Arts', in William David Spencer and Aida Besançon Spencer, eds, *God Through the Looking Glass: Glimpses from the Arts* (Grand Rapids, MI: Baker, 1998), pp. 99–115. In May, 1999, thanks to a generous decision of Gordon-Conwell Theological Seminary to take its faculty and spouses to Greece and Turkey, I was able to view the breath-taking mosaics of the ancient Church of Chora in Istanbul. I realized that the numerous blond-haired, blond-eyed (!) depictions of Jesus and the saints were not intended to comment on their actual appearance. Comprising hundreds of golden pieces, these mosaics represented the bright, rich, radiant glory of the Shekinah-filled God Among Us and the imparting of that glory to the saints touched by his divine light. Readers may find photographs of Chora's mosaics and frescos in Ali Kiliçkaya, *The Museum of Chora* (Ankara: Dônmez Offset, Mûze Eserleri Turistik Yayinlari, no date), e-mail: donmez@ada.net.tr

16. Readers interested in my comments on the ancient Greek magical papyri may consult my stylistic study comparing Jesus' prayers with his teaching style and with the pagan demotic texts in William David Spencer and Aida Besançon Spencer, *The Prayer Life of Jesus: Shout of Agony, Revelation of Love* (London: University Press of America, 1990), see pp. 264–5. The demotic prayers may be found in editor Hans Dieter Betz's essential work, *The Greek Magical Papyri in Translation Including the Demotic Spells* (Chicago: University of Chicago Press, 1986). The Greek historian Procopius (born c. AD 500) is the one who notes the letter was inscribed on the Edessan city gate (see Procopius, *History of the Wars*, II, 12, 26 (Loeb ed. I, pp. 368ff. according to an interesting discussion in Ernst Kitzinger, *The Cult of Images in the Age before Iconoclasm*, Dumbarton Oaks Papers, no. 8 (Cambridge, MA: Harvard, 1954), p. 103). Johannes Quasten in volume 1 of *Patrology* (Westminster, Maryland: Christian Classics, 150, 1983) notes that King Abgar Uchama reigned from 4 BC to AD 7, and again from AD 13 to AD 50. Since 'Augustine (*Cont. Faust.* 28, 4; *Consens. Ev.* 1, 7, 11) denies the existence of any authentic letters of Jesus, and the *Decretum Gelasiasnum* calls the letters in question apocryphal' he rejects them. E. von Dobschuetz in *Christusbilder* (= *Texte und Untersuchungen zur Geschichte der altchristlichen Literatur*, Neue Folge, III) (Leipzig, 1899), however, relates later legends of an image of Christ defending the city to 'nothing but a materialized proof of the ancient belief that the city of Edessa enjoyed the special protection of Christ', according to Kitzinger's summary. Giovanni Meille, elsewhere in his cited book, tells a story popularized by a 5th-century Armenian historian that King Abgar sent his secretary to sketch Christ, which proved a failed enterprise until Jesus washed his face with a towel and sent the impression to the king. Legends have it that, while this image or this letter or whichever protected Edessa, it could not be sacked. Quasten notes Caracalla did conquer Edessa in AD 216. Eusebius (Bishop of Caesarea AD 313–39) would have

recorded the correspondence from the archives at a date later than this, so at least one invasion succeeded. Still, the letter has enough historical attestation to have existed (in the ensuing years it has been lost to us when the archives burned). Whether it was authentic or not is uncertain, but it provides a fascinating historical footnote.

17. Cited in Giovanni E. Meille, *Christ's Likeness in History and Art*, p. 1.

18. C. C. Dobson, *The Face of Christ: Earliest Likenesses From the Catacombs* (Milwaukee: Morehouse, n.d.). Another helpful reference is Denis Thomas, *The Face of Christ*, Garden City, NY: Doubleday, 1979).

19. Elijah Muhammad, 'What the Muslims Believe', *The Final Call* 15, no. 17 (21 May 1996), p. 39. This has been a staple entry since the days when the magazine was called *Muhammad Speaks* (see, for example, 9, no. 27 (20 March 1970), p. 32; 14, no. 24 (21 Feb. 1975), p. 24, etc.).

CHRIST IN THE LEAST OF HIS BRETHREN

20. Mary Warner, 'The Shroud of Turin', *Analytical Chemistry* 61, no. 2 (15 Jan. 1989), p. 103A.

21. See Thomas Phillips, letter, *Nature*, 337 (16 Feb. 1989), p. 594. Those interested in other articles on the Shroud research from that period may consult a response by Robert Hedges on the same page and a commentary by Andy Coghlan, 'Neutron Theory Fails to Resurrect the Turin Shroud', *New Scientist* (25 Feb. 1989), p. 28; P. E. Damon, *et al.*, 'Radio Carbon Dating of the Shroud of Turin', *Nature* (16 Feb. 1989), pp. 611–14; M. Mitchell Waldrop, 'The Shroud of Turin: An Answer Is at Hand', *Science* (30 Sept. 1988), pp. 1750–1. The Warner and Waldrop articles contain further bibliographic references to articles in *Analytical Chemistry* and *Science*. Gary R. Habermas summarized subsequent research for lay readers in 'Cloaked in Mystery', *Christianity Today* (16 Nov. 1998), p. 80.

22. Archbishop Yesehaq, *The Ethiopian Tewahedo Church: An Integrally African Church* (New York: Vantage, 1989), p. 230.

23. Elijah Muhammad, 'What the Muslims Believe', *The Final Call*, p. 39.

Chapter Three: Selassie I as Jesus Returned

THE SECOND COMING OF CHRIST?

1. Euvin 'Don Carlos' Spenser, 'Just a Passing Glance', *Just a Passing Glance* (Washington, DC: RAS: 3008, 1984), record. It is also available on RAS Records' widely circulated *The Real Authentic Sampler* (Washington, DC: RAS: 3301, 1988), compact disc.

2. Michael Rose and Derrick Simpson's 'I Love King Selassie' was originally released in 1977 and is available on Black Uhuru's *Black Sounds of*

Freedom (London: Greensleeves: 23, 1981), record, the live album Black Uhuru, *Tear it Up* (New York: Mango: 9696, 1982), record, Michael Rose's solo album *Be Yourself* (Cambridge, MA: Heartbeat: 187, 1996), compact disc, as well as in numerous collections.

3. Ajai Mansingh and Laxmi Mansingh, 'Hindu Influences on Rastafarianism', in *Caribbean Quarterly Monograph: Rastafari*, ed. Rex Nettleford (Kingston: University of the West Indies, 1985), p. 108.

4. Ras Michael and the Sons of Negus' 'New Name' appeared on *Kibir Am Lak: Glory to God* (Kingston, Jamaica: Top Ranking: no number, no date), record. It was gathered on the collection Ras Michael and the Sons of Negus, *Rally Round* (Ho-Ho-Kus, NJ: Shanachie: 43027, 1985), record. Lyrics used by permission of Ras Michael Henry, granted 14 July 1993.

SELASSIE THE LION AND JESUS THE LAMB

5. Junior Murvin, 'Judas and Jesus', *Muggers in the Street* (London: Greensleeves: 70, 1984), record.

6. Some Rastas who reject the substitutionary atonement of Christ and also equate the pagan, emperor-worshipping Pontius Pilate and Pagan Rome with the Christian's Pope and Roman Catholic Church have developed their own views of what Christians are 'after', when positing Jesus as 'a leader', as Rasta intellectual Imani Tafari-Ama informed me:

> Mind you, some people, just to play angel's advocate now, see the whole crucifixion thing as a contrivance of the Catholic, the Roman system. To them, they find Jesus as a means of absolving themselves from having murdered this man, so that when they turn around and say, the same one that they endorsed to be killed, to be crucified. Yes? Because you follow the Bible story is Pilate's facilitation of the crucifixion that allowed it to happen, right? And then it's the same Catholic church that turn around and make the crucifix a holy thing. So, that, you said to yourself, by some sleight of hand here, what happened?

7. Millard Faristzaddi, *Itations of Jamaica and I Rastafari* (Miami: Judah Anbesa, 1987), p. 7.

8. Alex Walker, 'Kings of Kings', on Ras Michael, *Zion Train* (Lawndale, CA: SST: 168, 1988), record.

9. Alex Walker, 'I and I Praise Rastafari', on Ras Michael, *Zion Train*.

10. Ras Michael, Insert, *Zion Train*.

11. Ras Michael, 'He Is Risen', *Know Now* (Newton, NJ: Shanachie: 64019, 1989), record. Lyrics quoted by permission of Ras Michael Henry, granted 14 July 1993.

12. Ras Michael, 'Marriage in Canaan', *Know Now*. Lyrics quoted by permission of Ras Michael Henry, granted 14 July 1993.

13. T. 'Ijahman Levi' Sutherland, 'Jesus Selassie I Keepeth My Soul', *Africa* (Washington, DC: RAS: 3203, 1984), record.

14. Israel Vibration, 'Give I Grace', *The Best of Israel Vibration* (Kingston, Jamaica: Sonic Sound: no number, 1978–80), record.
15. Winston Hubert 'Peter Tosh' McIntosh, 'Creation', *Bush Doctor* (New York: Rolling Stones Records: COC39 109, 1978), record.
16. Bunny (Wailer) O'Riley, 'Blackheart Man', *Blackheart Man.*
17. Itals, 'Rastafari Chariot', *Brutal Out Deh* (St. Louis, MO: Nighthawk: 303, 1981), record.
18. Keith/Kerri 'King Chubby' 'Junior' Byles, Jnr. 'Jordan', *Jordan* (Cambridge, MA: Heartbeat: 45, 1988), record.
19. Henry 'Peter Broggs' James, 'I A Field Marshall', *Cease the War* (Washington, DC: RAS: 3022, 1987), record.
20. Johnny Clarke, 'Every Knee Shall Bow', *Originally Johnny Clarke* (Bronx, NY: Clocktower: 0108, n.d.), record.
21. David 'Ziggy' Marley, 'Pains of Life', *One Bright Day* (Beverly Hills, CA: Virgin, 1989), record.
22. Occasionally, Rastas recapture the vision of Leonard Howell, who conceived of Haile Selassie ruling not only in Ethiopia, but establishing 'the Black Supremacy on triumphant soil of the world's capital' in 'the new Bible Land, the Isles of Springs. The same country that the Anarchy called Jamaica British West Indies' (*The Promised Key*, p. 13). Howell, himself, may have tried to establish such a rule when he eventually declared himself 'Haile Sellassie', as we shall see. Other Rastas have occasionally run for political office. Ras Sam Brown, for example, stood as the Black Man's Party's independent candidate for Western Kingston in the 1961 election (see details in Leonard Barrett's excellent *The Rastafarians* (Boston: Beacon, 1988), second edn, pp. 148–56). Most ambitious is the *Rastafari Manifesto: The Ethiopian-African Theocracy Union Policy: EATUP/True Genuine Authentic Fundamental Indigenious Original Comprehensive Alternative Policy: FIOCAP* by JAHRASTAFARI Royal Ethiopian Judah-Coptic Church Issemble of Elders and Illect of JAHRASTAFARI: Haile Sillase I Theocracy Government of 11 Welcome Avenue, Kingston 11, which attempts to outline an entire theocratic monarchical government for Jamaica under 'The Most High & Almighty Jah; source of all benefits; above all, possessing all power to direct all things according to his sole will who has yet established Jah law: and placed all creation in submission to it' (p. 67). (Those interested might note that Patrick Taylor of York University has attempted an assessment of EATUP ('Rastafari, the Other, and Exodus Politics: EATUP') in *Journal of Religious Studies* 17 (1991), pp. 95–107. In my mind, reading through the massive *EATUP et al.* document, I am reminded of the theonomy movement in the United States, which is an ultra-conservative movement which would like to change the democacy of the USA into a theocracy.

Many intriguing articles, chapters, books have been written analysing the political dimensions of Rasta (or its 'Ministry of Social Change', as Texas University Professor Darren Middleton subtitled his treatment in

The Modern Churchman 31, no. 3). These have yielded some interesting insights, for example, Katrin Norris appears to suggest that non-repatriation oriented Rastas supported Millard Johnson's 'blackman's party', launched one week after the mission to Africa left in April, 1961 (see pp. 57–8 in Katrin Norris, *Jamaica: The Search for an Identity* (London: Oxford University Press, 1962). Famed candidate for Parliament Ras Sam Brown contributed his own 'Treatise on the Rastafarian Movement' in the *Journal of Caribbean Studies* 6, no. 1 (1966) and years later recorded his tenets in *Teacher* (Washington, DC: RAS: 3074, 1991), compact disc. Among noteworthy full-length treatments are Denison University Professor Anita M. Waters, *Race, Class, and Political Symbols: Rastafari and Reggae in Jamaican Politics* (New Brunswick, NJ: Transaction, 1985), Horace Campbell, *Rasta and Resistance: From Marcus Garvey to Walter Rodney* (Trenton: Africa World Press, 1987) and the aforementioned Ken Post's Marxist interpretation *Arise Ye Starvelings* (see also his 'The Bible as Ideology: Ethiopianism in Jamaica, 1930–38' in Christopher Allen and R. W. Johnson, eds, *African Perspectives: Papers in the History, Politics and Economics of Africa Presented to Thomas Hodgkin* (London/Cambridge: Cambridge University Press, 1970), pp. 185–207), among others.

Most Rasta musicians use their lyrics and music to make powerful political statements, as the United Kingdom's Steel Pulse did in *Handsworth Revolution* (New York: Mango: 9502, 1978), record, and *Tribute to the Martyrs* (New York: Mango: 9568, 1979), record, or Ranking Ann in 'Kill the Police Bill' on *A Slice of English Toast* (Washington, DC: Ariwa: 002, 1991), compact disc, or as Jamaicans do from protesting the particular (as Joseph Hill attacked a police search in 'Five to One Strip Me' on Culture's *Culture in Culture* (Cambridge, MA: Heartbeat: 67, 1991), record) to the general (as Peter Tosh pleaded for 'No Nuclear War' (Hollywood, EMI America: 46700, 1987), record, or Michael 'Mikey Dread' Campbell for no 'World War III' on *Beyond World War III* (Somerville: Heartbeat: 02, 1981), record).

23. Bob Marley, Neville Willoughby, *Bob Marley Interviews* (Kingston, Jamaica: Tuff Gong, no number, 1981), audiocassette.

DID HAILE SELASSIE CONSIDER HIMSELF BLACK AND DIVINE?

24. Marcus Garvey, *More Philosophy and Opinions of Marcus Garvey*, vol. 3, p. 236.
25. Ibid., p. 242.
26. See, for example, Cain Hope Felder, *Troubling Biblical Waters* (New York: Orbis, 1989), for a careful discussion (see, particularly, p. 34). To further muddy the waters, Selassie himself was such a scholar that he even carefully qualified the Solomonic claims made for his lineage in an

interview he granted *Project '67*, a Canadian news programme. When the interviewer made the statement: 'You are descended, Your Imperial Majesty, from King Solomon and The Queen of Sheba', Haile Selassie ignored the translator to reply in his own voice in English:

> This is just our history, ancient history. The Queen of Sheba, she go to visit Solomon – King Solomon. She makes him one son. She returns back to her country. And our history says since that time we descend from King Solomon . . .

Obviously versed in the dispute, he was careful to attribute the lineage claims to tradition: 'our history says'. ('The Conquering Lion of Judah: A Profile Study of His Imperial Majesty, Haile Selassie I, Emperor of Ethiopia', *Project '67*, Writ., Prod. and Trans. Edward Habib (vid?), Ex. Prod. Harry J. Boyle, Int. Bill McNeil (vid?), Narr. Larry Glover, Elwood Glover, broadcast in Canada, c. June, 1967. I am indebted to Judy Mowatt for giving me an audiocassette of this broadcast.)

27. See, for example, the notes to *The NIV Study Bible* (*New International Version*), Kenneth Barker, gen. ed. (Grand Rapids: Zondervan, 1985; London: Hodder & Stoughton, 1987), note on Genesis 10.28.

28. See the discussion in Edward Ullendorff, *Ethiopia and the Bible* (London: British Academy, 1968), pp. 131–45. An interesting contemporary perspective is that of Charles B. Copher in his chapter 'The Black Presence in the Old Testament' in Cain Hope Felder, *Stony the Road We Trod* (Minneapolis: Fortress, 1991), who decides, 'Whatever her location, however, she must be included in the black presence' (p. 158). Whether Hamite or Semite, to Copher, she is a ruler of colour.

29. How would one, then, understand his famous speech, adapted to music by Bob Marley as 'War', wherein the emperor lectures that until skin colour is no more important than eye colour war will exist? Even if he considered himself fully a Semite, he would still speak out, as emperor, on behalf of all the people he ruled, two thirds of whom were considered Hamitic, with more melanin in their skin tone and features termed 'negroid'.

30. Robert E. Hood, *Must God Remain Greek?: Afro Cultures and God-Talk* (Minneapolis: Fortress, 1990), p. 91. In his forthright way, Orlando Patterson announced to Rasta readers in 1964 that their fixation on Haile Selassie was due to 'a total involvement in the society and a passionate need to be accepted by it' that fundamentally had 'no desire to change the social system but merely the present relationship within it', wishing a reversal of positions wherein 'the present black men should be transformed into white men and the whites into blacks'. He discerned this need 'subtly implied in the Rastafarian doctrine by the fact that it was Ethiopia of all the nations of Africa the cult chose to conceive as heaven, and an Ethiopian to be their God'. How did the selection of Ethiopia lead him to his conclusion? 'Ethiopians, as is well known, are not Negroes, certainly not the elite group who are the ones of whom the cultists have

photographs. One only has to take a look at a photograph of Haile Selassie himself to see his clearly defined Caucasian features, though of semitic mould.' Whether or not Selassie himself agreed with Professor Patterson was a subject of hot debate in the 1930s.

31. Haile Selassie I, *Selected Speeches of His Imperial Majesty Haile Selassie First: 1918–1967* (Addis Ababa: The Imperial Ethiopian Ministry of Information Publications and Foreign Languages Press Department, 1967), p. 645.

32. Stan Jackson, Director of Administration, Billy Graham Evangelistic Association, Minneapolis, MN, letter to the author, 22 May 1996.

33. Haile Selassie I, *Selected Speeches*, pp. 646–7.

34. Ibid., pp. 650–1.

35. Ibid., pp. 639, 642.

36. Ibid., p. 634.

37. Ibid., p. 618.

38. His Imperial Majesty, Haile Selassie I, 'Building an Enduring Tower', in Carl F. H. Henry and W. Stanley Mooneyham, eds., *One Race, One Gospel, One Task: World Congress on Evangelism, Berlin 1966*, official reference volumes: papers and reports (Minneapolis: World Wide Publications, 1967), pp. 19, 21.

39. Ibid., pp. 19, 20.

40. *Project '67*, 'The Conquering Lion of Judah: A Profile Study of His Imperial Majesty, Haile Selassie I, Emperor of Ethiopia'.

41. '(The Lutheran Laymen's League Presents a Special Program on) The Celebration of Christmas in Ethiopia', *Bringing Christ to the Nations: The Lutheran Hour*, Int. in Addis Ababa the Rev Dr Oswald Hoffmann, broadcast c. Dec 1968. I am indebted to Clinton Chisholm and Judy Mowatt for giving me a copy of this broadcast on audiocassette.

SELASSIE I AS AMBASSADOR FOR JESUS

42. Abuna Yesehaq to Barbara Blake Hannah, quoted in Clinton Chisholm, 'Rastafarianism Evaluated' (Kingston, Jamaica: Chisholm, 1990), audio-cassette.

43. Archbishop Yesehaq, *The Ethiopian Tewahedo Church*, p. 204.

44. Ibid., p. 208.

45. Ibid., p. 202.

46. Ibid., p. 206.

47. Ibid., p. 208.

48. Ibid.

49. Ibid., p. 207.

50. Ibid., p. 212.

51. To take just a brief sampling among some of the Rastafari that I interviewed and whom I quote in the present volume, Ras Michael told me, 'My Mother was an Anglican.' Michael Rose confided about his

parents, 'They used to go to Catholic Church. That's where they used to send me. They use to say, "Trim. Go to church. Trim church"' (see his song, 'Push, Push'). Frederick 'the Maytal' 'Toots' Hibbert told me he was reared in 'a clapping church like the Seventh Day Adventist. Then I went to different churches, you know?' Alvin Keith Porter of the Itals told me his father was 'Methodist'. The members of Black Uhuru told me they were reared around a 'Catholic convent'. Ansel Cridland explained, 'There were Christians at I birth ... Them used to go to church. And Sunday day them would like see me go to church.' Byron Antonio Beckford told me his parents went to the Church of the Open Bible, which is a thriving Jamaican Protestant denomination, and on and on. Leonard Barrett reports a similar discovery among the Rastas with whom he spoke, 'About 90 percent of the members interviewed were from Protestant or Catholic churches or Pentecostal sects. The minority who said they had no church connection did acknowledge that they came from Christian homes.' Leonard Barrett, *The Rastafarians*, p. 3.
52. Archbishop Yesehaq, *The Ethiopian Tewahedo Church*, pp. 220–1.
53. Ibid., p. 224.
54. Ibid., p. 225. Not only was Emperor Haile Selassie opposed to ganja, but so was Marcus Garvey, who called it 'a dangerous weed'. Anaesthetizing oneself with cannabis is diametrically opposed to Garvey's pragmatic realism and he recommended 'serious steps be taken to suppress this ganja habit' (see his editorial, 'The Dangerous Weed' in the *New Jamaican* (13 August 1932)). For all Christians who follow Paul's direction in Ephesians 5.18 to avoid 'debauchery' and be filled with the Holy Spirit rather than the 'spirits' of intoxicating substances, ganja presents a barrier to fellowship. While Rastas regularly accuse Caribbean Christians of hypocritically indulging anyway – Peter Tosh even claimed to have seen a 'parson selling it' (see Roger Steffens, 'In the Tracks of the Stepping Razor: The Peter Tosh Biography' in *Peter Tosh: Honorary Citizen* (New York: Columbia: C3K 65064, 1997, p. 47)) – a growing number of Rastas have declared ganja a tool of the oppressor to keep them sedated and have repudiated its use. One of the most outspoken statements is Mutabaruka's song 'Dispel the Lie', which attacks ideas such as that Rastas can only achieve clarity and discover 'jah' when smoking a 'chalice' in a 'palace' (see among other lyrical uses of this popular pro-ganja image Peter Tosh's own song 'Buk-in-hamm Palace' on *Mystic Man* (Kingston, Jamaica: Intel-Diplo/New York: Rolling Stones Records: COC 39111, 1979)). For Mutabaruka, 'no god' is seen in a 'cloud of smoke', and identifying Rastafari as a 'drug religion' that encourages 'youths' to 'get high' is 'a misconception' and 'a lie' that was 'sent by babylon' (Mutabaruka, 'Dispel the Lie' (Newton, New Jersey: Shanachie: 43083, 1991)). What would make a Rasta change his position so dramatically on cannabis? For Mutabaruka, it was the realisation that the 'Drug Kulcha' is turning the Jamaican youth into a 'Johnny Drughead', as he titled two of his most influential songs. As he explained

to Shivaun Hearne of the *Jamaica Journal*, 'Herbs that was here for how much years was never really a problem but we can see the mark of guns and drugs and what it doing now. You hear bout murders now that you only used to say, "Bway it woulda neva happen inna Jamaica."' ('Mutabaruka Talks to Shivaun Hearne,' *Jamaica Journal* 16, no. 2 (March 1992) p. 50). Haile Selassie made no mistake in rejecting it.

55. Ibid.
56. Ibid., pp. 226–7.
57. Barbara Makeda Lee (Blake Hannah), *Rastafari: The New Creation*, second edn (Kingson: Jamaica Media Productions, 1981), p. 34.
58. Ibid., p. 54.
59. Ibid., p. 34.

Chapter Four: Haile Selassie As a Crucified Christ

WOULD GOD DIE TWICE?

1. Joseph Owens, *Dread: The Rastafarians of Jamaica* (Kingston, Jamaica: Sangster, 1976), p. 109.
2. Quoted in 'Would You Believe Rasta Theology?', *High Times* (Sept. 1976), p. 102.
3. Jon Bradshaw, 'The Reggae Way to "Salvation",' THE NEW YORK TIMES MAGAZINE (14 Aug. 1977), p. 28.
4. William A. Blake, 'Beliefs of the Rastafari Cult', Nov. 1961, The West Indies Collection, Jamaica Theological Seminary, Kingston, Jamaica, p. 8.
5. Archbishop Yesehaq, *The Ethiopian Tewahedo Church*, p. 225.
6. Neil Spencer, liner notes to the album *Peter Tosh: The Toughest, The Selection 1978–1987* (Hollywood: Capital: 90201, 1988), record.
7. Pableto 'Pablo Moses' Henry, 'I Am a Rastaman', *We Refuse* (New York: Profile: 1295, 1990), record.
8. Stephen Davis and Peter Simon, *Reggae International* (New York: Rogner & Bernhard, 1982), p. 102.

HAILE SELASSIE DID NOT DIE

9. Stephen Davis, *Bob Marley* (Garden City, NY: Doubleday, 1985), p. 168. In the final pages of his book *Dread* (pp. 256–79), Joseph Owens listed a wealth of responses he recorded on cassette at a Rasta reasoning in Portland Cottage, Clarendon a week after reports of Haile Selassie's death were announced in *The Gleaner*.
10. Mihlawhdh Faristzaddi, *Itations of Jamaica and I Rastafari: The Second Itation* (Miami: Judah Anbesa, 1991), p. 117.

11. See the Koran, chapter 4, 'Women', verses 150–160. See also chapter 3, 'The Family of Imran', 40–55.

The Passion of Selassi I

12. Joseph Hill, 'Sufferer', *Three Sides to My Story* (Newton, NJ: Shanachie: 43088, 1991), compact disc.
13. Mihlawhdh Faristzaddi, *Itations of Jamaica and I Rastafari: The Second Itation*, p. 117. In 1980 Bob Marley lamented:

> I defend Haile Selassie but right now in Ethiopia they don't like any talk of Selassie. The government there don't like Rasta either because them bring off propaganda and want to change to a kind of Russian tradition. So I man say it's nice to go there but I don't really feel the strength is there. Not until things change with the government and the people become the people again (Bob Marley, in Ian McCann, ed., *Bob Marley in His Own Words* (London: Omnibus, 1993), p. 37).

After a January 1984 tour of Ethiopia, singer Freddie McGregor, famous for such Rasta reggae classics as 'Brotherman', 'Rastaman Camp', 'Zion Chant', and 'Chant Down Babylon', still observed:

> But no lion is to be seen in Addis Abbaba wearing a scepter. I myself had on a RAS Records jacket, and I couldn't wear it, because the lion had a scepter on it. So that alone show me that things there are wrong (Freddie MacGregor to Roger Steffens, liner notes, *All in the Same Boat* (Washington, D.C.: RAS: 3014, 1986)).

14. Ansel Cridland, 'No Money Lover', the Meditations, *Wake Up!* (Kingston, Jamaica, 1978), record.
15. Ras Seymour McLean, letter to the author, 11 June 1997.
16. 'The Looting of the Ethiopian Church on 13 April 1868, by the British Army', *Magdala Campaign: News Letter of Ras Tafari International Consultants* 1, no.1 (1997), p. 1.
17. 'British Stole Ethiopian Church Relics', *The Voice* (10 Sept. 1996). See also Colette Hibbert, 'Jamaican Heads Ethiopian Inquiry', *The Gleaner* (11–17 Sept. 1996), p. 2.

God as Man, Man as God: Selassie Was Just a Human

18. Please see my brief critiques, 'Does Anyone Really Know What Time It Is?: On Calendars and the Apocalyptic Imagination', *Christianity Today* (17 July 1995), p. 29, and 'The Year 2,000? On Whose Calendar?' *North Shore Sunday* (14 Feb. 1999), p. 9. An excellent resource is Robert G. Clouse, Robert N. Hosack, and Richard V. Pierard, *The New Millennium Manual: A Once and Future Guide* (Grand Rapids: Baker, 1999).
19. Sylvia Thrupp, ed., included George E. Simpson's article 'The Ras Tafari

Movement in its Millennial Aspect' in her collection *Millennial Dreams in Action: Studies in Revolutionary Religious Movements* (New York: Shocken, 1970). A careful discussion of Jamaican apocalyptically-oriented figures is included in Barry Chevannes, *Rastafari: Roots and Ideology.*

20. L. Festinger, H. Riecken, and S. Schachter, *When Prophecy Fails* (Minneapolis: University of Minnesota, 1956). See an analysis in Gregory A. Kimble and Norman Garmezy, *Principles of General Psychology*, second edn. (New York: Ronald, 1963), pp. 592ff.

21. Gordon D. Kaufman, *Systematic Theology: A Historicist Perspective* (New York: Scribners, 1968), p. 422.

22. Jon Bradshaw, 'The Reggae Way to "Salvation"', p. 28.

23. Karlene Faith, 'One Love – One Heart – One Destiny: A Report on the Ras Tafarian Movement in Jamaica', in *Cargo Cults and Millenarian Movements: Transoceanic Comparisons of New Religious Movements*, ed. G. W. Trompf (New York: Mouton De Gruyter, 1990), p. 307.

24. Ibid., p. 306.

25. Ibid., p. 309.

Chapter Five: The 'Eastern' Christ of Rastafari

SELASSIE AS ARCHETYPE

1. Dennis Forsythe, 'West Indian Culture through the Prism of Rastafarianism'. TS (Mona: Department of Sociology, University of the West Indies, 1979), p. 3. I have chosen to quote mainly from the original typed and mimeographed paper, rather than the later *Caribbean Quarterly* monograph entry or the book, because it represents most clearly his immediate thinking after the removal of Selassie I.

2. Ibid., p. 6.

3. Ibid., p. 10.

4. Ibid., p. 12.

5. Ibid., p. 20.

6. Ibid., pp. 14–15.

7. Ibid., p. 25.

8. Ibid., p. 32.

9. Ibid., p. 41.

10. Ibid., p. 42.

11. Ibid., p. 41.

12. 'This Man Is Seeing God and God Says He Smokes Only the Best. This Man is Bob Marley and He Smokes With God', *High Times* 13 (Sept. 1976), p. 47. Later in the interview, Marley paralleled the plight of Jesus with that of the Rastafari: 'Is jus' like de Rastaman. Like Christ. Why did de whole worl' crucify? Him find, say in dis time de Rastaman is de only

truth.' For Bob Marley Rastas' present outcast condition but future elevation by Jah were illustrative of Jesus' saying 'de first shall be de las' and de las first' (Matthew 19.30, 20.16; Mark 9.35, 10.31; Luke 13.30) (p. 148). Such remarks make an easy dismissal of Jesus in Marley's thought, on the basis of diatribes like 'Get Up Stand Up', problematic. As the lyric from 'Time Will Tell' with which I opened Chapter 1 indicates, Marley was engaged in dismantling the old image of Jesus in order to reconstruct a depiction of Christ as a dreadlocked sufferer, analogous if not continuous with present day Rastafarians.

13. Dennis Forsythe, 'West Indian Culture through the Prism of Rastafarianism', p. 43.
14. Ibid., p. 44.
15. Ibid., p. 48.
16. Ibid., pp. 49–50.
17. Ibid., p. 52 (see also p. 50).
18. Ibid., p. 56.
19. Ibid., p. 59.
20. Ibid., pp. 59–60.
21. Ibid., p. 60.
22. Manley 'Big Youth' Buchanan's 'Every Nigger is a Star' can be found on Big Youth's *Everyday Skank: The Best of Big Youth* (London: Trojan: 189, 1980), record. This is not to be confused with Sly and the Family Stone's 'Everybody is a Star', which is completely different, coming at the racism issue from an inclusive, rather than black pride, angle.
23. One Rasta, Brother Baia, told Barry Chevannes he 'recalled how the Salvation Army used to make much of the song, "[The] Lion of Judah shall break every chain/And give us the victory again and again,"' until the Rastafari movement took root, when 'quietly I don't hear Salvation Army sing that again' (Barry Chevannes, *Rastafari: Roots and Ideology*, p. 118). A number of early Rastafarian chants can be found on such treasures as Count Ossie and The Mystic Revelation of Rastafari's *Grounation* (Kingston, Jamaica: MRR Records, no number, no date), record, and The Church Triumphant of Jah Rastafari and Haile Selassi I Theocracy Government's *Churchical Chants of the Nyabingi* (Heartbeat: 20, 1983, 1997), compact disc. That Christian gospel reggae has begun again to celebrate 'the Lion of Judah' who 'shall break every chain' is evidenced by Evangelist Douglas and The Evangelites' resounding declaration in their stirring 'Jesus Say Yes' *Jesus Say Yes* (Miami, Florida: DE Ministries: 001, no date).
24. Dennis Forsythe, Rastafari: For the Healing of the Nation (Kingston: Zaika, 1983), p. 10.
25. H. Spencer Lewis, *Rosicrucian Questions and Answers, With Complete History of the Rosicrucian Order* (San Jose, CA: Rosicrucian Press, 1929), pp. 54–5. Lewis' explanations of Alchemy (pp. 197–8) and a myriad of similar issues are in this volume. A biographical sketch appears in H. Spencer Lewis, *Rosicrucian Manual*, sixth edn. (San Jose, CA:

Rosicrucian Press, 1934), pp. 129–31. See Forsythe's acknowledgement of the 'secret knowledge' he is sharing being 'guarded and kept alive over the years by such people as the Free Masons, the Rosicrucians, the Alchemists, etc.' in *Rastafari: For the Healing of the Nation*, p. 14.

26. H. Spencer Lewis, *Rosicrucian Questions and Answers*, p. 56.
27. H. Spencer Lewis, *Rosicrucian Principles for the Home and Business* (San Jose, CA: Supreme Grand Lodge of AMORC Printing and Publishing Department, twelfth edn., 1961), pp. 229–35.
28. Dennis Forsythe, *Rastafari: For the Healing of the Nation*, p. 10.
29. Ibid., p. 14.
30. Dennis Forsythe, 'West Indian Culture through the Prism of Rastafarianism', p. 61.
31. Dennis Forsythe, *Rastafari: For the Healing of the Nation*, p. 19.
32. Ibid.
33. Ibid., pp. 19–20.
34. Ibid., p. 166.
35. Ibid., p. 20. J. M. Robertson, *Pagan Christs* (New Hyde Park, NY: University Books, 1967).
36. Dennis Forsythe, 'West Indian Culture through the Prism of Rastafarianism', pp. 64–5.

JESUS AS AN ENLIGHTENED TEACHER

37. See, for example, A. C. Bhaktivedanta Swami Prabhupada's commentary *Bhagavad-Gita As It Is* (London: Bhaktivedanta Book Trust, 1968), pp. 22, 207, 145. Interviewer Beverley Scott was presented this position by a Rastafarian who affirmed that 'god is a living man', providing 'transformation' in 'the telepatic communication of the theocratic order or government which is earth's rightful ruler. This is the government which give the spiritual law and the ministerial law of the land.' Selassie, he explained, was both divine and human: 'Title of Jah Rasta was really given to Emperor Haile Selassie through the line of David. Not only that, but he does things like you and me.' He also believed in the 'Prime-over [who] is the invisible force'. He explained, 'People talk of Jesus as the Messiah, but I am tota[lly] convinced that he is not the Messiah.' When she asked, 'Who is he?', he replied simply, 'A teacher'. The 'messiah', he explained, is 'Jah Rasta. When we chant in our time of togetherness the power of Jah comes down – the invisible force.' Holding so much content for Selassie, this Rasta had little place left for Jesus spiritually, so the human label 'teacher' was affixed as a catch-all category for the words and works of Jesus' observable ministry. While 'Teacher' is a term of great respect (near the end of his life the distinguished Rastafarian leader Sam Brown was honored with a compact disc titled *Teacher*, which contained his comments on numerous topics (Washington, DC: RAS: 3074, 1991)), the title contains no divine dimension. Beverley Scott,

'Interview with a Rastafarian: (Dread)' 18 March 1993, The West Indies Collection, Jamaica Theological Seminary, Kingston, Jamaica.

38. Ajai Mansingh and Laxmi Mansingh, 'Hindu Influences on Rastafarianism', in *Caribbean Quarterly Monograph: Rastafari* ed. Rex Nettleford (Kingston, Jamaica: University of the West Indies, 1985), p. 103.

During my own research, Ghanaian scholar Dr Edward Osei-Bonsu, while on a study leave to the seminary where I teach, told me that locks are mainly seen in Ghana (from which many of Jamaica's ancestors were kidnapped) in association with fetish shrines:

> The fetish priest dreadlocks do not come across this size [as the Jamaican Rasta style]. It's almost like a crown. They don't cut them. I don't know why it just grows like that. It is not to be cut. I haven't seen them cut it. Yes, they call them dreadlocks. The only place you see the dreadlocks, then, is on the fetish priest, or a child who the parents couldn't have a child and they had one through the fetish. So, until puberty, the child wears dreadlocks in honor of the spirit. I grew up with two young boys. They were peers. They were dreadlocked because the mother could not bear children and then she went to the fetish priest and so they give them a different name. 'Dreadlocks' was the English word. The Twi word is MPESEMPESE.

But these fetish locks are much thinner in style than the heavy Rasta dreads. Today, because of the international impact of Jamaican Rastafari, rebounding back on one of its chief ancestral countries, thick locks do appear and the Asante call them 'Rasta'. Mainly in Ghana, they are sported by footballers and other sports figures, and on musicians as well as on the few open Rastas, so that is why the Asante call them that:

> Normally, we don't use this English word 'dreadlocks.' So we call it 'Rasta.' Even if you ask most people, they wouldn't be able to give you the right word for it. Some say locked hair, but some say Rasta. So that the main word they use is Rasta. And you know that our ladies braid their hair that way. They braid their hair in that hairstyle, and that hairstyle is called Rasta. And so that is why I said that we don't look at it as religion. You see mad people in the street like that because they don't comb their hair or bathe and it just comes out like that. And so, when I [first] saw people like that [with the thick locks], I considered them as mad, crazy people.

But, the style of thick locks, freed as it is from the traditional thinner locks' religious connotations, has since become popular in Ghana as well as in many other parts of Africa. The possiblility remains that today's thick Nazarite locks may be the product of Jamaicans' cultural memories of the Asante practice of locks (though thinner) setting one aside, that is, making one holy, to a religious shrine by a religious sign.

39. Barry Chevannes, *Rastafari: Roots and Ideology*, p. x.

40. N. Samuel Murrell, 'Who is Who in the Rasta Academy: A Literature Review in Honor of Leonard Barrett', in Murrell, Spencer, McFarlane, eds., *Chanting Down Babylon: The Rastafari Reader*, p. 439. In his co-

authored chapter with University of the West Indies Professor Clinton Hutton in the same volume, the statement is even stronger:

> Without a clear understanding of the sources of Rastafarian psychological thinking, as outlined above, serious errors like that of Ajai Mansingh and Laxmi Mansingh (discussed in Neil J. Savishinsky's 'African Dimensions of the Jamaican Rastafarian Movement,' Chapter 7, below) are inevitable. Having erroneously posited that Hindu influence constituted the spiritual and intellectual core of Rastafari, the Mansinghs asserted that 'the basic concepts, philosophy, beliefs, rituals and codes of Rastafarianism' are founded on 'parochial Hinduism' (p. 46).

41. Marcus Garvey, *More Philosophy and Opinions of Marcus Garvey*, vol. 3, pp. 111–12.
42. Ibid., p. 112.
43. Bankie Banx's 'Remember Bob' is on *Soothe Your Soul* (New York: Redemption Records: RA 102, 1982), record. *Reggae Sunsplash '81: A Tribute to Bob Marley* (Los Angeles: Electra: E1-60035, 1982), record; Toots & the Maytals, *Live at Reggae Sunsplash* (Silver Spring, MD: Sunsplash Records: RS 8901, 1983), record; Judy Mowatt, *Black Woman* (Ho-Ho-Kus, NJ: Shanachie: 4301, 1983), record; Ziggy Marley and the Melody Makers' 'Lying in Bed' is on *"Time Has Come . . .": The Best Of* (Hollywood: EMI Manhattan: 90952, 1988), record, 'Unuh Nuh Listen Yet' is on *Play the Game Right* (Hollywood: American EMI: ST 17165, 1985), record; 'This One' is on *Joy and Blues* (Beverley Hills, CA: Virgin: 0777 7 87961 2 1, 1993), compact disc. Black Uhuru's 'Emotional Slaughter' is on the same album that has their excellent 'Let Us Pray', *Live in New York City* (Franklin Lakes, NJ: Rohit: RBU 88000, 1988), record. Brigadier Jerry's 'Tribute to Bob Marley' is found on *On The Road* (Washington, DC: RAS: 3071, 1990), record, and Papa Finnegan and Junior Ranking's on *Two the Hard Way* (Cambridge, MA: Heartbeat: 23, 1983–84), record. Mikey Dread's salute is on *SWALK* (Cambridge, MA: Heartbeat: 09, 1982), record; Carlene Davis' on her *Songs of Freedom* (France: Lagoon: LG2 1076, 1993), compact disc; and the I-Three's on *Beginning* (Hollywood: EMI America: ST 17222, 1986), record. Mother Cedella Marley Booker collects 'Mother Don't Cry' and 'He's a Rastaman' on *Awake Zion* (Salem, MA: Rykodisc ROIR: 10204, 1990), compact disc. Monty Montgomery's 'Irie' is collected on *This is Reggae Music, Volume 4* (New York: Mango: 59850, 1989), record. Joseph Hill distributes his 'A Double Tribute to the O.M.' on *Lion Rock* (Somerville, MA: Heartbeat: 12, 1982), record, and his 'Psalm of Bob Marley' on the Culture album *Good Things* (Washington, DC: RAS: 3048, 1989), compact disc.
44. Stephen Davis, *Bob Marley*, p. 255.
45. Amy Wachtel, 'Brother Bob Marley: Light of the Trinity', *Reggae Report*, 15, no. 4 (1997), p. 23.
46. For the Native American embracing of reggae, see Renata Golden, 'Reggae Inna Hopiland', *The Reggae & African Beat* 3, no. 5 (Oct.

1984), pp. 13–14. See also Roger Steffens' 'Bob Marley, Rasta Warrior', in N. Samuel Murrell, William David Spencer, Adrian McFarlane, eds., *Chanting Down Babylon*, p. 264, for mention of the Havasupai. Particularly, see the letter by Native American JoAnn P. Thorne in *The Beat* 14, no. 3 (1995), p. 55, which credits Bob's words with opening her 'heart' so that, 'I have also had a vision of H.I.M. standing before me dressed in kingly robes. He had a crown and His arms were outstretched and beckoning to me.'

47. Sanjay Dev's contribution to the article 'Voices: Bob Marley's Worldwide Impact', *The Beat* 14, no. 3 (1995), p. 56.

48. The First Presleyterian Church of Elvis the Divine, founded on the internet from 'revelations' claimed by the Reverend Mort Farndu (formerly Marty Rush) and Dr Karl Edwards (a.k.a. Ed Karlin) was a '90s cyberspace phenomenon, the 'spiritual' complement to all those 'incarnational' stacks of 'religious Elvis' books such as Greil Marcus' *Dead Elvis*, Ted Harrison's *Elvis People*, Louie Ludwig's *The Gospel of Elvis*, John Strausbaugh's *E: Reflections on the Birth of the Elvis Faith*, among many more. When the University of Mississippi hosted a first international conference on Elvis Studies in 1995, respected Lehigh University religion professor N. J. Giradot decided to offer a course entitled 'Jesus, Buddha, Confucius, and Elvis', inviting Presleyterian Church leaders to hold a two day 'revival on campus'. The Rev Farndu began by 'E-vangelizing students' during the day, then holding a camp meeting in the chapel at night with an Elvis impersonator, readings from a 'New and Improved Testament', sermons on 'the blessings of fatty foods' and Elvis' 'Second Come Back', healings in Elvis' name, and a list of 31 commandments of things to consume (double fudge brownies, Dristan, etc.). See N. J. Giradot, 'But Seriously: Taking the Elvis Phenomenon Religiously', *Religious Studies News* (Nov. 1996), p. 11. For the Reformed Druids joke turned cult, see Margot Adler's list of neo-pagan organizations in her occult directory in *Drawing Down the Moon* (Boston: Beacon, 1986).

49. Roger Steffens, 'The Queen Mother & The Anti-Christ: Cedella Booker and David Koresh', *The Beat* 13, no. 3 (1994), p. 58.

50. 'Reggae Is Now' can be found on Ziggy Marley and the Melody Makers' albums *Play the Game Right* and *'Time Has Come . . .': The Best of Ziggy Marley and the Melody Makers*.

51. Roger Steffens, 'Behind the Scenes with Bob: The "Clean Up Woman" Comes Clean – Betty Wright', *The Beat* 15, no. 3 (1996), pp. 53–6.

52. Stephen Davis, *Bob Marley*, p. 255.

SELASSIE, JESUS, HOWELL, AND HENRY AS 'GODS'

53. Ajai Mansingh and Laxmi Mansingh, 'Hindu Influences on Rastafarianism', p. 105.

54. Marcus Garvey, *Philosophy and Opinions*, vol. 1, p. 44.
55. Shivaun Hearne, 'Mutabaruka Talks to Shivaun Hearne', *Jamaica Journal* 24, no. 2. Answering a question about what impacted his dub poetry, Mutabaruka said, 'The influence now come bout dis Black Power ting, yu know. 'Cause when I used to go school, Marcus Garvey Junior used to teach me in school and he had his organization and we used to join the organization' (p. 49).
56. Marcus Garvey, Junior, quoted in 'Would You Believe Rasta Theology?', *High Times* (Sept. 1976), p. 59.
57. Marcus Garvey, *Philosophy and Opinions of Marcus Garvey*, vol. 2 (New York: Arno/New York Times, 1969), pp. 27–33.
58. Ajai and Laxmi Mansingh, 'Hindu Influences on Rastafarianism', p. 108.
59. Ibid., p. 109. For other theories on possible meanings of Howell's pseudonym, see endnote 9 of my commentary on *The Promised Key* in Murrell, Spencer, McFarlane, eds., *Chanting Down Babylon: The Rastafari Reader*, pp. 386–7.
60. Ajai and Laxmi Mansingh, 'Hindu Influences on Rastafarianism', p. 108.
61. M. G. Smith, Roy Augier, and Rex Nettleford, *The Ras Tafari Movement in Kingston, Jamaica* (Kingston: Institute of Social and Economic Research, University College of the West Indies, 1960), p. 8.
62. Karlene Faith, 'One Love, One Heart, One Destiny', p. 316.
63. Barrington Chevannes, 'The Repairer of the Breach: Reverend Claudius Henry and Jamaican Society', in Frances Henry, ed., *Ethnicity in the Americas* (The Hague: Mouton, 1976), p. 267.
64. 'Aakhun' George W. Singleton, BA, DH, *Esoteric Anatannuology, Egyptology and Rastafariology: The Defalsification of Ancient Predynastic and Dynastic Egyptian History, Chronology, Culture and Spirituality* (Indianapolis: Blacquendian Royal Coop Association/BRCA Enlightenment Publications, 1997) pp. xvii–xviii.
65. Ibid., p. 189.
66. Ibid., p. 57. Of course, the fact that annuls this whole system is that 'Rasta Fari' was *not* the name 'given by his parents on the birth day he arrived'. Tafari was his given name. Ras was a title he later achieved.
67. Ibid., pp. 57–8.
68. Peter Tosh, 'I Am That I Am', *Equal Rights* (New York: Columbia: 34670, 1977), record.
69. Ras Tesfa, *The Living Testament of Rasta-For-I* (New York(?): Ras-J-Tesfa, 1980), p. 48. Ras Tesfa expounded further on his inclusive approach to Rastafari in an interview with Ellen Oumano, 'Ras Tesfa: Poetry in Motion', *Reggae & African Beat* 5, no. 5/6 (1986), p. 41.

> So, in the process of time we've had Confucius, Jesus of Nazareth, Mohammed, Nostradamus, Haile Selassie and so on. Now these evolved souls are the manifest spirit of God that walks on earth. They're the closest thing to perfection there is, and these evolved souls are the teachers who put

you in tune with the spirituality of life. These are the God-men that walk the earth. These are the ones who guide you, physically and spiritually, back to the source.

70. Ras Tesfa, *The Living Testament of Rasta-For-I*, p. i.
71. Ibid., p. 17.

Chapter Six: God as Man

The Humanity of God

1. Leonard Howell, *The Promised Key*, p. 4.
2. Ibid., p. 10.
3. Ibid., p. 3.
4. Ibid., p. 10.
5. Lyrics used by permission granted by Patrick 'Tony Rebel' Barrett, 8 November 1993. 'Creator' can be found on Tony Rebel's superb *Vibes of the Time* (New York: Chaos/Columbia OK 53455, 1993), compact disc, which includes such pieces as 'Success' (which speaks about helping God 'bear the cross' of progress), 'The Voice & the Pen' (which keys off the spiritual 'Go Down Moses'), 'Nazerite Vow' and others.
6. Joseph Smith, Sermon, *The Journal of Discourses*, vol. 6. All Mormon quotes are gathered by Walter R. Martin in *The Kingdom of the Cults* (Minneapolis: Bethany Fellowship, 1965), p. 178. The sermon by Joseph Smith is listed in vol. 6 of the 26-volume series *Journal of Discourses by Brigham Young, His Two Counselors, the Twelve Apostles and Others, Reported by G. D. Watt* (Liverpool: E. D. and S. W. Richard, 1854–86).
7. Joseph Fielding Smith, ed., *The Teachings of the Prophet Joseph Smith* (Salt Lake City, Utah: Deseret, 1938), p. 345.
8. Joseph Smith, Jr., *Doctrine and Covenants: The Pearl of Great Price* (Salt Lake City: The Church of Jesus Christ of Latter Day Saints, 1953), Sec 130:22.
9. Brigham Young in *The Journal of Discourses*, vol. 3, p. 50.
10. Bob Marley and Peter Tosh, 'Get Up, Stand Up', *Burnin'* (New York: Island: 9256, 1973), record.
11. Joel Lawson, 'From Jesus Christ to Rastafari', *Rasta Vibrations: A Magazine of Reality and Culture* no. 7 (July/August, 1995), p. 12.
12. Ibid., p. 11.
13. Ibid., p. 19.

Dread Jesus as Only a Man

14. Stuart Hamblen's 'Partners With the Lord' has been collected on his Harmony records LP *Hymns Sung By Stuart Hamblen* (New York: Columbia/Harmony: HL7009, 41082, no date), record. Hamblen is best

known for his classic 'It's [It Is] No Secret (What God Can Do)', a version of which was recorded by Ras Michael and the Sons of Negus on their album *Rastafari* (London: Grounation/Vulcan: GROL 505, n.d.), record. 'One of Us' is on Joan Osborne's Relish (New York: Blue Gorilla/ Mercury/Polygram: 314 526 699-2, 1995), compact disc.

15. An excellent collection of these later Wailing Souls' songs has been released as *Wailing Souls: The Very Best Of . . .* (Newton, NJ: Shanachie: 48019, 1990), compact disc.

16. Robert Hill, 'Leonard P. Howell and Millenarian Visions in Early Rastafari', p. 30.

17. Leonard Howell, *The Promised Key*, p. 6.

18. 'Send Down the Rain', 'Redemption Song', and 'Africans Keep Your Culture' are all included on *Majek Fashek: Prisoner of Conscience* (New York: Mango: 539 870-2, 1989), compact disc.

19. 'So Long', 'Religion is Politics', 'Holy Spirit', 'I Come From De Ghetto', and 'Send Down the Rain' are on Majek Fashek and the Prisoners of Conscience, *Spirit of Love* (New York: Interscope: 7-91742-2, 1991), compact disc.

20. 'Together as One', a title cut on African audiocassettes, has been included on Lucky Dube, *Captured Live* (Newton, NJ: Shanachie: 43090, 1991), compact disc. 'Jah Live' is on *Prisoner* (Newton, NJ: Shanachie: 43073, 1990), compact disc.

21. 'King of Kings' is on Sonny Okosuns' *African Soldiers* (New York: Profile: 1414, 1991), compact disc, as is 'Mohammed'.

22. 'Come Back Jesus' from *Apartheid is Nazism* (Shanachie's 43042) has been collected on *The Best of Alpha Blondy* (Newton, NJ: Shanachie: 43075, 1990), record. Alpha Blondy and the Solar System's *The Prophets* is released by EMI (Hollywood: EMI/Capital: C1-91793, 1989), record.

23. Musical Power and the Root Vibrators, 'Rasta No Go Dirty' on *Tribute to Sam Okwaraji* (Lagos(?): Sammy Sparkle All Stars Records: SSAS 0068, no date), record.

24. Ras Kimono's 'Rastafari Chant' is collected, along with a number of outstanding African reggae pieces (including Majek Fashek's 'African Unity', Sonny Okosuns' classic 'Fire in Soweto', Alpha Blondy's 'Cocody Rock', Lucky Dube's 'Prisoner', Victor Essiet and the Mandators' 'Thanks and Praises') on *Fly African Eagle* (Newton, NJ: Shanachie: 45033, 1997), compact disc. EMI also has an excellent African reggae compilation *Reggae Africa* (Culver City, CA: EMI/I.R.S.: 7243 8 28187 2 4, 1993), compact disc, as have several other companies over the years (e.g. Heartbeat's record *Black Star Liner: Reggae From Africa* (16: 1983)). Reggae by Africans and others is included on Ras' *Mup: Reggae Around the World* (Washington, DC: RAS: 3050, 1988), record, and tucked in with other African music on a host of samplers, some quite affordable like Celluloid's *New Africa* (New York: Celluloid: 6110, 1985), record, LaserLight's *Pop Music From Africa* (Los Angeles: LaserLight: 15 285, 1990), compact disc, etc.

25. Victor Essiet and the Mandators, 'Thanks and Praises' on *Power of the People: Nigerian Reggae* (Cambridge, MA: Heartbeat: 156, 1994), compact disc, lyrics published by V. E. Music, administered by 58/59 Music Publishing, BMI., used by signed permission of Victor Essiet, 5 October 1995. Besides this fine collection, Victor Essiet has released a number of albums in Nigeria since *Sunrise* (his first reggae album in 1979), *Imagination* three years later, *Crisis* three years after that, and *Rebel* (whose cover photo art can be seen on page 36 of an informative article by Roger Steffens on African reggae, 'Reggae: The Deliverance of Nigeria', *The Beat* 10, no. 5 (1991): pp. 34–7). For articles on the African roots of Rastafari readers may consult Neil J. Savishinsky, 'African Dimensions of the Jamaican Rastafarian Movement' in Murrell, Spencer, McFarlane, eds., *Chanting Down Babylon: The Rastafari Reader* (also of interest are some of his other intriguing studies: 'Rastafari in the Promised Land: The Spread of a Jamaican Socioreligious Movement Among the Youth of West Africa', *African Studies Review* 37, no. 3 (Dec. 1994), 'The Baye Faal of Senegambia: Muslim Rastas in the Promised Land?', *Africa* 64, no. 2 (1994), 'Transnational Popular Culture and the Global Spread of the Jamaican Rastafarian Movement', *New West Indian Guide/Nieuwe West-Indische Gids* 68, nos. 3 & 4 (1994)). See also Leonard E. Barrett, 'African Roots in Jamaican Indigenous Religion', *The Journal of Religious Thought* 35, no. 1 (Spring/Summer, 1978), N. Samuel Murrell, 'Beyond the Locks of Rastafari: Cultural Identity with the African World', paper delivered at the 17th Annual & 1st International Conference of the National Council for Black Studies, Accra, Ghana, West Africa, July/August 1993. Readers who want to understand the background of the Black diaspora in the West Indies should read Orlando Patterson, *The Sociology of Slavery: An Analysis of the Origins, Development and Structure of Negro Slave Society in Jamaica* (Madison, NJ: Farleigh Dickinson University, 1969).

Jesus as the White Man's Myth

26. Ras Seymour McLean, letter to the author, 11 June 1997.
27. Leonard Howell, *The Promised Key*, p. 9.
28. George E. Simpson, 'Political Cultism in West Kingston, Jamaica', *Social and Economic Studies* 4, no. 2 (1955), p. 142. See also Professor Simpson's article, 'Some Reflections on the Rastafari Movement in Jamaica: West Kingston in the Early 1950s', *Jamaica Journal* 25, no. 2 (Dec. 1994), pp. 3–10, which has also been reprinted in Murrell, Spencer, McFarlane, eds., *Chanting Down Babylon: The Rastafari Reader*, pp. 217–28.
29. Len Garrison, *Black Youth, Rastafarianism, and the Identity Crisis in Britain* (London: Centre for Learning Resources, 1979), p. 28.

30. Ernest Cashmore, *Rastaman: The Rastafarian Movement in England* (London: Counterpoint/Unwin, 1979), p. 63.

JESUS AS THE WHITE MAN'S CONDITION

31. Cashmore, *Rastaman*, p. 58.
32. Ibid., p. 105. 'Jim Squashey' is collected on *Everyday Skank: The Best of Big Youth* (London: Trojan: 189, 1980), record.
33. George Liele's inspiring story can be found in many places, including Clement Gayle's fine booklet, *George Liele: Pioneer Missionary to Jamaica* (Kingston: Jamaica Baptist Union, 1982). A number of the books on Rastafari detail its relations with the Afro-Caribbean faith, including Barry Chevannes, *Rastafari: Roots and Ideology*, pp. 17–33, Leonard Barrett, *The Rastafarians*, pp. 20–28, Ivor Morrish, *Obeah, Christ and Rastaman* (Greenwood, SC: Attic, 1982), pp. 17–67, Peter B. Clarke, *Black Paradise: The Rastafarian Movement* (Wellingborough, Northamptonshire: Aquarian, 1986), pp. 25–6, K. M. Williams, *The Rastafarians* (London: Ward Lock Educational, 1981), pp. 7–11, Horace Campbell, *Rasta and Resistance* (Trenton: Africa World Press, 1987), pp. 24–6, among many others. The forthcoming introduction to Afro-Caribbean religions by N. Samuel Murrell and Ennis Edmonds promises to be an updated and authoritative compendium of information.
34. Readers who wish accessible single volume collections of information about Jesus Christ and the apostles outside of the New Testament records may consult such resources as F. F. Bruce, *Jesus and Christian Origins Outside the New Testament* (Grand Rapids: Eerdmans, 1974), Henry Bettenson, ed., *Documents of the Christian Church* second edn. (London: Oxford University Press, 1963), Eusebius, *The History of the Church*, second edn., trans. G. A. Williamson (London: Penguin, 1989), among other collections. General readers interested in an accessible summary of the quests may consult Richard France's entry 'Historical Jesus, Quest of', in Alister E. McGrath, ed., *The Blackwell Encyclopedia of Modern Christian Thought* (Oxford: Blackwell, 1993), pp. 260–6.
35. Hugh Schonfield, *The Passover Plot* (New York: Bernard Geis, 1965), p. 160. Schonfield had been developing his theories for many years. See his *The Lost Book of the Nativity of John: A Study in Messianic Folklore and Christian Origins With a New Solution to the Virgin-Birth Problem* (Edinburgh: T. & T. Clark, 1929), *The Authentic New Testament: Edited and Translated From the Greek for the General Reader by Hugh J. Schonfield* (Aberdeen: Dennis Dobson, 1955), *After the Cross* (London: Tantivy, 1981).
36. Hugh Schonfield, *The Passover Plot*, p. 162.
37. Ibid., p. 167.
38. Michael Baigent, Richard Leigh, and Henry Lincoln, *Holy Blood, Holy*

Grail (New York: Delacorte, 1982). D. H. Lawrence, 'The Man Who Died,' *St Mawr and The Man Who Died* (New York: Vintage, 1953), pp. 161–211. Michael Moorcock, 'Behold the Man,' in Roger Zelazny, ed., *Nebula Award Stories Number Three* (New York: Pocket, 1970), pp. 84–192. 1967 is the original date of this story. That Rastas looking for ways to undercut the presentation of Jesus as God do find these speculations interesting can be evidenced by Imani Tafari-Ama's observation to me:

> Then I would want to introduce Michael Baigent's and them theology about the Merovingian dynasty – you know, the whole thing of the holy blood and the holy grail? I find that a fascinating thesis, that Jesus didn't really die, or Yeshua, or whatever name we would give him in this context. But, that as a coverup, he really procreated, which would be an aberration to the divine image, that he didn't have sex and all this thing. And that this holy blood line has been perpetrated in history. And, therefore, that is what gives the Templars, for example, their raison d'être. So, I don't think it is impossible that this could have been a historical reality. But, in order to maintain the mystification that keep people eyes closed to even delving into certain gnostic truths – you know? – then, you keep these truths as heretic and as secret. So that only people who are into these secret societies and whatever like lodges and this would have access to certain information about something that might have been earthshattering.

Despite appealing to the Rasta aversion to any death (including Jesus'), the programme of humanizing Jesus and devaluing his divinity may lead even thinking Rastas to countenance such fantastical reconstructions two millennia removed and nearly as many 'cultures' later over those first-hand witness accounts from the culture and time period that are recorded in the biblical records.

39. Abelard Reuchlin (as Hevel V. Reek), *The True Authorship of the New Testament* (Kent, WA: Abelard Reuchlin Foundation, 1979), p. 1.
40. Ibid., cover.
41. Ibid., p. 1.
42. Ibid.
43. Ibid., p. 2.
44. Ibid., inside cover. Though their work may be motivated by similar concerns, to confuse the work of these three commentators would be to commit a great error. For example, while Reuchlin considered the whole New Testament a fabrication, Schonfield wrote an entire book, *The Bible Was Right: An Astonishing Examination of the New Testament* (London: Signet, 1959), summoning up corroborating historical data to substantiate those New Testament claims he could accept.
45. William A. Blake, 'Beliefs of the Rastafari Cult', p. 9.

FREEING JESUS FROM THE CHAINS OF MYTH

46. Readers who would like to learn more about the *Meginnāh* and other uses of song in Scripture are directed to my exploration of popular song in the Bible as well as in popular culture in William David Spencer and Aida Besançon Spencer, eds., *God Through the Looking Glass: Glimpses From the Arts* (Grand Rapids: Baker, Carlisle: Paternoster, 1998). 'You Can't Fool Me Again', a 1969 limited release, can now be found on *Peter Tosh: Honorary Citizen* (New York: Columbia Legacy: 65064, 1997), compact disc. 'Crystal Ball' is on *Mystic Man* (New York: Rolling Stones Records: COC 39111, 1979), record, and is also available on Capital/Parlophone/EMI's greatest hits package *Peter Tosh: The Toughest* (C1-90201, 1988), as well as on Peter Tosh's own label Intel-Diplo in Jamaica. 'Stand Firm' is on the album *Bush Doctor* (New York: Rolling Stones Records: COC 39 109, 1978). 'Rightful Ruler', which also features U-Roy on his first recording, is now available in the *Peter Tosh: Honorary Citizen* collection. Both 'Recruiting Soldiers' and 'Jah Seh No' are on *Mystic Man*. 'Nah Goa Jail' and 'Come Together' are from *No Nuclear War* (Hollywood: EMI: ELT 46700, 1987). Tosh claimed to have seen a 'parson selling' ganja (see Roger Steffens, 'In the Tracks of the Stepping Razor: The Peter Tosh Biography', in *Peter Tosh: Honorary Citizen* booklet, p. 47). He would often indulge in diatribe where he attacked the church by attacking Jesus (as opposed to Yesus). At the One Love Peace Concert he attacked 'Bartholomew de los Cassis' (Bartolomé de Las Casas), the priest who recommended blacks be imported to work in the New World to ease Arawak slavery in a memorable outburst:

> Bartholomew de los Cassis, who was the first guy come 'round with dem cross 'round him neck fe come trick black people and say right now black people is Israel, so if we want hold them the only thing we can hold them with, is fe tell them say, see the cross there, and fe follow Jesus, him soon come back.
>
> Look how bloodbath long we there, a wait 'pon Jesus! All now, to bloodbath. All the war in the earth, Jesus can't do a thing 'bout it ... Is I and I have to come together with love, seen. (Quoted in Roger Steffens, 'In the Tracks of the Stepping Razor: The Peter Tosh Biography', in *Peter Tosh: Honarary Citizen*, p. 48.)

One can find Las Casas' bitter self-recrimination in his *History of the Indies*, III: 129, trans. and ed. by Andree Collard (New York: Harper, 1971), wherein he 'soon repented and judged himself guilty of ignorance. He came to realize that black slavery was as unjust as Indian slavery and was no remedy at all, even though he had acted on good faith, and he was not sure that his ignorance and good faith would excuse him in the eyes of God.'

Those who wish to read my fuller thoughts on the conflict between true Christianity and exploration in the name of Christ in the evil subjugation of the Americas may consult my chapter on the 'God of Power versus God of Love: United States of America' in Aida Besançon Spencer and William David Spencer, ed., *The Global God* (Grand Rapids, Baker, 1998).

47. Bob Marley and Peter Tosh, 'Get Up, Stand Up', *Burnin'*, and again on Peter Tosh's *Equal Rights* (New York: Columbia: AL 34670, 1977), record. See a similar sentiment in Jimmy Cliff's title track for the soundtrack of the film *The Harder They Come* (Los Angeles: Mango: 9202, 1972), record, though Cliff has moved religiously between Rastafari and Islam.

48. Ziggy Marley and the Melody Makers, 'Wrong Right Wrong', *Jahmekya* (Beverly Hills, CA: Colgems-EMI/Ziggy Music, 1991), compact disc. In his biography of Bob Marley, Stephen Davis quoted Danny Sims acknowledging the prior claim of Jesus on Bob Marley: 'There was no "Jah" in the music Bob was making back then [the 1960s]. It was all "Jesus" this and "Lord" that' (p. 76). In fact, the Wailers as a group were nurtured in a Christian church. Timothy White reports: 'Having no guitar of their own, they had been using an ancient acoustic at the Ebenezer Church in Trench Town, practicing with it in the church hall. The nervy Peter went to the rectory and persuaded the minister to load him the guitar on a long-term basis' (*Catch a Fire: The Life of Bob Marley*, p. 151). Peter Tosh himself told Roger Steffens he developed his talent in 'Sunday school, in a choir, playing piano. If they needed someone to hold a high note and no one could find it, I could' ('In the Tracks of the Stepping Razor: The Peter Tosh Biography', *Peter Tosh: Honorary Citizen*, New York: Columbia: C3K 65064, 1997, p. 42).

49. 'Crazy Baldhead' is on Bob Marley and the Wailers' *Rastaman Vibration* (Los Angeles: Island 9383: 1976), record.

50. 'Cornerstone' can be found on numerous collections of earlier material like Trojan's *Soul Rebels*, available from London's Receiver Records (106, 1987), record, Masters' *The Bob Marley Collection* (005185) record, out of Holland, or, of course, on the definitive *Songs of Freedom* compact disc multi-set out from Tuff Gong/Island (512 280-2, 1992), which preserves much Wailers material.

51. 'Careless Ethiopians' from Toots and the Maytals *Knock Out!* album (New York: Mango: MLPS 9670-B, 1981), record.

52. Frederick Toots Hibbert, 'Hallelujah' and 'Matthew Mark', *Never Grow Old: Presenting the Maytals* (Kingston: Studio One: JBL 1113, no date), record.

53. Mutabaruka's 'I Am De Man' appears on *Blakk Wi Blak ... K ... K ...* (Newton, NJ: Shanachie: 43083, 1991), compact disc, 'God is a Schizophrenic' on *Any Which Way ... Freedom* (Newton, NJ: Shanachie: 43061, 1989), record, 'Say' on *Check It!* (Chicago: Alligator: 8306, 1983), record.

54. John Moodie, *Hath ... The Lion Prevailed ...?*, p. 26.

55. Ibid.

56. F. G. Ried Pastor, 'Is Mussolini a Papal Henchman?', *Plain Talk* (20 July 1935), p. 7.
57. L. F. C. Mantle, 'The Italo-Ethiopian Conflict', *Plain Talk* (19 Oct. 1935), pp. 7–8.
58. L. F. C. Mantle, 'Diffusion of Ethiopic Knowledge Needed', *Plain Talk* (28 Sept. 1935), p. 7.
59. L. F. C. Mantle, 'The Italo-Ethiopian Conflict: "Things that Affects us Here"', *Plain Talk* (2 Nov. 1935), p. 11.
60. Tekla Mekfet, *Christopher Columbus & Rastafari: Ironies of History . . . and Other Reflections on the Symbol of Rastafari* (St Ann, Jamaica: Jambasa, 1993), p. 69.
61. L. F. C. Mantle, 'The Italo-Ethiopian Conflict: "Things that Affects us Here"', p. 11.

JESUS AS A PROPHET

62. A roundup listing of a multitude of global reggae groups can be found in my chapter 'Chanting Change Around the World: The Global Mission of the Rastafarian Arts', in Murrell, Spencer, and McFarlane, eds., *Chanting Down Babylon: The Rastafari Reader*.
63. 'Let's Give Praise and Thanks' is available on the Melodians, *Sweet Sensation* (New York: Mango: 162-539 635-2, 1980), compact disc.
64. William A. Blake, 'Beliefs of the Ras Tafari Cult', p. 9.
65. O'Neal A. Walker, 'A Brief Study of Rastafarianism,' Nov. 1975, The West Indies Collection, Jamaica Theological Seminary, Kingston, Jamaica, p. 5.

Chapter Seven: Roots Christianity

THE TRINITIES IN RASTAFARI

1. Marcus Garvey, *More Philosophy and Opinions*, vol. 3, p. 78.
2. Joseph Hill, 'Marriage in Canaan' and 'Rub-a-Dub Style' are on Culture, *Wings of a Dove* (Newton, NJ: Shanachie: 43097, 1992), compact disc; 'Sufferer' on *Three Sides to My Story* (Newton, NJ: Shanachie: 43088, 1991), compact disc; 'Jah Alone a Christian' on *Lion Rock* (Cambridge, MA: Heartbeat: 12, 1982), record, and as 'Christian' on *Culture at Work* (Newton, NJ: Shanachie: 43047, 1987), record.
3. An excellent recent example of Tony Rebel's superb work in dancehall is *Jah By My Side* (Kingston: Flames: 0001, 1997), compact disc, which includes such theologically intriguing songs as his presentation of Selassie as Jesus Returned 'Know Jah', 'Bible Chant', 'Think on These Things' and a host of others. One much more 'slack' oriented dancehall deejay who can follow his 'pum pum' offerings with a pious version of 'Amazing Grace' is Louie Rankin. Perhaps his most theologically

interesting moment came when he contributed a rap (called at the time 'toasting') extolling Jesus in Black Uhuru's 'One Love' on their excellent *Mystical Truth* (Glendale, CA: Mesa: R2 79044, 1992), compact disc. He identifies Jesus Christ as 'true love'. Who is Jesus to him? He explained to me:

> Selassie I. It was Jesus Christ who reveal himself in the same personality. Okay, so, in other words, Selassie I of Ethiopia I would say is the body of Jesus Christ ... So, it's the same person. I'm not looking at Selassie I in Ethiopian sense, Selassie I. It's Jesus. You understand? Jesus, who is in heaven that you praise ... I believe in Jesus Christ that we read in the Bible, let's put it like that. And I believe in Selassie I the same way, but I believe in him as Jesus, in that image.

4. Alvin 'Keith' Porter's 'In a Dis a Time' and 'Temptation' are on *The Itals: Early Recordings, 1971–1979* (St Louis, MO: Nighthawk: 310, 1987), record; 'Reggae Chariot' is on the Itals, *Brutal Out Deh* (St Louis, MO: Nighthawk: 303, 1981), record.
5. C. S. Lewis, *The Last Battle* (New York: Collier, 1956, 1970), pp. 164–5.
6. Ronnie Davis and N. Blake, 'Too Much Religion', Itals, *Easy to Catch* (Van Nuys, CA: Rhythm Safari: 57159, 1991), compact disc.

THE ANCIENT BRIDGE

7. One can read about the events that led up to this controversy written by an eyewitness at the council in Eusebius of Caesaria's *The History of the Church*. An interesting discussion of the issues involved can be found in J. N. D. Kelly, *Early Christian Doctrines*, second edn. (London: Harper and Row, 1960), pp. 223–51. See pp. 15–17 for Plotinus and Porphyry.
8. The Creed of Nicaea and its refinement adopted at Chalcedon, the Nicene Creed, can be found in Henry Bettenson, ed., *Documents of the Christian Church*, second edn. (London: Oxford University Press, 1963) pp. 25–6, as well as a letter from Arius to a supporter, Eusebius, bishop of Nicomedia, c. 321, p. 39.
9. Marcus Garvey, *More Philosophy and Opinions*, vol. 3, p. 66.
10. Haile Selassie I, *Selected Speeches of His Imperial Majesty Haile Selassie First*, 1918–1967, p. 639.
11. Ijahman Levi, 'The Church', *Are We A Warrior* (Island: 9557, 1979), record.
12. Sister Eleanor Wint and Ras Bas, 'A Contribution to Reggae and Rastafari', TS (Kingston, University of the West Indies, 1995), p. 1. Readers may read more insights by Sister Eleanor Wint, a Rastafarian who is a professor at the University of the West Indies, in conjunction with members of the Nyabingi Order, in her chapter 'Who is Haile Selassie? His Imperial Majesty in Rasta Voices', in Murrell, Spencer, McFarlane, eds., *Chanting Down Babylon: The Rastafari Reader*, pp. 159–65.

13. Margarett E. Groves, *Lamentation: The Voice of a New Poet* (Jamaica: Margarett E. Groves, 1989), p. 3.
14. Ibid., p. 5.
15. Silburn 'Mosiah' Morrison, *Rastafari: The Conscious Embrace* (Bronx, NY: Itality, 1992), pp. 14–15.
16. Ibid., p. 19.
17. Judy Mowatt, 'Who Is He?', *Love is Overdue* (Newton, NJ: Shanachie: 43044, 1987), record.
18. Tertullian, 'Adv. Praxean', in Henry Bettenson, ed., *Documents of the Christian Church*, p. 38.

'ROOTS CHRISTIANITY'

19. Brother Gad, 'Interview with Dr Vernon Carrington, Ms. Andrea Williams', *Running African*, Irie FM, Kingston, 13 July 1997, transcribed by Messian Dread of the Netherlands and printed with permission of Brother Gad (Manchester, UK, April 1998), on-line, available from Rastafari Links: http://web.syr.edu/~affellem/Gad.html, pages 3, 9.
20. Archbishop Yesehaq, *The Ethiopian Tewahedo Church*, p. 225.
21. Mutabaruka, 'Interview with Ian Boyne', MS of radio broadcast, Kingston, Jamaica, 12 May 1998, transcribed by Tom Frantz.
22. See Bob Marley, 'Talking Blues', Bob Marley and the Wailers, *Talking Blues* (New York: Tuff Gong: 422-848-243-1, 1991), record.
23. I have found evidence of the same strategy in play not only in Jamaica, but in the United Kingdom and the United States by Black Muslims seeking to enlist Rastas, whom they consider leaderless after the death of Selassie I. In Britain, the Muslim magazine *Sign of the Times* in its Feb–April 1997 issue, for example, published an excerpt from a speech Selassie delivered at a graduation ceremony in Ethiopia on 17 July 1959 and titled it 'The Need for Leadership by H.I.M. Emperor Haile Selassie I'. Accompanying the article was a beautiful drawing of the emperor in imperial regalia. Immediately following was an article by 'Hon. Minister Louis Farrakhan, leader of the Nation of Islam' urging Muslims to take over the leadership of educating the young. Several pages later an article in support of a dreadlocked inmate in prison was followed by columns on spiritual thoughts, enhancing one's creative force, and taking responsibility. This bid for enlisting Rastafarians into Islam was also noted by Bishop Joe Aldred of The Centre for Black–White Christian Partnership, a joint effort of the Council of Churches for Britain and Ireland, the Federation of Selly Oak Colleges, and the University of Birmingham, who reported, 'While in Sheffield I did notice a number of individuals with Rasta appearance who said that they frequented the Mosque. This syncretism was new to me.' He speculated, 'Their meeting point, I suspect, would neither be Selassie

nor Muhammed, but Afrocentrism' (Bishop Joe Aldred, letter to author, 4 June 1997).

Other observers who note the aggressive movement of the Nation of Islam in the United Kingdom include Shiloh Harmitt, who followed an observation that the 'black churches . . . have been ever slow to politicise the problems and needs of the black community on a wider scale', in the Birmingham-based *BBJ*, by pointing out: .

> A firm lead has been taken by the Nation of Islam. It's core appeal is evident among young blacks, and its popularity within youth culture has grown with the commercial revival of its once most radical proponent Malcolm X. Although its activities are marginalised within the black community, its message of black pride, self-discipline, hardwork and anti-drugs cannot go unnoticed. (Shiloh Harmitt, 'To Be Black & British: Is There a Way Forward?' *BBJ* (Autumn 1995), p. 33)

That the Caribbean community was attracted was also in evidence in the same issue when African Caribbean People's Movement (ACPM) spokes-person Eric McKenzie reported, 'When the Mohammed Ali Centre was threatened with closure we helped to keep the Centre in the hands of the community' (p. 24).

But not all Britons are so enthused about the influx of Islam. Many women are concerned about the obvious repression of women in Islam. As Kadija George noted in 'Politics of the Veil' in the summer/autumn 1996 issue of *Candace* magazine: 'The politics of the veil has been used in Iran as a basis to violate women. They are subjected to extreme penalties if they do not comply with the dress codes laid down by the clerical establishment' (p. 56). The article warns against all fundamen-talist restriction against women, whatever the religion, and not simply exchanging one set of repressive chains for another.

Another observer is Stanley Byfield, whose World Vision for Christ bookstore in London's Granville Arcade, Brixton, often serves Rastafarians hunting for the apocalyptically-oriented Schofield Reference Bibles. He notes: 'They're taking over a great part of Britain now. Yes. Yes. They're different. I think they're more militant than the Rastafarians. What we have in Britain now, you see, is a lot of Blacks going over to Moslems.' He sees the black population moving in either of two directions: 'You find most Blacks now, they're going over to the Moslems, you see? But, at the same time, a lot are coming to know Christ, which is a good thing. You get me? So, that's an anwer to prayer.'

In the United States, the Rev Olayiwola Awoyomi of the Celestial Church of Christ America Inc., an Africa-based Christian denomination now extending its missionary work into Newark, New Jersey, a large centre of the New York metropolitan area for both Rastafari and the Nation of Islam, reports having seen Black Muslims pay financial premiums to Rastafarians to attend mosques. After a few weeks, if the Rastas are obviously only coming for the money, their stipends are dropped. He sees a conscious campaign by Louis Farrakhan and the Black Muslims to recruit Rastafarians, whom these Muslims consider leaderless since the removal of their God, Haile Selassie.

Clearly, if Christians do not make an effort to assist Rastafarians in their movement toward emulating Haile Selassie I's devotion to Jesus, they may find sincere Rastas moving into Islam, which practises similar dietary laws and ritual restrictions on women, but which holds a divergent view of Jesus.

How divergent is Islam's view? Muhammed 'Ata ur-Rahim is an articulate Moslem apologist whose *Jesus: A Prophet of Islam*, published by London's Diwan Press, carries on his mission to explain Islam to Christians as well as to others. He writes:

> More and more people are now aware that the Christianity they know has little to do with the original teaching of Jesus. During the last two centuries, the research of the historian has left little room for faith in the Christian 'mysteries', but the proven fact that the Christ of the established Church has almost nothing to do with the Jesus of history does not in itself help Christians towards the truth.

What is the 'truth' about Jesus that he wishes to share? He quotes a Moslem tradition:

> He was a ruddy man inclined to white. He did not have long hair. He never anointed his head. Jesus used to walk barefoot, and he took no house, nor adornment, nor goods, nor clothes, nor provisions, except his day's food. His head was dishevelled and his face was small. He was an ascetic in this world, longing for the next world and eager for the worship of Allah.

For him, this short-haired, red and white, Allah worshipping, ascetical 'Jesus did exist. He was a man and a prophet of Allah' (Muhammed 'Ata Ur-Rahim, *Jesus: A Prophet of Islam*, second edn. (London: MWH, 1979), pp. 16, 2. This is the 'Jesus of history' offered by Islam to Rastafarians.

Black Muslims, however, reportedly have a different message, a dual one. While Louis Farrakhan publicly enlists Christian churches in demonstrations like his 'Million Man March' of 1995, he is said to term Jesus a 'paper messiah' when he speaks at mosques and, in an echo of Howell and Prince Emmanuel, to present himself as Allah's present messiah.

24. Mutabaruka, 'Interview with Ian Boyne'.
25. Mortimer Planno, 'The Faculty of Interpretation: Bob Marley, Christ and Rastafari', speech delivered at the Social Sciences Lecture Hall, University of the West Indies, Mona Campus, Jamaica, 11 May 1998.
26. Reginald Allen, 'No Change for Born-Again Tommy: Yes Indeed!' *The Sunday Gleaner* (10 May 1998), 1E. Tommy Cowan's Talent Corporation Limited Agency is at Suite 3 1d Braemar Ave., Kingston 10 Jamaica, W.I. with e-mail at tcowan@toj.com. He has produced concerts and albums

not only with current Gospel reggae singers like Carlene Davis and Judy Mowatt but with many of the Rastafarian groups interviewed.

27. Djate Richards is noted for touring and session work as well as his own releases, particularly 1987's 'Rock With You' and 1992's 'Darling', now available from Little Sound Productions, 3948 Springleaf Pt., Stone Mountain, GA, 30083 (404-294-4590).

Conclusion

1. Abba Paulos, Patriarch of Ethiopia and Echegue of the See of St Tekle Haimanot, by fax to author from EOTC patriarchate private office, Addis Ababa, 19 November 1997. Having suffered imprisonment for his faith, Abba Paulos has brought a powerful, prophetic voice to the Ethiopian Church. At the All-African Council of Churches, held in October 1997, he spoke out against human rights abuses:

> We cannot continue to lament or witness the raging conflicts. We must learn to abhor the sight of bloodstained faces and mutilated bodies of our African brothers and sisters due to ethnic conflict or political settling of accounts.
>
> God did not create us so that we kill each other with hatred and sheer callousness. It is not and should not be part of the African culture to step over dead bodies and draw satisfaction from the misery of others. (Reuters, 'Church Leader of Ethiopia Hits Abuse of Rights', *The Boston Globe*, 5 Oct. 1997, p. A15.)

    Living and expressing such a message, Abba Paulos provides a powerful example of leadership for both Rastas and Christians to imitate.

2. Alex Walker, 'The Other Side of Rasta History', *The Sunday Herald*, Jamaica (21 March 1993), p. 35A.

3. Barbara Blake Hannah, 'Misunderstanding Rastafari', *The Sunday Herald*, Jamaica (4 April 1993), p. 5A.

4. Ian Boyne, 'Jamaica: Breaking Barriers Between Churches and Rastafarians', *One World* (May 1983), p. 4.

5. Ibid.

6. Stafford Ashani, 'Rasta Now', *Lifestyle*, no. 18 (Nov/Dec. 1991), p. 7.

7. Ibid., p. 9.

8. Ibid., p. 10.

9. Ian Boyne, 'Jamaica: Breaking Barriers between Churches and Rastafarians', p. 4. One of the most interesting attempts at dialogue is British Pentecostal theologian Robert Beckford's *Jesus Is Dread: Black Theology and Black Culture in Britain* (London: Darton, Longman and Todd, 1998), which was published just as the present book was being prepared for printing. While critics may grumble at Professor Beckford's loose handling of data (for example, he analyses Peter Tosh's lyrics in

400 Years as if they were Bob Marley's, misidentifies Alexander Bedward as Anthony, regularly misquotes song lyrics), yet what he does for Britain in *Jesus Is Dread* is reminiscent of the pioneering work of Father Joseph Owens, particularly in his article 'The Rastafarians of Jamaica' (Idris Hamid, ed., *Troubling of the Waters* (San Fernando, Trinidad: Rahaman, 1973)). While Father Owens' approach was more descriptive than analytical, being willing to conclude 'the early Christians of the first century have been resurrected in the adherents of the Rastafarian cult of Jamaica' (p. 165), twenty-five years later Robert Beckford is more analytical and sophisticated in his assessment of Bob Marley as archetypal Rasta thinker. That 'Marley, as a Rasta, declares Selassie divine' he calls 'problematic for two reasons: first, it reveals an uncritical approach to the text; second, it relies heavily upon an idealised and romanticised view of African history' (p. 123). On the praxis side he criticises Marley's 'promiscuous lifestyle, and his general failure to honour Black women in his music,' pointing out that 'any theological enterprise concerned with Black liberation in Britain must take seriously the multidimensional nature of oppression. That is, we must be not only concerned with racism but also with sexism' (p. 126). By looking past Bob Marley's shortcomings and focusing on his theological accomplishments, Beckford's intention is to clear the way for a true appropriation of what Rasta has to offer the overall enterprise of creating a black theology, namely its way of assessing truth-claims through 'personal experience', 'commitment to radical social change', urban mode of 'discourse' by reggae music (pp. 118–21), everyone of which, while grounded in the Bible, 'points us to a God of rhythm, in tune with the rhythms of Black life' (p. 129). Guided by the thought of mid-century German-American theologian Paul Tillich, and working with contemporary theology's tools of a Reader Response hermenuetic, where one interprets the Bible from one's social point of view, and Salvation History, wherein 'the Jesus of history becomes the Christ of faith for Black British men and women', he uses Dread Talk 'to find a meaningful way of describing Christ's activity in the world today' (p. 19). His title *Jesus is Dread* illustrates his attempt to appropriate from Rasta's black consciousness-centred point of view a way for Black British Christians to rethink their faith in a non-European model. 'Jesus' and 'Dread' have been linked for Rastas since before 1977 when the mystical Vivian 'Yabby You' Jackson with deejay Trinity released their self-identifying chant 'Jesus Dread' (recently rereleased on the definitive two-compact-disc set *Yabby You: Jesus Dread: 1972–1977* (Manchester, England: Blood and Fire: 021, 1997)). The title of the present book, *Dread Jesus*, reflects this movement among Rastas to see a 'Dread' or 'Rasta-like otherness' in the One Sent Among Us by the Over-All Creator. What Queen's College, Birmingham tutor in Black Theology Robert Beckford does, however, is attempt to construct a 'dread' identity from the Christian side, appropriating what he sees as the best of Rasta's interpretive tenets for a larger theological enterprise among people of color. In that sense, his is an intriguing step in the Rasta-Christian dialogue as well as in the formulation of a Black community-based Christian theology.

An interesting side note on Yabby You is that his breakthrough song, 'Conquering Lion', does not appear to be about Selassie, as many suppose, but about Jesus Christ. Released in the autumn of 1972, the song had originally been composed some five years earlier as the result of a street corner disagreement over ethics and the claims made by Jesus and those made for Selassie. Arguing with some 'Steppers' ('Rastaman . . . who locks them hair and go thief, but they claim say it is not them who thief, they say them take back some of what them father left the slave master'), Yabby You explained to London-based interviewer David Katz, 'I say, "Those things no right, for Jesus Christ say them things no right."' The reaction was instantaneous: 'The whole of them turn down on me, in a dispute, trying to show me which part of Rastafari is God.' Unimpressed with the Steppers' attempt to thrust Selassie into the Godhead, he remembers, 'When I come and I hear this Rasta argument, it look foolish to me. I can't see how the Almighty could be a man.' Instead he countered with his own declaration: 'Them keep saying to me, "Rastafari is the King of Kings and Lords of Lords." I say to them, "The King of Kings is Jesus Christ."' As a result:

> The Rastaman, them say me is not a Rastaman through me worship Jesus Christ. Them give me a name, so Rastaman can know me different, and them call me Jesus Dread. Trinity, me did bring him as a dj, he was a dj with sound like Big Youth, but him was a baldhead, so we make him do it. Them think say I am ashamed over it; I proud of it, to know I is not a Rastaman dread, I is a Jesus dread.

The resulting twenty-seven years of recorded chants by this dreadlocked patriarch of conscious reggae may well provide Black Christian theologians like Robert Beckford with a subsequent 'canon' for future work as archetypal examples of what he is seeking to do through *Jesus is Dread*: describe Jesus Christ in valid, biblical terms highlighted by representatives of indigenous black movements (like Rastafari) (David Katz, 'Yabby You: The Prophet Speaks', *The Beat* 14, no. 2 (1995), pp. 50–51).

10. John Harlow, 'Dead Singers Given New Voice by Hi-tech Clone', *The Sunday Times*, London (11 May 1997), 4.

11. Kay Kaufman Shelemay, 'The Musician and Transmission of Religious Tradition: The Multiple Roles of the Ethiopian Dâbtâra', *Journal of Religion in Africa* 22, no. 3 (1992), pp. 254–5.

Interviews

John Aboyeji, Gordon-Conwell Theological Seminary, c. Spring, 1991, by telephone, c. Autumn, 1993

Femi Adeyemi, by telephone, c. Autumn, 1993

Olayiwola Awoyomi, Heathrow Airport, London, 29 May 1997

Clement 'Bankie Banx' Banks, by telephone, 19 March 1992, 16 Oct. 1992, 15 Nov. 1992

Patrick 'Tony Rebel' Barrett, Cool Runnings tour bus, Boston, MA, 8 Nov. 1993

Byron Antonio Beckford, on the beach, Montego Bay, Jamaica, 31 Dec. 1990

Anthony 'Anthony B' Blair, by telephone, 11 Nov. 1998

Manley 'Big Youth' Buchanan, House of Blues, Cambridge, MA, 10–11 March 1997

Stanley Byfield, World Vision for Christ Bookstore, Granville Arcade near Coldharbour Lane, Brixton, London, 13 May 1997

Clinton Chisholm, by telephone, 24 April 1997

Tommy Cowan, Family Church on the Rock, Kingston, Jamaica, 17 May 1998

Ansel Cridland (of the Meditations), by telephone, 21 May 1993, 2 Nov. 1996

Richard Custerbeck, Southern Baptist Theological Seminary library, Louisville, Kentucky, Winter, 1981

'D', Caribbean Graduate School of Theology, Kingston, Jamaica, Jan. 1991

Garth Dennis (of Black Uhuru), Middle East Restaurant, Cambridge, MA, 31 March 1993

Dean Ellis, All Tone Records, Granville Arcade, Brixton, London, 13 May 1997

Victor Essiet (of the Mandators), by telephone, 17 Sept. 1995

Majek Fashek, Loon Mountain State Park, Loon Mountain, NH, 22 Aug. 1992

Marcel Goffe, by telephone, 28 May 1998

Cuthbert Gustav, Jefferson County (KY) Adult Literacy Center at St Augustine School, Louisville, KY, Autumn, 1979

Barbara Blake Makeda Lee Hannah, National Prayer Breakfast, Kingston, Jamaica, 17 Jan. 1991

Joseph Hill (of Culture), Catch a Rising Star Club, Cambridge MA, 8 Oct. 1992

Ras Michael Henry, Susse Chalet, Cambridge, MA, 14 July 1993, by telephone, 15 July 1993

Frederick 'Toots' 'The Maytal' Hibbert, by telephone, 16 June 1997

Ras Isha (Elijah), in a yard in Negril, Jamaica, 24 Oct. 1995

Monica 'Maniah Mani' Lambett, at her stand in Brixton Market off Coldharbour Lane, London, 13 May 1997

Neville 'Bunny Wailer' O'Riley Livingston, in a car park, Kingston, Jamaica, 1 Jan 1991

David 'Ziggy' Marley, by telephone, 27 Oct. 1993

Ras Alan Martin (of United Negro Improvement Association (UNIA)), Social Sciences Lecture Hall, University of the West Indies, Mona, Jamaica, 11 May 1998

Winston 'Pipe' Matthews (of the Wailing Souls), Cool Runnings tour bus, Boston, MA, 8 Nov. 1993

Judy Mowatt, Caribbean Graduate School of Theology, Kingston, Jamaica, 12 May 1998

Edward Osei-Bonsu, at my home in MA, c. Spring, 1995

Oluwole Peku Ojitiku, Loon Mountain State Park, Loon Mountain, NH, 22 Aug. 1992

Mortimer (Mortimmo, Martimo) 'Kumi' Planno, Social Sciences Lecture Hall, University of the West Indies, Mona, Jamaica, 11 May 1998

Alvin 'Keith' Porter (of the Itals), by telephone, 1 July 1997

Louie Rankin, Middle East Restaurant, Cambridge, MA, 31 March 1993

Djate 'Jahtee' Richards, Catch a Rising Star Club, Cambridge, MA, 8 Oct. 1992

Lindon 'Half Pint' Roberts, House of Blues, Cambridge, MA, 10–11 Nov. 1998

Michael (Mykal Roze) Rose, Sheraton Commander Hotel, Cambridge, MA, 25 Feb. 1993

Derrick 'Duckie' Simpson (of Black Uhuru), Middle East Restaurant, Cambridge, MA, 31 March 1993

George Eaton Simpson, by telephone, 24 April 1997

Ras Siam (Sam), in a yard in Negril, Jamaica, 24 Oct. 1995

Tracey Singleton and Sons of Negus, Susse Chalet, Cambridge, MA, 14 July 1993

Somala of Dominica, Catch a Rising Star Club, Cambridge, MA, 8 Oct. 1992

Euvin 'Don Carlos' Spenser (of Black Uhuru), Middle East Restaurant, Cambridge, MA, 31 March 1993

Imani M. Tafari-Ama, office of Clinton Chisholm, Hagley Park Plaza, Kingston, Jamaica, 15 May 1998

Junior Taylor, Sheraton Commander Hotel, Cambridge, MA, 25 Feb 1993

Andrew Tosh, Middle East Restaurant, Cambridge, MA, 31 March 1993

For Further Reading

Barrett, Leonard E. Sr., *The Rastafarians*, rev. (Boston: Beacon, 1977, 1988)

Beckford, Robert, *Jesus Is Dread: Black Theology and Black Culture in Britain* (London: Darton, Longman and Todd, 1988)

Cashmore, Ernest, *Rastaman: The Rastafarian Movement in England* (London: Unwin, 1979)

Chevannes, Barry, *Rastafari: Roots and Ideology* (Syracuse: Syracuse University Press, 1994)

Davis, Stephen and Peter Simon, *Reggae International* (New York: Rogner and Bernhard, 1982)

Douglas, Kelly Brown, *The Black Christ* (Maryknoll, NY: Orbis, 1994)

Faristzaddi, Millard, *Itations of Jamaica and I Rastafari* (Miami: Judah Anbesa, 1987)

Faristzaddi, Mihlawhdh *Itations of Jamaica and I Rastafari: The Second Itation* (Miami: Judah Anbesa, 1991)

Forsythe, Dennis, 'West Indian Culture Through the Prism of Rastafarianism', in Nettleford, ed., *Caribbean Quarterly Monograph: Rastafari*

Forsythe, Dennis, *Rastafari: For the Healing of the Nation* (Kingston: Zaika, 1983)

Garrison, Len, *Black Youth, Rastafarianism, and the Identity Crisis in Britain* (London: Centre for Learning Resources, 1979)

Garvey, Marcus, *Philosophy and Opinions of Marcus Garvey*, vol. 1 (New York: Arno/New York Times, 1968)

Garvey, Marcus, *Philosophy and Opinions of Marcus Garvey*, vol. 2 (New York: Arno/New York Times, 1969)

Garvey, Marcus, *More Philosophy and Opinions of Marcus Garvey*, vol. 3, eds. E. U. Essien-Udom and Amy Jacques Garvey (London: Frank Cass, 1977)

Hill, Robert, 'Leonard P. Howell and Millenarian Visions in Early Rastafari', *Jamaica Journal* 16, no. 1 (Feb. 1983)

Howell, Leonard (under the pseudonym 'G. G. Maragh'), *The Promised Key* (Accra, Gold Coast: Dr. Nnamdi Azikiwe, Editor of *The African Morning Post*, Head Office, no date, c. 1935), reprinted with commentary by W. D. Spencer, 'The First Chant: Leonard Howell's *The Promised Key*', in Murrell, Spencer, and McFarlane, eds., *Chanting Down Babylon: The Rastafari Reader*

McCann, Ian, ed., *Bob Marley: In His Own Words* (London: Omnibus, 1993)

Mansingh, Ajai, and Mansingh, Laxmi, 'Hindu Influences on Rastafarianism', in Nettleford, ed., *Caribbean Quarterly Monograph: Rastafari*

Moodie, John, *Hath ... The Lion Prevailed ...?* (Boynton Beach, Florida: Hath the Lion Enterprise, 1992)

Murrell, Nathaniel Samuel, Spencer, William David, and McFarlane, Adrian Anthony, eds., *Chanting Down Babylon: The Rastafari Reader* (Philadelphia: Temple University Press, 1998)

Nettleford, Rex, ed., *Caribbean Quarterly Monograph: Rastafari* (Kingston, Jamaica: University of the West Indies, 1985)

Nicholas, Tracy and Bill Sparrow, *Rastafari: A Way of Life* (Garden City, N.Y.: Doubleday, 1979)

Owens, Joseph, *Dread: The Rastafarians of Jamaica* (Kingston: Sangster, 1976, 1993)

Rogers, Robert Athyli, *The Holy Piby* (Woodbridge, N.J.: Athlican Strong Arm Company, 1924)

Selassie I, Haile, *Selected Speeches of His Imperial Majesty Haile Selassie First: 1918–1967* (Addis Ababa: The Imperial Ethiopian Ministry of Information Publications and Foreign Languages Press Department, 1967)

Smith, M. G., Augier, Roy, and Nettleford, Rex, *The Rastafari Movement in Kingston, Jamaica* (Kingston: Institute of Social and Economic Research, University College of the West Indies, 1960)

Yesehaq, Archbishop, *The Ethiopian Tewahedo Church: An Integrally African Church* (New York: Vantage, 1989)

Index

The Society for Promoting Christian Knowledge (SPCK) has as its purpose three main tasks:

- **Communicating the Christian faith in its rich diversity**
- **Helping people to understand the Christian faith and to develop their personal faith**
- **Equipping Christians for mission and ministry**

SPCK Worldwide serves the Church through Christian literature and communication projects in over 100 countries. Special schemes also provide books for those training for ministry in many parts of the developing world. SPCK Worldwide's ministry involves Churches of many traditions. This worldwide service depends upon the generosity of others and all gifts are spent wholly on ministry programmes, without deductions.

SPCK Bookshops support the life of the Christian community by making available a full range of Christian literature and other resources, and by providing support to bookstalls and book agents throughout the UK. SPCK Bookshops' mail order department meets the needs of overseas customers and those unable to have access to local book-shops.

SPCK Publishing produces Christian books and resources, covering a wide range of inspirational, pastoral, practical and academic subjects. Authors are drawn from many different Christian traditions, and publications aim to meet the needs of a wide variety of readers in the UK and throughout the world.

The Society does not necessarily endorse the individual views contained in its publications, but hopes they stimulate readers to think about and further develop their Christian faith.

For further information about the Society, please write to:
SPCK, Holy Trinity Church, Marylebone Road,
London NW1 4DU, United Kingdom.
Telephone: 0171 387 5282